PENNSYLVANIA Medical Malpractice

A Guide for the Health Sciences

PENNSYLVANIA Medical Malpractice

A Guide for the Health Sciences

Hugh F. Hill, M.D., J.D.

Series editors

James A. Rapp, J.D., and Roy T. Rapp, M.D.

THE C. V. MOSBY COMPANY

ST. LOUIS • WASHINGTON, D.C. • TORONTO 1988

MOSBY

A TRADITION OF PUBLISHING EXCELLENCE

Editors: **Thomas A. Manning, Terry Van Schaik**
Assistant Editor: **Patricia L. Gregory**
Project Manager: **Mark Spann**
Design: **Liz Fett**

Printed in the United States of America

The C.V. Mosby Company
11830 Westline Industrial Drive, St. Louis, Missouri 63146

Library of Congress Cataloging-in-Publication Data

Hill, Hugh F.
Pennsylvania medical malpractice.

Includes index.
1. Physicians—Malpractice—Pennsylvania. I. Title.
[DNLM: 1. Malpractice—Pennsylvania—legislation.
W 44 H646]
KFP326.3.H55 1988 346.74803′32 88-1824
ISBN 0-8016-4251-5 347.4806332

GW/MV/MV 9 8 7 6 5 4 3 2 1

FOREWORD

Few areas of civil litigation engender as much controversy and hostility among the participants as medical malpractice lawsuits. The patient-plaintiff or the deceased's family believes the preventable injuries were caused by the physician-defendant's lack of skill and personal concern; the doctor feels his professonal competence and integrity are being challenged and his livelihood threatened. The opposing experts are often subjected to scathing cross-examination and bitter personal attacks, and the attorneys genuinely or theatrically attempt to either dramatize or downplay the unfortunate circumstances, depending on their respective roles, with a keen awareness of the high stakes involved in the outcome. With more than 20,000 new malpractice actions filed against doctors and hospitals each year in the United States, and high six- and seven-figure verdicts no longer rare, it is understandable that the medical community is apprehensive, distraught, and fearful, sometimes to the point of irrational fear and illogical defensive posturing.

Too many individual writers and commentators, medical and legal groups, and political figures have unwittingly fanned the flames of the national problem by injudicious and inaccurate attacks on the ethics, motivation, and honesty of one profession or the other, blindly failing to recognize that such emotional, barbed rhetoric will only agitate and worsen a complex, multifaceted societal dilemma. There are no simplistic solutions to the medical malpractice quagmire that would be reasonable, equitable, and feasible in a democratic, technologically advanced, large, and heterogenous country like ours. Those who profess to have a facile, implementable answer that would be just and fair for both injured patients and physicians are either unduly influenced by their particular bias or unaware of how the civil justice system must function in our society.

This series of books dealing with medical malpractice cases, statutes, and various related issues in each jurisdiction represents a unique approach that is designed to explain and clarify the substantive and procedural aspects of malpractice lawsuits for physicians and other health care practitioners with special emphasis on the history, development, and current status of this category of personal injury legal actions in the various states. The physician-attorney Rapp family deserves special recommendation for this innovative approach.

This particular book by an acknowledged medical-legal expert, Dr. Hugh Hill, a practicing emergency room physician who is also an attorney, deals with malpractice litigation and case law in the Commonwealth of Pennsylvania. The volume admirably and successfully accomplishes the goals set forth by the author and editors in their respective prefaces. A great deal of practical, useful information is presented in an interesting, understandable, and most importantly, objective manner that is clearly tailored for the doctor who has no formal legal education. The categorization of cases, logical explanations, helpful references, and salient commentaries make this volume extremely worthwhile for all health care professionals who would like to know more about how malpractice cases are spawned; what the general and specific legal requirements in Pennsylvania are for a plaintiff to pursue such legal actions; how juries in different parts of the state have dealt with these cases through the years; what patterns have emerged that permit a reasonable degree of predictability to be applied to future cases; and, of utmost concern and interest, how malpractice lawsuits can be intelligently and reasonably avoided or their incidence diminished.

Hospital administrators, medical educators, and other health care professionals such as dentists and nurses, as well as practicing physicians, will learn a great deal from this well-structured text with its orderly compilation of cases, statutes, and cross-references.

These cases do not just happen in some haphazard, fortuitous, totally unrelated fashion. To know and understand the most frequently occurring primary and secondary etiologic factors in these medical malpractice lawsuits is unquestionably the most intelligent and logical way to avoid becoming a defendant in such an unpleasant and traumatic experience.

Cyril H. Wecht, M.D., J.D.
Chairman of the Board of Trustees
of the American Board
of Legal Medicine

AUTHOR'S PREFACE

Health care professionals *can* learn more about the law of medical malpractice. That they *should* learn more is so often repeated as to no longer be seriously questioned. There is a plethora of offerings available to those wishing courses, texts, newsletters, etc., but the demand for information on the subject appears insatiable. The need for quality, effective resources is clear. What the health provider should do with this information is, I believe, still a subject of controversy.

Every doctor, nurse, therapist, and administrator—every professional in the field of health care—is capable of comprehending legal factual information and understanding legal principles. The law is not such a tangled web as to defy all but expert analysis. Law is a living part of our society, the result of real people trying to deal with real problems. A historical approach may facilitate understanding, but it is not necessary. Also unnecessary are cross-correlations and knowledge of other areas of the law. Medical malpractice law, for itself and in its current manifestation, can be profitably approached by an inquiring mind, even one trained in the sharp logical dissections and empiric skepticism of health science.

We are reminded unmercifully of the importance of malpractice law and our study of it. It is traditional to begin malpractice lectures and treatises for health professionals with a grim litany of the horrors currently faced and even more dread and dire predictions of the future. We have tried to keep this to a minimum. *It is all true,* but it is already widely known and we assume some rationally based interest on the reader's part. Besides, the news gets so much worse so fast that any statistics and projections are quickly out of date.

The interest rightly focused on the subject stimulates much publishing. But with this book and its series companions, The C. V. Mosby Company has not just added to a growing literature. The series represents a qualitative step in available texts on medical malpractice. Every state's malpractice law is different, but publishing houses in these individual jurisdictions have not seen a sufficient potential market to justify books that focus on this area of law and for this audience. C. V. Mosby, with its fine tradition of medical publishing, performs a real service in offering primers in specific states' law of malpractice. I am grateful for the opportunity to be part of this innovative, daring, and important project.

On a personal note, let me caution against certain potential effects of malpractice consciousness-raising. The malpractice problem is so severe as to justify a little constructive hysteria, but not sufficient to excuse trading on fear. As health care providers, in whom enormous public trust still resides, we must not allow the defensive measures we take against the threat of malpractice to negatively affect our patients. Risk management and quality assurance should be clearly distinct goals. Good quality care protects our patients—good risk management protects ourselves, our colleagues, and our institutions. The one follows the traditional rationale of the healer by acting in the patient's best interests; the other is self-oriented. By keeping these worthy goals distinct in our minds, we can be aware of conflicts between them. We can avoid putting patients to risk and expense not justified by the patient's own needs, risk and expense we are tempted to cause to protect ourselves. There are measures we can take ethically to reduce malpractice risk, and first among them is the acquisition and integration of information.

Finally, a word about the making of this book. Most of the work, all of the organization, and certainly the inspiration must be credited to the Rapp family. The Pennsylvania edition is adapted by me to this state's own law, and any errors are my own. I wish to thank my family for their support and sacrifice during the writing and editing process.

Hugh F. Hill III, M.D., J.D.
Bethesda, Maryland

EDITOR'S PREFACE

The traditional learned professions—theology, law, and medicine—have the mutual potential of doing significant good or committing awesome mischief. This potential is never greater than when members of these professions either join forces or come into conflict with one another.

Attorneys and doctors presently find themselves in such conflict. The name of this divisive force is *medical malpractice.* For these professionals, the survival of their professions as they currently exist is at risk. Attorneys, who have conceived and nurtured a legal system with such features as the contingent fee, believe they are merely providing a forum for injured patients to be adequately compensated for injuries suffered at the hands of doctors. Doctors, on the other hand, see the legal system as a monster towering over every health care provider: after years of training to save lives and improve the quality of life, medical decisions must be weighed against their legal impact and potential liability.

Most doctors perceive attorneys as their natural enemies. Instead of seeing attorneys as sincerely interested in justice or improved patient care, doctors consider attorneys unemotional and interested only in the money they can net out of a case. Indeed, after being adversaries by day, the attorneys on each side may be evening dinner companions.

To label all attorneys generically when referring to medical malpractice is unfair. Many fair-minded attorneys would never initiate a frivolous suit with hopes of settling the case for its nuisance value, but others are so economically motivated that they would, as the saying goes, sue their own mothers. Reciprocally, some doctors, dentists, and other health care providers should be drummed out of health care.

A logical approach to cleaning up both of these camps would be to combine efforts and concentrate on our mutual concern—the patient. To do this, doctors must not only do the best they can medically but fulfill their legal obligations as well. In doing so, doctors can help to avoid malpractice. If malpractice is claimed, they can defend actions effectively and therefore have increased their chance of winning the case. Fulfilling legal obligations requires that doctors gain a working knowledge of the legal system—particularly in the state and locality in which they practice.

Doctors have seldom taken the time or had the interest to learn much about the law. Yet the law affects their practices daily. It regulates whether they can practice medicine, how they are to practice medicine, and when they are guilty of malpractice.

Most health care providers have many questions about the law, especially as it pertains to medical malpractice. After all, it is likely every doctor will have several malpractice claims or suits brought against him during his career. The books in this series have been written to answer many of these questions and to prepare doctors better to deal with these claims. We also intend these books to assist doctors who may be called upon to testify in medical malpractice cases in which they are not being sued.

We do not intend the books in this series to be definitive texts on medical malpractice. Rather, we have basically outlined things that a nonlawyer health care provider should know about the legal aspects of medical malpractice. This basic introduction should be expanded and updated by collecting and reading a personal library and attending pertinent seminars. This is particularly important because the law, like medicine, is ever-changing. Although we usually refer to doctors, this book covers malpractice law for virtually any health care provider.

Each book in this series follows the same organizational plan, but each explains medical malpractice laws and issues as they pertain to the individual state. Attorneys practicing or licensed in each state have written the books, and we are thankful for their contributions and expertise.

James A. Rapp
Roy T. Rapp

CONTENTS

A NOTE ON LEGAL CITATIONS

To allow further reading or research on matters discussed in this book, we have included at the end of each chapter citations to Pennsylvania statutes and cases, as well as other references. The law and the rules are constantly changing, growing, being refined, and sometimes reversing direction. These changes, in addition to stimulating the reader's interest (we hope), often require research. Sufficient information is given in each citation to find the case in the most popular compilations (called reporters); sometimes cross-referencing with the assistance of a librarian will be needed. Statutes compiled by number are straightforward, as are major texts and law reviews. We expect that most readers will be novices to the law library, and we want to explain what we are referencing.

The majority of citations in this book are to statutes, administrative rules, or court cases.

Statutes are laws passed by the Pennsylvania legislature or the United States Congress and then published in books. This Commonwealth's legislated laws are collected in a set of books called the Pennsylvania Statutes Annotated. *Annotation* is the glossing of the bare statute with case decisions referring to that law and sometimes with other information. The laws are divided into titles and each title into sections, designated by the symbol §. Citations herein are to the Purdon collection, designated by volume numbers (as 42 Pa. C.S.A.) followed by section numbers. While a major section is devoted to laws governing the health professions, statutes affecting health practice and practitioners are scattered throughout. The abbreviation "et seq.," for "et sequentia," which means "and that which follow," can be used where reference is made to a group of consecutive paragraphs or sections. (Lawyers are criticized for their fondness for Latin and obscure phrases, but doctors of medicine are not well-positioned to object to another profession's use of the arcane.) Statutes adopted by the United States Congress are similarly compiled in a set of books called the United States Code, or U.S.C.

Administrative rules are closely related to statutes. These rules are also sources of law. They implement, apply, or interpret statutes. For example, the State Department of Health, carrying out its duties prescribed in statutes written by the state legislature, has promulgated rules affecting health practice. The rules are issued pursuant to Pennsylvania's laws governing administrative procedure. (In brief, proposed rules are published for a mandatory period to allow notice and comment, then amended, finalized, or withdrawn.) Administrative rules published by state agencies are collected and published as the Pennsylvania Code. For example, 27 Pennsylvania Code §27.2 lists diseases that must be reported. The list is created to effectuate a legislative enactment—35 Pa.C.S.A. § 521.4. Rules adopted by United States government agencies are similarly codified and published in the Code of Federal Regulations, or C.F.R.

Most medical malpractice law comes from actual controversies and the reports of judicial decisions in those cases. The publication of these case reports is important to the law's tradition of stare decisis, following case precedent and deciding similar cases in similar ways. This doesn't refer to fact decisions, such as which of two versions of events are true. The decisions followed as precedent are those of judges making rulings on the law in higher, or appellate, courts. For example, all of Pennsylvania's courts are bound to follow the State Supreme Court's ruling on whether or not an unwanted child can sue for a failed sterilization. The Supreme Court didn't decide whether or not an individual child or an individual doctor would win the case; the Court decided whether or not the suit could be tried. Parallel court decisions are not binding, but are often used to support a particular result. Appellate decisions are officially published, trial court decisions rarely so.

References to case reports adhere to a standard form. The names of the parties are given, followed by citations to collections, or reporters, where the court's opinion on that case may be found. The party bringing the case before that particular court is usually named first. Thus a doctor defendant who lost at trial and appealed may be listed first in the report of the appellate opinion. Multiple parties are not all listed, a common circumstance in medical malpractice cases where, often, all involved professionals and institutions are sued. A case may be cited as Patient v. Dr. X, et al., for example, giving the name of only one of the defendants. The citation concludes with the year in which the case was decided. Other verbiage is commentary by the authors of this book and not part of the reference. Example: Incollingo v. Ewing, 444 Pa. 263, 282 A.2d 214 (1971). The names of the parties are given first. The first reference is to the official state case reporter, volume 444; the court's opinion begins on page 263. Most of the cases cited in this book refer only to the regional reporter, in this example volume 282 of the Atlantic second series, beginning on page 214. The regional reporters are published by the West Publishing Company and contain opinions from many states in the area; these reporters are more commonly available in the law libraries accessible to health professionals. Cross indexing and the assistance of a law librarian will probably be required the first few times a case is sought in other reporters. Where the name of a court is not given, such as Pa. Super.

(Pennsylvania Superior), the report refers to a decision by the State Supreme Court.

The reader is encouraged to venture into the nearest law library. Handle a few of the reporters; thumb through them and sense the great variety of problems addressed by Pennsylvania's courts. Health care professionals can comprehend much by reading the law and in less time that it takes a lawyer to, for example, work through the Kreb's cycle.

THE MEDICAL MALPRACTICE CRISIS

Where doctors are

1

Synopsis

Malpractice, a crisis of the mind and heart

What is the number one issue on the minds of health care professionals today? Consider any single issue. Measuring by degree of concern, number of mentions at professional conferences, amount written for the professions (if "throw-away journals" are included), and intensity and foci of lobbying and reform efforts, malpractice is at or near the top of everyone's list. At any gathering of doctors, social or professional, the subject is likely to come up. The education of professionals about the law of malpractice is now a growth industry; indeed, the publication of this book is the result of concerns about malpractice. The intensity of feelings about the subject and the importance it now has threaten to overwhelm and dominate doctors' professional lives. **Otherwise conscientious health professionals can be heard seriously discussing what they must do to protect *themselves*, even when that protection involves some medically unnecessary discomfort, expense, or risk for the patient.**

What is it about malpractice that provokes such fear and loathing? The obvious answers are money considerations and threat to professional survival. Perception of a wider threat is involved, too, as more and more suits are brought and publicized. Statistically, physicians can all anticipate being sued. Nonphysician health care professionals are also experiencing increased exposure to malpractice suits. The monetary amounts involved in these cases seem to be rising astronomically—a deluge of million-dollar cases floods the courts. But more is involved.

There must be more involved than money and risk to reputation; something more terribly threatening must be part of the angst associated with this issue. Money is—only money. For example, physicians are notoriously casual about financial matters. Doctors reasonably expect a good income and expect it to continue. Physicians are thought of as more likely than other professionals to invest recklessly. Many doctors are not good businessmen, and with good reason—the doctor's training and psyche are not bent to business. The doctor who is clever and successful in business is unusual enough to stand out. Further, the monetary risk in Pennsylvania is limited. Insurance is generally still available, albeit expensive, and the patient compensation fund appears solid. Insurance above the fund's limit of $1 million is also available. Clearly, the malpractice insurance crisis as the decade of the 80s closes is less severe in the Commonwealth of Pennsylvania than in some other states. The risk of personal financial loss as a result of a malpractice judgment is basically no worse than it was 20 years ago.

The reputational injury associated with a malpractice case is not new either. Even in middle-sized communities, a surgeon not yet well-established whose patient dies under the knife can face the choice either of moving on or of needing a long time to live the death down. The practitioner whose patient gets an unexpected bad result receives damaging word-of-mouth publicity, regardless of the cause of the bad result.

Doctors are accustomed to functioning in high-risk situations. To a professional aware of the life-or-death nature of day-to-day decisions, does the risk of being sued add that much to the stress? Yes, being sued is personal, while the patient's death is his or her own. But only the most hardened and selfish healer fails completely to empathize. Most practitioners are affected by their patients' misfortunes, and many agonize over what could have been done differently.

Is there a mob psychology involved? Does the barrage of news on the subject beget its own fear? Is there a self-fulfilling prophesy at work? Perhaps, but health care professionals have an historical pattern of positive response to crisis. From the time of the great pioneer physicians, doing what they could during the plagues of previous centuries, to the AIDS epidemic of today, exposure to personal risk has been a part of the ethics of healing professions. The patient's best interests are of more importance to the practitioner than the practitioner's own interests. Not just during times of crisis, but in every routine clinical decision, it is the patient's needs against which the choice is made. The fear of a malpractice suit is the professional's own.

If indeed the response to the "malpractice crisis" is in any way overdone when compared with the obvious reasons for that response, then two explanations can be cited. These explanations involve the psychology of malpractice suits. **Being sued for malpractice strikes at the very heart of the healer's *raison d'etra.*** The threat of suit puts barriers and distance between the patient and the health professional and thus diminishes any secondary gains in the relationship.

A malpractice suit, or even the threat of a malpractice suit, necessarily involves a specific damning accusation. The patient or family member must necessarily accuse the doctor of causing an injury to the patient. Someone must allege that the patient is somehow worse off at the hands of the practitioner.

The accusation of negligence is there, too, the assertion that the doctor somehow did wrong. But most health professionals had to come to terms with the possibilities of judgment errors and imperfections during their training. We all must forgive ourselves our various shortcomings daily. What is hard to accept is that these shortcomings might actually hurt someone who has trusted us. Doctors have a strong aversion to considering even the possibility that their own negligence caused injury.

To any healer, the thought of injuring a patient is anathema. People daily make themselves vulnerable to their doctors; trust is necessary to the therapeutic relationship. The healer administers dangerous drugs, performs frightening surgery, and pronounces sentences of doom all in the patient's best interest. The justification for all of these horrors is that the patient will be bettered thereby. Health care professionals continually put their patients at risk of injury or death to avoid some grim possibility or to gain some clear advantage for the patient. It is not an exaggeration to say that acting to benefit the patient is not only the justification for the healer's interventions but also the meaning and heart of the profession. The claim that something the practitioner did or failed to do hurt the patient attacks this most basic of precepts.

The specter of malpractice inevitably raises barriers between the patient and the health professional. The specter is invoked, and the patient becomes a source of threat to the doctor. If something goes wrong, and sometimes even if it doesn't, the patient can sue, causing incredible grief and distress. No one can relate to the potential source of such a disaster without that potential affecting the relationship. To the patient, it's the doctor who stimulates the lawsuit by "malpracticing"; to the doctor, it's the patient who triggers the whole sequence by going to a lawyer.

Thus malpractice is more than just a monetary and reputational threat. A lawsuit for negligence strikes at the core of the health practitioner's professional existence. The fear of such a suit damages and even destroys the doctor's relationship with patients.

What is "malpractice"?

What is this horror that burdens not just society's healers, but society itself? What seemingly insane fate has created and perpetuated such a dread? Following the background information in this chapter, subsequent chapters of this book lay out the characteristics of malpractice in detail and with specificity for Pennsylvania. A preliminary general and brief review of how we got to where we are will help the reader to understand the nature of the beast and to gain a greater perspective on it.

Put simply, malpractice is the failure of a doctor to act like a reasonable doctor. It involves the lack of the necessary amount of skill and care, and through this lack or failing a patient is injured. How much skill and care is necessary? The technical answer is that amount of skill and care expected of a reasonable practitioner of the same school and specialty in the same or similar circumstances.[1] The practical, albeit circular, answer is that amount of skill and care that will keep you from losing a lawsuit. This practical answer indicates how lawyers look at the problem: is there some basis for a suit? is there some basis for defending against a suit?

History and rationale

Why do we as a society allow suits for medical malpractice? We not only allow them, we provide courts as a forum for deciding them and we provide means to enforce the resulting judgments. What is the justification for the legal system taking money from the practitioner and giving it to the patient?

Most doctors say that they could practice better medicine and take better care of patients if the plague of malpractice suits was lifted. Most plaintiff's lawyers say that malpractice is a necessary scourge to force health care practitioners to be careful, to do the right thing. But that is not the reason society provides courts and enforcement for malpractice plaintiffs.

Historically, courts grew as a means of extending governmental and religious authority and, importantly, as a means of dispute settlement. The more ancient methods of settling grievances were disruptive and dangerous. Shakespeare described it thus: "Two households, both alike in dignity, In fair Verona, where we lay our scene, From ancient grudge break to new mutiny, Where civil blood makes civil hands unclean."[2] Feud, vendetta, and dueling were all still practiced only a little over a century ago. Violent civil strife put the society at risk of injury to innocents and disrupted commerce.

Settling grievances between citizens was, even among tribal peoples, usually the prerogative and duty of the sovereign. Subordinates were delegated this responsibility and began to function as judges. In most cultures, judges strove for consistency, following precedent and deciding similar cases similarly. This predictability encouraged use of the courts for dispute settlement. When an individual or group felt itself aggrieved, courts were a means to redress.

In the eighteenth and nineteenth centuries, English judges consistently began to find a duty of care beyond that of the ordinary citizen toward his fellows. This higher duty was expected of those in whom special trust was placed and to whom people were vulnerable. In those days the duty was applied to common carriers, such as stagecoach operators, and to innkeepers. Out of this line of cases, as well the line of commercial contract cases, grew the early law of medical malpractice.

Historically, then, civil suits were promoted to discourage violent means of dispute resolution. Malpractice law developed from legal reasoning applied to those persons with special responsibilities. But what rationale, what justification, is there today for malpractice lawsuits?

The same policy considerations applicable to all negligence law are involved in medical malpractice. As a society, we do not wish to see persons who are innocent victims solely bear the burdens of their injuries. *Compensation* is the rationale for awarding money to the successful plaintiff in a lawsuit. The justification for taking that money from the unsuccessful defendant in a lawsuit is the fault, error, wrong, or negligence of the defendant. Although it seems not so to many doctors, ours is still a fault-based system of compensation. Lawyers ask, who should suffer the cost of the loss, the person who caused it or the victim? The degree of fault is not, at least theoretically, considered. A minor fault resulting in a major disaster still triggers all the liability for that outcome. Law school professors commonly cite the example of the hemophiliac as an individual who can be seriously harmed by a friendly intentioned slap on the back.[3] Despite those good intentions, suit can be brought for injuries from that slap, that unpermitted touching.

Although lawyers are not heard discussing it often, the same rules governing suits for professional negligence apply to nonmedical professionals. Of course, lawsuits against all types of health care providers follow the same legal procedures and are decided by the same legal (not medical) standards.[4] Architects, engineers, lawyers, and other professionals are all liable to negligence claims. Doctors have noted with glee the rise in rate of legal malpractice cases and legal malpractice premiums.

Medical malpractice case reporting

As the above historical review points out, statutes are not the only source of "law." Judges decide cases and their opinions are also a source of the law, giving precedent and instruction to subsequent judges and to lawyers.

But the published cases must be read with an understanding of why and how they are selected for publication. The formal legal reporting system focuses on appealed cases—not on trials. When deciding a case on appeal, the higher level courts (the "appeals" courts) often assume the truth of one side or the other's argument. This is because most legal challenges ask an appellate judge to reverse something that was decided previously. Often, the appellate judge can't do this unless there was an obvious error, abuse of judicial discretion, or no basis at all for the ruling of the trial (or lower appellate) court below. As a specific example, consider requests for reversals of a jury's verdict. The trial judge and the appellate court can be asked to review and change or throw out the jury's finding after a trial. The verdict has to be fatally flawed before it will be reversed. Because of the importance of trial by jury in our system, there must be something terribly illogical with the verdict before a judge will take the decision out of the jury's hands—such as when a jury decides that a doctor was not negligent but awards money to the patient anyway.

If the appeal claims a factual error, there must be no possible basis for the jury's decision before it will be changed. The jury's decision must have been flagrantly contrary to the evidence and an injustice must have been done before the trial judge or appellate court will reverse on the basis of a factual error. The reviewing court assumes and sometimes recites the evidence as favorably as possible in support of the decision below and only then examines the evidence. **Thus when the case is reported, it seems slanted.** Media reports, taken from case reports, don't often take this intentional bias into account. The report can look as if the doctor was terrible and did everything wrong, or as if the doctor was a saint and the claim was frivolous from the beginning.

Another reason for caution in reading case reports is the bias of whoever is doing the reporting. This hazard is obvious when two or more doctors are discussing lawsuits. Health professionals often get each other worked up, topping each other with horror stories of how unfair the system was in this or that case. Although it's less easy to recognize, published reports can also reflect the writer's strong prejudice.

The malpractice crisis

Although many doctors regard suits for professional negligence as a blight on only recent decades, the problem is not new. The Pennsylvania Supreme Court confronted its first medical malpractice case at least as far back as 1853.[5] At least one medical historian has concluded that we are in the second American medical malpractice crisis, the first occurring a century ago.[6]

No doctor—or other professional—will seriously contend that any profession is completely free of malpractice. But the extent and impact of medical malpractice as a cause of patient injuries have been grossly exaggerated in the public perception. Only a miniscule percentage of treatments result in malpractice complaints. Most complaints never become suits, and a high percentage of suits are won by doctor-defendants.[7] Nevertheless, patients are filing suits at a frenzied rate.

The crisis is one of availability of insurance

The increased frequency of medical malpractice suits and increased losses paid by medical malpractice insurers have been well documented.[8] In Pennsylvania, personal injury jury verdicts (not only medical malpractice) run higher than national averages.[9] Malpractice verdict awards tend to average 2 to 3 times the amount for other personal injury claims.

At one time, doctors paid little attention to a rise in incidence of malpractice claims. "That's why I have insurance," they'd retort. But insurance carriers have had to raise rates to shocking levels. Critics of the industry (often the plaintiff's bar) argue that companies are making record profits and have themselves created a crisis in order to be free to raise rates and to affect public policy.[10] But the reduced number of carriers writing malpractice coverage and the bankruptcy of a few companies are not feigned.

Industry analysts suggest that malpractice insurers were caught at the intersection of rising frequency and severity of claims, inadequate premiums and strong market share competition, and falling rates of return on investments. The AMA's own figures showed a shocking increase in number of annual malpractice claims per 100 physicians. In the region that includes Pennsylvania, the rise was more than fourfold.[11] The rise in jury awards disproportionately affected certain kinds of cases. One study showed that, over a 2-decade period, little or no increase occurred in median awards for comparable injury in cases of workplace injury, auto accident, injury on property, etc. However, for medical malpractice and product liability cases, a significant increase occurred.[12] Over one recent 10-year period, medical malpractice verdicts increased 475%![13]

While costs rose, insurance companies were caught with obligations created during a period of fierce competition for premium dollars. In the glory days of unprecedented high investment return rates, insurers could make a profit just by holding the premium for a few years, even if the entire premium was eventually paid out in losses. Losses totaling 105% and even 110% of premium income were acceptable. This opportunity sucked more players into the market and tempted companies to compete more aggressively by holding down premiums and lowering underwriting standards. But as the losses continued to skyrocket, the return on investment fell.[14] The insurers were caught. Doctor-owned and -oriented companies entered the market but soon found themselves having to assess big premium increases to make up lost ground caused by early ephemeral profit margins—margins that disappeared when claims began to come in.[15] Understandably, the number of carriers willing to take risks in this volatile market decreased, and the ones that stayed attempted to avoid high-risk practitioners.

Why here and now?

Most of the proffered explanations for the increased frequency of medical malpractice claims fall into two categories: public awareness and expectations and liberalized legal rules. It wasn't so long ago that death was understood to be the natural result of the mortal condition. Now, it seems to the harassed doctor, the first thought on the minds of patients and families whenever anything goes wrong is "Who's fault is it?" Health practitioners are both the beneficiaries and victims of the successes of modern health science. Even today, some patients revere doctors, in part because science can do so much more than even a generation ago. But these same miraculous advances have generated inflated public expectations. Patients and families are less inclined to accept passively heretofore routine occurrences as God's will or fate. The newly diagnosed cancer patient asks why it wasn't picked up earlier; the surgical patient with a less-than-perfect result asks if anything could have been done differently; the parents of the child with a congenital abnormality wonder if some drug caused the problem. There is a powerful motivation for these inquiries—money.

A factor that cannot be quantified, but should not be underestimated, is public awareness of the possibility of winning large verdicts in lawsuits. Each new case spawns others. Plaintiffs' lawyers are fond of publicity both during and after a case. Plaintiffs' lawyer groups spend vast resources in an effort to inform the public of their right to sue, a thinly disguised business promotion scheme. In every major city there are ads for legal services, often explicitly soliciting malpractice cases. If the patient or responsible family member hasn't been exposed to this relentless drumbeat of reminders, some friend or relative has and suggests a lawsuit.

Liberalization of the rules of law governing medical malpractice cases has substantially increased the opportunities for patients to win large amounts of money. Although Pennsylvania has not done so, many states have allowed experts from far away to testify as to a national standard of care. The statute of limitations—the time within which suit must be started—has been effectively lengthened by changing the beginning of that time. Instead of being figured from the time of the act, the statute of limitations is now figured from the time of discovery of the problem. Many legal reforms have enhanced access to courts, liberalized pleading requirements, fortified discovery procedures, and generally favored plaintiffs.

Many doctors point to lawyers as the reason for the medical malpractice problem, citing evidence such as the excessive number of attorneys graduating from law schools annually. While the number of hungry lawyers may play a role, the bar is at fault in another way: patients' legal representation has improved significantly. The huge contingency fees won by patients' lawyers have attracted some of the best lawyers into the field. These specialists, as well as the legal generalists who can catch a malpractice case, spend both their time and money unstintingly in pursuit of a victory. Ethical rules prohibiting advancing money to clients to pay for the expenses of the lawsuit have been changed, and successful firms maintain huge "war chests" to apply to new cases.

Reform efforts

Patient advocates as well as doctor partisans decry the current system, not just for unfairness but for ineffectiveness as well. Only 28 cents of the malpractice premium dollar get to injured patients; only 12.5 cents of that dollar reimburse the victim for economic losses not otherwise compensated.[16]

Efforts to reform the system in Pennsylvania have met with mixed success. The Health Claims Arbitration Act was declared unconstitutional, but the catastrophic Patient Compensation Fund was allowed.[17] Much more can be done. Tort reform should be on every doctor's mind at election time. Some of the potentially most helpful changes are the most likely ones to be aggressively combated by patient/plaintiff attorney groups. The sacred cows in the legal system are numerous.[18] For health care professionals and patient care advocates (who are concerned about what the malpractice problem is doing to health care delivery), the following are the areas of greatest concern and opportunity:

The legal system persists in allowing the contingent fee. Under this arrangement, an attorney typically receives 1/3 to 2/5 of an injured person's recovery. While this may have been necessary in the past when truly just cases were not pursued because the injured patient lacked resources, today we have approached the opposite extreme—truly frivolous cases are litigated. In the past, the percentage of cases won by patients at trial was much lower than today. The judge was more likely to reduce the occasional outrageous verdict, and the chances of collecting on these verdicts were fewer—insurance coverages were lower, and the individual doctor was less wealthy. Big rewards for the successful patient's lawyer seemed more justified under past conditions. Neither past nor present attorneys are anxious to work for nothing; ***attorneys take cases on because of their potential for income to themselves, not the relative merit of the patient's claim.*** Since the middle of the last century only lawyers in the United States have enjoyed the contingency fee. England, France, and most other countries consider it illegal and unethical.[19]

The legal system does not make a losing party pay a winning party's attorney fees. The American rule makes each party pay its own legal fees, win or lose, with very few exceptions. A change is needed and could be accomplished by legislation. If a doctor wins a claim brought against him by a patient, the doctor should be able to collect reasonable attorney fees from the patient (or from the patient's attorney, if the attorney is paying expenses for the patient). Likewise, if the patient wins, the patient should collect reasonable attorney fees from the doctor—reasonable, not contingency percentages. This change not only would make the contingent fee unnecessary but also would encourage patients and doctors to resolve meritorious cases equitably through settlement.[20]

The legal system discourages claims for malicious prosecution against a patient or his attorney for filing a case that is without merit or for filing carelessly or casually. As a practical matter, patients and their attorneys can file suits with virtual impunity. Pennsylvania law will allow recovery against a patient for bringing a case only if it can be shown that the patient brought suit for malicious reasons and that the physician had property seized or went to jail as a result.[21] The patients'/plaintiffs' bar feels that no harm comes from shaking the tree to see if something will fall out (such as a nice check for the claim's nuisance value). The damage to the doctor's reputation that results from frivolous suits goes without possibility of redress in the current system.

Damage awards are often excessive. To award a patient out-of-pocket expenses in a malpractice case, such as the cost of remedial surgery, is one thing, but to award exaggerated amounts for pain and suffering and the like is quite another. Possibly because insurance is available, litigants have developed and courts have allowed rather grandiose notions of the damages that should be paid to compensate a patient in medical malpractice cases.[22] Widespread publicity, encouraged by the plaintiffs' bar, makes "megaverdicts" more likely in subsequent cases.

The statute of limitations has been stretched too long. A troublesome fact for insurance companies and doctors is that the statute of limitations is open-ended regarding obscure causes of injury. Patients are expected to exercise reasonable diligence to discover the cause of injury, but if this requirement is satisfied, the time within which they must bring suit remains open. Some other states have retained the older rule of giving patients a limited period to sue from the time of the malpractice itself. Uncertainty and open-ended liability adds significantly to the costs of insuring Pennsylvania physicians.

The disease that health care providers must confront is the medical malpractice crisis. The disease is promoted and spread by a legal system that not only has encouraged unreasonable expectations of doctors but also excessively compensates injured patients. This book discusses in an informative and informed way the pathophysiology of the disease. The prophylaxis and treatment will be addressed. At the conclusion, the reader will be less fearful, better informed, and more prepared to meet and deal with the problem of medical malpractice.

Doctors and other health care providers can start to deal with the malpractice crisis and its attendant disruptions in four general ways:

- Repair and improve the doctor-patient relationship.
- Practice defensively in cognizance of the requirements that courts have placed on health care providers.
- Study and become familiar with malpractice law.
- Work for legislation to correct a flawed personal injury compensation system.

Our purpose in the following chapters is to provide doctors and other health care professionals with a basic, nonlegalistic overview of these topics. Of course, the medical malpractice crisis is of national scope, but our emphasis here is on Pennsylvania law. Many works are available that address the problem generally and on a national level—this book is a specific as possible about Pennsylvania. A bibliography is given in Chapter 8.

The organizational framework is itself an attempt to demonstrate a lawyer's approach to the subject. Exposure to this way of thinking may be provocative or even infuriating, but the framework reflects the facts. This is what is happening. It is what is happening in the courts of Pennsylvania. It is what could happen to you.

The basis of any negligence suit is an assertion of fault causing injury. Let's first focus on the fault. What is expected of doctors?

Endnotes

1. Donaldson v. Maffucci, 397 Pa. 548, 553-4, 156 A.2d 835, 838 (1959).
2. Prologue, Romeo and Juliet. In Act I, Scene 1 of the play, Prince Escalus stops the street fight between Capulet and Montague: "Rebellious subjects, enemies to peace, Profaners of this neighbor stained steel, . . . If ever you disturb our streets again, Your lives shall pay the forfeit of the peace."

3. This is referred to as the "thin skulled plaintiff" rule. Osteogenesis imperfecti might be a better example of such vulnerability.
4. For convenience, the terms *doctor* and *physician* are often used in this book. Almost everything contained herein has at least some applicability to all health care professionals. Also the masculine gender is used throughout, in the older style. Reference is meant to both men and women, and no disrespect is intended.
5. McCandless v. McWho, 22 Pa. 261 (1853).
6. Dale Smith, Ph.D., address at Suburban Hospital, Bethesda MD, August 26, 1987.
7. Gots, R.: The Truth About Medical Malpractice, 23, New York, 1975, Stein & Day. Previous publications have indicated a physician win rate of 75%, but these figures are probably out of date now. Most objective attorneys in the field agree that 50% is closer to the truth.
8. *See generally* United States General Accounting Office, *Medical Malpractice: Insurance Costs Increased but Varied Among Physicians and Hospitals* (1986). American Medical Association Special Task Force on Professional Liability and Insurance, *Professional Liability in the '80's: Report 1* at 7, citing Best's Insurance Management Reports (October 1984).
9. Personal Injury Verdict Survey, Penn. Ed., Jury Verdict Research, 1986. In 1986, Pennsylvania's personal injury verdicts were 5% above the U.S. average. When laid out against a national distribution curve, Pennsylvania's personal injury verdicts are within one standard deviation of the national median 51% of the time, 6% are below one standard deviation, and 43% are above. *Id.*
10. Rutigliano, J.: Insurance Crisis for Doctors? Fact, Fantasy, or Fiction? Trial **22**:28, 1986.
11. *Professional Liability Report 1*, at 15, American Medical Association (October 1984).
12. Peterson, Mark A., Compensation of Injuries: Civil Jury Verdicts in Cook County, Rand Report R-3011 ICJ, The Institute for Civil Justice, The Rand Corporation, 1984. All categories showed an increase when significant lost income was factored into the damages, but more so certain categories, including malpractice. Interestingly, malpractice verdicts for comparable injuries have, on the average in this study, consistently exceeded verdicts for product liability cases. Work-related injury cases were higher than malpractice verdicts for the same injury, but over the period of this study (1960s and 1970s) the relationship inverted, with malpractice verdicts higher at the end.
13. Derived from 'Current Award Trends,' p. 18, Jury Verdict Research, Solon, OH, January 1985.
14. Professional Liability Report 1, *supra* n. 10, at 7.
15. In 1984, for example, Pennsylvania's three leading carriers were Pennsylvania Medical Society Liability (29.6% of state's market), Phico (27.9%), and Med. Protective (19.4%). The previous year, premium increases for Pa. Med. Soc. Liab. and Phico were 30.8% and 26.1% respectively.
16. Jeffery O'Connell, address at the Urban Institute's conference: Medical Malpractice, Can the Private Sector Find Relief?, February 21, 1985.
17. 40 Pa. C.S.A. Sect. 1301 et seq. (Purdon 1986).
18. *See generally* AMA Special Task Force on Professional Liability and Insurance, *Professional Liability in the '80's: Report 3* at 11-14 (1985).
19. 71 ABA Journal at 38 (December 1985), comments of Grant P. DuBois. Older American legal ethics suggested the contingency fee only when the client truly could not afford a lawyer otherwise. Rules forbidding the patient's lawyer to pay expenses of a suit have only recently been eliminated.
20. When attorney fees are awarded to the winner, the attorney-client agreement regarding fees will usually not dictate the amount awarded. For example, a losing doctor would not be required to pay the fee produced by a contingency fee arrangement. Instead, a reasonable fee would be determined based on various factors, of which the time devoted to the case would be most significant. Cf. *Robak v. United States*, 658 F.2d 471 (1981). The rule whereby costs are paid to the winner without exception

for contingencies resulted in the horror of million-dollar verdicts with $400,000 in fees added. This situation existed in at least one state (Florida) until a recent rule change.

21. See Chapter 7 regarding suits for malicious prosecution.
22. See American Medical Association Special Task Force on Professional Liability and Insurance, *Professional Liability in the '80's: Report 1* at 12 (October 1984).

ELEMENTS OF MEDICAL MALPRACTICE CLAIMS

What's expected of doctors

2

Synopsis

Medical malpractice law is generally based on traditional tort law principles. Alternative theories, such as breach of contract, are seldom raised. Although it may seem to be a distinct area of law, malpractice should be viewed in the context of tort.

Broadly speaking, a tort is a civil or private wrong, other than breach of a contract, for which a court will provide a remedy in the form of an action for damages.[1] When the courts provide a remedy, someone can bring a lawsuit on that basis. Criminal law, unlike tort law, is concerned with the protection of interests common to the public at large, often exacting a penalty from the wrongdoer. Tort law compensates individuals, rather than the public, for losses suffered.[2]

Negligence theory of tort liability

Generally

Various tort liability theories exist. The lawyer must have a theory to bring a case to the court (and then prove all the required elements of that theory to win). In medical malpractice cases, negligence is usually the applicable tort theory. Unlike an intentional tort, such as assault and battery, negligence may be based on omissions or failures to act.[3] Negligence does not require that the doctor intended the result. Under some unusual circumstances, a doctor may be liable for an intentional tort, sued for money damages, and prosecuted for a criminal offense as well. In the typical case, however, the doctor can be sued only for money damages. Although the patient's lawyer may make allegations concerning the practitioner's intentions, all that need be proved is failure to meet the standard of care in malpractice cases.

The negligence theory in medical malpractice—as in other cases—requires that four elements be established:

- The health care provider who is sued must have incurred a duty to care for the patient—*a doctor-patient relationship.*
- The provider must have failed to perform or have breached that duty by deviating from the standard of care—*negligence.* The "negligent" act or omission is the heart of the legal theory of "negligence." With few exceptions, the standard of care must be established by the expert testimony of other health care providers.
- The patient must have been injured—*damages.*
- The negligence of the provider must be the reason for or proximate cause of the injury or damages—*causation.*

Duty: The doctor-patient relationship

The doctor's obligation to care for a patient arises by virtue of the doctor-patient relationship. A doctor has no duty or obligation to accept a patient.[4] However, once the doctor accepts the patient, a doctor-patient relationship exists, and the doctor has the duty to adhere to a certain level of care.

Duty is easily found in most malpractice cases. A physician-patient relationship can be established even casually and the doctor required to follow through on the patient's care. For example, a doctor examining a child injured at an athletic event has established a physician-patient relationship. Duty can also attach as a result of the health care provider holding himself out as available. The public's reasonable reliance on that availability will trigger the duty, such as that of an emergency department. In a case in another state, the making of an appointment established the relationship.[5]

Breach of duty: standard of care

The doctor who fails to provide the level of care required under the law will be liable for damages resulting to the patient. The level of care by which the doctor's conduct is measured is legally termed the *standard of care*. Violation of this standard establishes the second required element—negligence.

Generally, in tort law the standard of care by which a person's conduct is measured is "reasonable care" as exercised by a "reasonable person." When instructing a jury, courts try to elaborate on the characteristics of a "reasonable person" and what constitutes "reasonable care." In the end, however, the jury determines what a reasonable person would do under the circumstances of the case presented. Custom is relevant but is not determinative of whether "reasonable care" has been exercised. For example, the custom in a particular community may be to jaywalk. Yet a jury could (and probably should) find that a person is negligent when jaywalking.

In medicine, the standard of care by which a doctor's conduct is measured is somewhat different. While again "reasonable care" is the fundamental standard that must be met, it is the care as exercised by a "reasonable doctor." Generally, that standard is defined as constituting the skill and care customarily exercised by doctors in the same line of practice under similar circumstances. Application of the standard of care in a malpractice case should result in the doctor's care of a patient being compared with that customarily rendered by other doctors in the same situation. Furthermore, the practice to be compared has been limited to that of doctors in the same or at least a similar community within the state. This is known as the "locality rule." The locality rule derives from the notion that a doctor should be held to the standard of care existing in that doctor's own community. American courts developed this rule in the nineteenth century to protect the rural doctor, who was presumed to have less education and less access to facilities, equipment, and information than a doctor practicing in a large urban area.

The locality rule has been attacked as outmoded for a number of reasons. Some attorneys argue that application of the rule can deny an injured patient compensation even where the treatment was clearly negligent, because the treatment was consistent with the practices prevailing in a doctor's own community.[6] Attorneys (and at least one court) have said that an entire medical specialty may be negligent.[7] Some suggest that a "conspiracy" or "veil of silence" among doctors in a community could deny a patient the expert medical testimony essential to the case.[8] Attorneys complain that doctors' inherent peer empathy blinds them to peer negligence and that fear of "professional" retribution muzzles physicians able to see negligence. Finally, attorneys point out that because broad opportunities for continuing education are now available, doctors should be held to a similarly broad, even national, standard. Because of these and other criticisms of the locality rule, patients' attorneys have attempted to hold every doctor to a national standard, regardless of the area or facility where the doctor practices. In other words, a small-town doctor is supposed to exercise the same care as the most proficient doctor in a huge metropolitan center.

Pennsylvania's highest courts have not resolved the locality rule issue. At present, the standard applied to health care professionals in the Commonwealth is that of practitioners "in the same or similar locality. . . ."[9] This standard has been strictly construed. One case involved a witness excluded from testifying in a similarly sized Pennsylvania community, even though the two towns were only 22 miles apart.[10]

A federal court has predicted that Pennsylvania will change to a national standard, at least for specialists.[11] That court sensed an opening in a footnote to an earlier Pennsylvania Supreme Court opinion, which seemed to suggest that the locality rule might be reconsidered.[12] Thus a member of the American Academy of Family Practice may be held to a national standard and a noncertified generalist may not.

Under the same or similar locality rule, medical experts must be familiar with the practice in the locality (or a similar community) of the doctor sued before they can testify about the standard of care in a malpractice case. This is the cause of vitriolic attacks on the rule. Without the rule's limits, patients could bring in expert witnesses from anywhere to testify against Pennsylvania doctors. But the federal court case cited above indicates (1) that federal courts applying Pennsylvania law will likely use a national standard for specialists until told otherwise by a Pennsylvania court, and (2) that the rule might be changed to a national standard by Pennsylvania's own courts. Most states use a national standard.

To be on the safe side, if at all possible doctors should gear their practices to conform to what would be considered acceptable nationally, unless a higher local level of practice exists. Where doctors do not follow a practice that would be considered acceptable nationally, they must have a good reason for not doing so and document it.

Small-town practitioners must never let an attorney's appeal to professional vanity trap them into suggesting that they are as good as the most eminent metropolitan practitioner. The attorney will use this ploy to try and make a higher standard of care apply to the small-town doctor. The advantage of a locality rule should not be thoughtlessly sacrificed.

To establish the standard of care, a patient's attorney must usually present expert testimony.[13] This is done by asking experts hypothetical questions,[14] during which experts are asked to assume the facts presented in a case or that are reasonable inferences from the established facts.[15] The experts are then asked to express opinions based on these assumptions or upon the patient's records. The opinions state what is or is not within the standard of care for medical practice under the circumstances assumed.

What is this magical "standard" on which the law judges and the expert testifies? Much confusion exists, even within medicine, about the meaning of "standard of care." Some well-meaning physicians insist on only the very highest standards; others relate it to their own practices, exclusively. A few believe the phrase should apply to whatever was done with good intentions. But the standard of care is none of these.

The *standard of care* is a legal term of art, when used in a medical malpractice case. It has a stated meaning, but not an exact one. The legal definition is not dependant on common or idiosyncratic understandings, nor on lay dictionaries. In Pennsylvania, "standard of care" means the practitioner must "possess and employ in the treatment of a patient the skill and knowledge usually possessed by physicians in the same or a similar locality, giving due regard to the advanced state of the profession at the time of the treatment. . . ."[16] A specialist is held to a higher standard than a generalist.[17] Beyond this, an expert is permitted to testify about his or her opinion on whether or not the defendant acted within the skill and knowledge usually possessed.

Exceptions exist to the requirement of an expert testimony to establish medical malpractice.[18] One exception encompasses cases in which the doctor's conduct is considered so grossly negligent or the treatment provided is so common that a layman can evaluate it readily.[19] An example of this exception is a case involving sponges or instruments left in the patient's abdomen during surgery.[20] Another exception involves cases in which established instructions or rules are not followed. For example, the fact that a doctor did not follow a drug manufacturer's explicit instructions about the proper administration of a drug, or FDA indications, may be presented as evidence of negligence. Similarly, a doctor may be considered negligent in disregarding rules established by the hospital or clinic in which the doctor practices.[21]

The expert witness usually must be of and licensed in the same "school of medicine" as the allegedly negligent doctor.[22] This means that a medical doctor can testify about the standard of care of another medical doctor, but usually not to the standard of care of a chiropractor. The law thus recognizes different schools of medicine and does not favor one over another.[23]

This position is in keeping with Pennsylvania's strong adherence to the "two schools of thought" doctrine. In this Commonwealth, the jury in a malpractice case is instructed that where experts differ, the jury can find both of differing methods or responses proper.[24] Although intuitively obvious, this rule has been described as "the bane of the plaintiff's medical malpractice bar."[25]

The judge decides whether or not to allow an expert to testify based on the witness' background and qualifications.[26] But the impact of that testimony, the "weight" it is given, is up to the jury.[27] The expert's opinion is opinion; it should not be regarded as ultimately conclusive.[28]

Breach of duty: Theories of liability

The doctor who has a duty to a patient will be negligent if he or she violates or breaches that duty. Attorneys describe violations of a doctor's duty by various theories of liability or causes of action; these are the forms medical malpractice may take, and they are discussed in detail in Chapter 3.

Although many patients equate bad medical results with breach of the standard of care, it is important to recognize that merely showing a bad result is not proof of malpractice.[29] A patient must demonstrate that the doctor did not do what the average, reasonable doctor in good standing, practicing in the same or a similar community, would have done in a similar case. Proof of a bad result or a mishap does not equate with a lack of skill or negligence. If a doctor has given a patient the benefit of his best judgment—assuming that judgment conforms to that ordinarily used by reasonably well-qualified doctors in similar cases—no legal negligence exists, even if that judgment is mistaken.[30]

The Pennsylvania Supreme Court also has recognized that malpractice is not demonstrated just because a patient shows that another doctor would have acted differently from the doctor sued.[31] Rather, medicine is a profession that involves the exercise of individual judgment within the framework of established procedures. Differences in opinion may, in fact, indicate that more than one response to a clinical situation meets the applicable standard of care.[32]

Damages

To recover damages in a malpractice case the patient must have incurred an injury. Mistake without injury is no more compensable than a bad outcome without fault. Although *damage* is sometimes used to refer to the injury, the term in law properly refers to the amount sought or awarded for the injury. Damages are the pecuniary or money compensation given to pay the patient for the losses suffered.

Several types of damages exist. Common categories include:

- General damages. These are the necessary and logical consequence of a particular injury. The law presumes they exist with only limited proof. For example, it generally follows that the patient having a surgical instrument removed in a second operation will have some additional pain and suffering as a result. That pain and suffering constitute a general damage. General damages usually include physical and mental disability, loss of enjoyment of life, and pain and suffering.[33]
- Special damages. These are a natural result of an injury but do not inevitably result from it; they require detailed proof. For example, if a surgeon leaves an instrument in a patient, the patient will incur the costs of having another operation to remove the instrument. The cost

of that additional operation is a special damage. Special damages have traditionally included loss of time; impairment of future earning capacity, hospital, medical, and nursery expenses; the cost of drugs; and aggravation of a preexisting condition.[34]

- Compensatory damages. This is a term that may include special and general damages, which are categories of compensatory damages. The term simply refers to any money intended to restore the patient to the position occupied before the occurrence of the injury complained of or to compensate the person for the loss.
- Punitive or exemplary damages. These are damages designed to punish a person sued and to deter others from similar conduct.[35] They are over and above the damages to compensate a person for his loss and are commonly awarded in cases of intentional torts. They are an anomaly in negligence, a system otherwise intended to compensate. A claim of punitive damages can raise special concern for a person who is sued because insurance to cover punitive damages may not be included in the policy. The risk also exists that a court might disallow insurance coverage of a punitive damage award as contrary to public policy. If insurance paid an award, it would defeat the avowed purpose of punitive damages.

"Pain and suffering" is typically a substantial element of damages in medical malpractice awards.[36] Patients almost always demand it as part of their claim.[37] This element has two aspects: "pain," which is often equated with physical or physiological body processes and is said to involve the specific perception of different forms of stimulation intense enough to injure the body at least minimally or transiently[38]; and "suffering," which is essentially mental anguish and includes worry, concern, grief, humiliation, embarrassment, depression, and other unpleasant mental reactions.[39] Examples include the pain and suffering associated with deafness or partial paraplegia following a postlaminectomy infection[40] and mental distress caused to the parents of a child born with neurofibromatosis.[41]

Causation

It is not enough for a patient to show a breach of the standard of care and injury. The patient must also establish that the doctor's breach proximately caused the injuries. If the doctor's treatment or lack of treatment did not cause the patient's injury, the doctor is not liable.

To win, a medical malpractice plaintiff must prove a "direct causal link" between the alleged negligence and the harm suffered.[42] "Proximate cause" is another legal term of art. The Pennsylvania Supreme Court explained it to mean the point at which legal responsibility attaches for harm done to another person.[43] The causal connection can be established by evidence that the negligence was a "substantial factor in bringing about" the injury.[44]

When doctors consider the "cause" of something, they usually think in scientific or absolute terms. Something either was or was not the cause. But as the Court's explanation above indicates, the law requires much less to establish causation. A patient does not need to show that a doctor's malpractice was the sole or only cause of injury.[45] The patient need only demonstrate that the doctor's action or inaction more probably than not caused the injury.[46]

Experts are usually asked to express an opinion on causation, as well as whether or not the standard of care was met. Generally, the expert is asked to testify to "reasonable medical certainty" regarding the causal connection between asserted negligence and injury.[47] Speculation is not permitted; absolute scientific certainty is not required. The jury is asked to decide causation by the measure of "more probably than not," but the expert must be more certain.

Causation can be shown by proof that the defendant negligently terminated the patient's chances for survival:

Example

Kenneth Hamil's wife called the hospital late at night to say that her husband had severe chest pains. The supervisor had her bring him in right away. However, the electrocardiograph wouldn't work and a second machine couldn't be found. Mrs. Hamil took her husband to a physician's office, where he died while an ECG was being taken. The estate sued the hospital and the doctor ordering the ECG at the hospital.

At trial, the plaintiff's expert testified that Mr. Hamil had a 75% chance of survival if admitted and treated. He did not testify that the negligence, to a reasonable degree of medical certainty, caused the death. The defendants asked for and received a directed verdict in their favor because cause had not been established.

The Pennsylvania Supreme Court, on appeal, said that the jury should have been allowed to decide the case. If there was any substantial possibility of survival and the defendant destroyed it, he is answerable, the Court said. Evidence of causation "to a reasonable degree of medical certainty" was unnecessary.[48]

Summary statement of theory

To recover in a medical malpractice case, the patient, using expert testimony, must establish the standard of care against which the doctor's conduct is measured. The patient must then prove that the doctor deviated from and fell below that standard and that this deviation caused the injury or damage to the patient.[49]

Breach of contract

Medical malpractice claims most often are brought in the context of tort law. However, a contract theory sometimes is raised. Under this theory a patient argues that a contract existed with the doctor for care, in return for which the patient paid the fee. By failing to competently care for him, the doctor is said to have violated or breached that contract. The patient then seeks damages. Because damages are normally more limited under contract law than tort law, breach of contract claims are usually raised merely as an additional or alternative theory of relief.[50] Parties are free to contract for a specific result and must be cautious to avoid this trap.[51]

Endnotes

1. Keeton, W.: Prosser and Keeton on the Law of Torts (ed.5) at 2, St. Paul, Minn., 1984, West Publishing Co.
2. *Id.* at 5-6. Punitive damages are, of course, an exception to these policy considerations. See below, Punitive or Exemplary damages.
3. *Id.* at 160.
4. Craddock v. Gross, 504 A.2d 1300, 1302 (Pa.Super. 1986). Not so in civil law countries, however. Under the common law in England and in the United States, there is no basic duty to treat. Regardless of the ethics involved, one cannot be successfully sued for failure to aid someone to whom one owes no duty.
5. Lyons v. Grether, 218 Va. 630, 632-4, 239 S.E. 2d 103, 105 (1977).
6. The standard is not determined only by what is done or common practice. Davis v. Kerr, 239 Pa. 351, 358 86 A. 1007, 1010 (1913). But "(w)hat usually is done may be evidence of what ought to be done,. . ." Texas & Pacific R. Co. v. Behyer, 189 U.S. 468, 470 (1903). Opinion by Holmes, J. But most often quoted is Judge Learned Hand: "(I)n most cases reasonable prudence is in fact common prudence; but strictly it is never the measure; a whole calling may have unduly lagged in the adoption of new and available devices. It never may set its own tests, however persuasive be its usages. Courts must in the end say what is required; there are precautions so imperative that even their universal disregard will not excuse their omission." The T.J. Hooper, 60 F. 2d 737, 740 (2CA 1932).
7. Helling v. Carey, 83 Wash.2d 514, 518-9, 519 P.2d 981, 983 (1974). Gates v. Jensen, 92 Wash.2d 246, 253-4, 595 P.2d 919, 924 (1979).
8. Belli, An Ancient Therapy Still Applied: The Silent Medical Treatment, 1 Vill.L.Rev. 250 (1956).
9. Donaldson v. Maffucci, 397 Pa. 548, 554, A.2d (1959).
10. Fala, The Law of Medical Malpractice in Pennsylvania, U.Pitt.L.R. 203, 212 (1974), citing Arnold v. Koehler, 39 Wash. 19 (Pa.Comm.Pl. 1958).
11. Kubrick v. U.S., 435 F.Supp 166, 188, aff. on other gnds., 581 F.2d 1092, rev. on other gnds., 444 U.S. 111, remanded 614 F.2d 770 (1977). The Federal District Court interpreted earlier cases as requiring a "similar" location standard for generalists. *Id.*, citing Donaldson, above n.9.
12. Incollingo v. Ewing, 444 Pa 263, 276 n.6, 282 A.2d. 214 n.59 (1971). It is unusual for a court's opinion to point out what it is not saying. From such miniscule germinations, mighty growths of change in the law have sprung.
13. Brannan v. Lankenau Hospital, 490 Pa. 588, 417 A.2d 196, 199-200 (1980).
14. Ranieli v. Mutual Life Ins. Co. of America, 271 Pa.Super. 261, 413 A.2d 396, 398 (1979).
15. These facts must be "established", or offered in evidence, already—prior to being presented to the expert, or the parties must have agreed or "stipulated" to them.
16. Donaldson, supra n.9, at 397 Pa. 553-4, 156 A.2d 839.
17. Pratt v. Stein, 298 Pa.Super. 92, 444 A.2d 647, 708 (1982).

18. *See generally* Chapter 4, regarding ways through which a plaintiff may avoid the need for expert testimony.
19. James v. Harrisburg Polyclinic Hospital, 496 Pa. 465,470-4, 437 A.2d 1134, 1136-9 (1981).
20. Davis v. Kerr, 289 Pa. 351, 355-8, 86 A. 1007, 1009-10 (1919). Long before the Pennsylvania Supreme Court explicitly applied res ipsa loquitur to medical malpractice, it shifted the burden of proof to defendant in a retained gauze pad case.
21. These written standards can substitute for expert testimony to establish the proper standard of care.
22. McHugh v. Audet, 72 F.Supp 394, 399 (1947).
23. For example: A case against a dentist: McCartney v. Hyman, 134 Pa.Super 524, 4 A.2d 581, standard of "his profession" applied, 584, but a physician allowed to testified that dentists are competent to treat mouth infections, 584 (1939). A case involving a nurse: Baur v. Mesta Mach. Co., 405 Pa. 617, applies "prudent nurse" test, 621, but a physician allowed to testify as to that standard and that it was not met, 625-6, 176 A.2d 648, 687, 687-9 (1961).
24. Furey v. Thomas Jefferson University Hospital, 325 Pa.Super. 212, 472 A.2d 1083, 1089-90 (1984).
25. Farage and McBride, Tort Law, 56 Pa.B.A.Q. 1, 35 (Jan. 1985).
26. Long v. Frank, 14 Leb. 118 (Pa.Com.Pl. 1972). Taylor v. Spencer Hosp., 222 Pa.Super. 17, 292 A.2d 449, 452 (1972).
27. In re Jones, 432 Pa. 44, 50, 246 A.2d 356, 361 (1968).
28. See Chap. 7, infra, for the procedure involved.
29. Salis v. U.S., 522 F.Supp 989, 994 (D.C.Pa. 1981). But this doctrine is under attack by attornies who argue that infrequent bad results should allow an inference of negligence, i.e. that rarity suggests impropriety. Fala, supra n.10, at 225-8.
30. Smith v. Yohe, 412 Pa. 94, 98, 194 A.2d 167, 170 (1963).
31. Hodgson v. Bigelow, 335 Pa. 497, 504, 7 A.2d 338, 435 (1939).
32. Trent v. Trotman, 508 A.2d 580, 584-5 (Pa. Sup. 1986).
33. Louissell, D., Williams, H., and Kalisch, J.: Medical malpractice at 18.03, New York, Matthew Bender & Company, Inc.
34. *Id.*
35. Medvecz v. Choi, 569 F.2d 1221, 1227 (3CA 1977). Even when punitive damages can be sought in medical malpractice cases, they are seldom awarded. The primary reason attorneys claim them is to terrify the defendant. They also expand the scope of information that the patient's attorney can obtain before trial or present at trial. When punitive damages are sought, for example, the attorney can force the doctor to disclose his income tax returns and assets because the financial resources of the doctor would be relevant in determining just how much in punitive damages should be awarded to assure that the award was enough to "punish" the doctor.
36. In Pennsylvania, there must be a physical injury or physical manifestation of the emotional injury before the plaintiff can recover this form of damages. c.f., Boarts v. McCord, 511 A.2d 204, 208-9, citing Restatement of Torts Sect. 436A.
37. In the 1986 GAO survey, size of pain and suffering awards were identified as excessive by a majority of professional provider groups surveyed. Further indication of this concern appeared in the identification of another major problem—awards/settlements were thought excessive in relation to economic costs arising from the injuries. Medical malpractice, No Agreement on the Problems or Solutions, GAO/HRD-86-50, Feb. 1986.
38. Louisell, supra n. 33.
39. *Id.*
40. Pratt v. Stein, 298 Pa.Super. 92, 444 A.2d 674, 699 (1982). Verdict for $1M included only $294K in "real" losses.
41. Speck v. Finegold, 497 Pa. 77, 80, 439 A.2d 110, 111-2 (1981).
42. Salis, supra n. 29, at 995.
43. Hamil v. Bashline, 481 Pa. 256, 264-66, 392 A.2d 1280, 1284 (1978).
44. *Id.*
45. Reichman v. Wallach, 306 Pa.Super. 177, 452 A.2d 501, (1982).

46. Hamil, supra, n. 38, at 1284-5.
47. McMahon v. Young, 442 Pa. 484, 486, 276 A.2d 534, 535 (1971). The court can permit one expert to dispute another without doing so by reasonable medical certainty. Erkens v. Tredennick, 509 A.2d 424, 426 (Pa.Sup.Ct. 1986).
48. Adapted from Hamil, supra, n. 38. The proper way to deal fairly with the fact that Mr. Hamil was a very sick man when he arrived at the hospital was through the damages. He was deprived of the life span of a man his age with heart disease, not a healthy man his age.
49. Titchnell v. U.S., 681 F.2d 165, 166 (3CA 1982).
50. A contract theory traditionally has been used to avoid a problem with the statute of limitations. The statute of limitations for medical malpractice cases is 2 years in Pennsylvania, while the statute of limitations for contracts is 6 years. *See* 42 Pa.C.S.A. Sect. 5524.
51. Shaheen v. Knight, 11 Pa.D&C.2d 41, 44 (Comm.Pl. 1957). When a result has been guaranteed, a contract theory might be used to avoid the necessity of an expert witness. *See* Chapter 3, regarding the need of expert witnesses in medical malpractice cases. With HMO's, IPA's, PPO's, and OWA's (Other Weird Arrangements) becoming more prevalent, contract theories may resurface in malpractice cases. It is a particular problem in operations to sterilize—surgeons must be careful to avoid the implication that there is a contract to produce sterility.

FORMS OF MEDICAL MALPRACTICE

Why doctors are sued

3

Synopsis

Defensive Medicine

Consent
- Assault and Battery: The General Consent Requirement
- Informed Consent
- Consent by or for Minors
- Living Will Declarations
- Unauthorized Postmortem Procedures

Diagnosis
- Misdiagnosis
- Delayed Diagnosis
- Failure to Refer
- Negligent Referral

Treatment
- Negligent Treatment
- Delayed Treatment
- Refusal to Treat
- Guaranteed Results and Warranties

Medical malpractice is conduct that falls below the standard of care, but this statement means little in the abstract. Thus doctors should be aware of the *forms* that medical malpractice usually takes. Attorneys often refer to each form as a "cause of action." These are informal categories of accusations made against the practitioner. Lawyers think in these terms and categories. A patient has a cause of action if facts and circumstances exist that theoretically establish a right to recover damages from a doctor. Facts that fit a particular form give the patient a chance to win. Very simply, and from a legal viewpoint, the forms of medical malpractice are why doctors are sued.

Defensive medicine

In reading about and considering the forms of medical malpractice, doctors should ponder what "defensive medicine" techniques can be adopted to avoid medical malpractice claims or to establish that care was not negligent. Although some people criticize the idea of defensive medicine, most doctors consider it a matter of "survival medicine"; doctors must practice this type of medicine to survive the legalities of current practice. This is not to suggest that patients need be put through medically unnecessary tests or treatments or to suggest that medically needed care be shunned for fear of suit. Throughout this chapter, readers should consider what they can do, consistent with the best medical ethics, to protect themselves, their fellow professionals, and their institutions. In Chapter 8, we offer suggestions for defensive medicine that parallel this discussion of the forms of medical malpractice, pointing out precautions that cost the patient nothing extra and add no risk of injury to the patient's medically indicated course.

Consent

Assault and battery: The general consent requirement

No physician may touch or have contact with a patient, such as during a surgical procedure, without receiving a proper consent.[1] A physician who touches or has contact with a patient without consent has committed battery.

Assault and battery are often expressed as linked torts. However, a doctor is very seldom accused of assault in connection with his medical practice. Assault ordinarily refers to the *apprehension* of touching or contact; battery refers to the touching or contact itself. To establish battery, a patient does not need to establish that the doctor intended harm. In fact, the doctor may have actually helped the patient. The basis of the action is merely failure to obtain consent.

Example

Irene Cooper's x-rays showed a suspicious filling defect in the wall of her hiatal hernia. Her physician recommended a gastroscopic examination and arranged for a consultant. Even though she had signed a blanket general consent form, both her attending physician and the consultant described the procedure. Ms. Cooper was not warned of collateral risks and was assured that the examination was a simple procedure and that there "should not be any trouble with it."

The flexible fiber gastroscope had then only been in use 5 years. Throughout those 5 years, there had been no reported perforations with the scope. The physician had used it 250 times without a problem.

Ms. Cooper began complaining of pain about 6 hours after gastroscopy. Emergency surgery was required to close the gastric perforation. Ms. Cooper recovered to bring suit against her attending physician and the consultant. There was no claim of negligent performance of the procedure, and the parties all agreed that the scope had caused the perforation. Ms. Cooper asserted that her consent had not been informed. At trial, there was testimony that the doctors gave good informed consent counseling, by medical professional standards. The judge told the jury the issue was: what would a reasonable medical practitioner do? The physicians won. Ms. Cooper appealed, claiming that the proper standard in Pennsylvania is: what would a reasonable patient need to know? The appeals court agreed and ordered a new trial. The court said expert testimony on informed consent issues wasn't needed. "(T)he primary interest in Pennsylvania jurisprudence in regard to informed consent is that of having the patient informed of all the material facts from which he can make an intelligent choice as to his course of treatment, regardless of whether he, in fact, chooses rationally."[2]

The case above also illustrates the importance of battery and informed consent lawsuits to the practitioner. Even if the procedure is indicated and properly performed, lack of consent can make the physician liable for injuries from complications—or even the normal sequelae—of the procedure. The patient gets a chance to convince the jury that a reasonable patient might not have had the procedure if there had been adequate disclosure.

Required consent may be given in several ways. It may be expressed in writing or in words. It can be implied by either the patient's behavior or the urgency of the situation.

- ***Expressed verbal or oral consent*** is a patient's articulated permission given verbally and not in writing. This consent is common in nonsurgical situations with rare, minor associated risks. A patient may say, "Doctor, would you check my blood pressure?" Or the doctor may say, "I need to examine you now," with the patient responding, "Fine."[3]
- ***Expressed written consent*** is a patient's authorization given in writing.[4] It is common in surgical situations or when other than routine treatment is provided. With the development of the informed consent doctrine, written consent has become common. Hospitals routinely require written consent on admission.
- ***Implied or assumed consent by the circumstances or behavior of the patient*** is consent that is not expressed but is presumed to exist by virtue of the facts or the actions of the patient. For example, if a doctor tells a patient, "I would like to examine your shoulder" and the patient removes his shirt without saying a word, it is reasonable to imply or assume that the patient has consented to the examination. Similarly, a patient who comes to the office complaining of a sore throat is requesting diagnosis and treatment. The doctor may touch the patient, do appropriate laboratory tests and, in the doctor's best judgment, give appropriate medication, both oral and intramuscular. Consent is implied or assumed if the patient does not object to what is being done.[5]

The issue of extent of consent is handled similarly regardless of form. If no limits are expressed, the physician may do what is necessary under the circumstances to effectuate the consented treatment.[6] But "blanket" consents, such as those signed on hospital admission, are not limitless in effect.[7] A new consent should be obtained for each new procedure.[8] Battery actions have been maintained in other states for removal of an organ incidental to a consented operation.[9]

- ***Implied or assumed consent by the facts, and in law,*** is consent that is not expressed but that the law presumes the patient would give, if able, for the treatment or surgery. The best example of this is emergency treatment or surgery. A patient's consent is thus not required when an emergency exists, either before or during treatment or surgery. However, the extent of therapy allowed under this exception to the consent requirement is limited to that necessary to deal with the emergency. Some sense of urgency must be involved. In one such case, the trial judge instructed the jury on the absence of the need for consent. He explained the general principle of the emergency exception and told the jury that they would have to "conclude that an **immediate** (emphasis in original) operation was necessary to save Mrs. Sipling's life or health, before this exception would be applicable."[10]

A patient usually may decline treatment even if that refusal is ill-advised. Courts have permitted patients to refuse not only treatment that would delay death but also treatment the absence of which would result in immediate death.[11] The patient must be capable of making the decision and informed of the risks of refusal. Refusal itself is not necessarily proof of diminished mental capacity.

Religion is often the basis for refusal of treatment.[12] Jehovah's Witnesses, for example, typically refuse to accept blood and blood products.[13] Christian Scientists may not seek treatment at all from a medical doctor. Patients may also refuse treatment for a variety of other reasons. If a patient declines recommended treatment of any sort, the doctor's record should state that treatment was refused and, ideally, should include a written waiver signed by the patient. The notation should state that the patient was advised of the consequences and that the patient's ability to recognize and appreciate these consequences was not impaired.

If the patient is not able to consent, a common practice is to have the patient's next of kin or whoever accompanies the patient consent to health care. This practice is advisable because it assures that the next of kin present has no objection to the health care being provided and that the circumstances require treatment. From a legal persepective, however, a person may not give valid consent for another without being authorized to do so. The most common examples of another person having legal authority to consent are cases in which a person is the patient's personal guardian or has power of attorney.

If the doctor doubts the competency of the patient refusing treatment, an effort may be made to have a personal guardian appointed for the patient with authority to consent to treatment. This particularly may be appropriate when nonroutine care or serious surgery is involved. It is unnecessary in emergencies. A doctor can ask a relative or friend of the patient to initiate guardianship or other proceedings.

Guardianship can be appropriate where mental, not physical, incapacity is present.[14] The court on "good cause" may appoint a guardian,[15] but the guardian's power to authorize treatment is still subject to the court's oversight.

Example

A 25-year-old girl's father went before the court requesting appointment as her legal guardian. He wanted to have her sterilized. The family physician testified that the girl was retarded and that her IQ was said to be 38. The father indicated that she had had an illegitimate child and was "the object of designing men." The lower court granted the father's petition.

On appeal, the Superior Court pointed to the Commonwealth's duty to protect its weaker members. Parents and guardians, it said, can't authorize sterilization without judicial permission. That permission should not be granted without clear and convincing evidence that sterilization is in the individual's best interest, regardless of society's interests.[16]

Where a patient's consent is required, the patient usually gives it himself. However, a patient may authorize another person—an agent—to consent to health care. To do so, patients execute "powers of attorney." Authorization of treatment is one of statutorily listed powers which may be specified for the attorney-in-fact.[17] Pennsylvania has joined other states making powers of attorney particularly useful because they are valid and binding even if the person granting them becomes sick or disabled.[18] The transfer of decision-making authority is "durable." This statute may avoid the need of a guardianship procedure for persons who have powers of attorney—someone is empowered to act without court approval. Without this statute (and as is the case in many states), powers of attorney cease to be valid if a patient becomes incompetent.

Authority to consent to health care is a power specifically and expressly granted in some forms of powers of attorney, but it usually will come within the scope of most forms even more generally written. If a patient has appointed an agent, the power of attorney should be carefully reviewed to determine the agent's authority, and a photocopy should be kept in the patient's file. The patient's personal consent also should be obtained whenever possible.

A court also has general authority to allow treatment and to direct that a patient submit to treatment even if the person is competent. Thus if special circumstances exist, such as when an individual's death would injure third parties (for example, by depriving minor children of a parent), courts have held that life-preserving treatment may not be refused.[19] A court may also allow treatment and direct that a patient submit to treatment where required by statute.[20]

Informed consent

A physician has a duty to inform the patient, in ordinary, understandable language, of the nature of the patient's ailment or condition, the risks and results of the proposed treatment or procedure, and the risks and results of any reasonable alternative methods of treatment, including failing to undergo any treatment at all. The adequacy of the consent hinges upon what a reasonable patient, in that patient's circumstances, would need to know.[21] This knowledge enables the patient to make an informed and intelligent decision on whether to submit to a proposed course of treatment or surgical procedure.[22] A doctor seeking a patient's consent should give the patient the opportunity to ask questions and should respond to the patient's concerns.

The requirement of an informed consent developed from the law of battery—an unpermitted touching. Initially, for example, courts would find that battery occurred even if "consent" was given, if that consent was given before the doctor had informed the patient of the risks involved in treatment or surgery. However, beginning around 1960 many courts recognized obtaining consent as one of the standards of professional conduct, so negligence and the informed consent doctrine generally displaced battery as the basis for liability.[23]

The informed consent doctrine is significant because if such consent is not obtained, a doctor can be liable for any adverse consequences of a procedure even if the procedure was appropriate and performed in a manner consistent with the applicable standard of care. Stated otherwise, a doctor is not negligent just because the outcome of a procedure is bad. However, if an informed consent is not obtained, the doctor will be liable for the bad outcome even though not negligent.

In Pennsylvania, expert medical testimony need not be presented to establish what should be explained when lack of informed consent is claimed.[24] A doctor has a duty to disclose those risks, results, or alternatives that a reasonable patient in the same or similar circumstances would have deemed significant in making a decision to consent.[25] Of course, once a rare complication results, it looms large and obvious in a jury's awareness. The doctor may also be caught on the horns of a dilemma in defending a suit for a rare complication: if the event was so unusual, doesn't that suggest negligence? if the event is one of those things that "just happens," why wasn't the patient warned of it?

As a general rule of thumb, risks of death and serious bodily harm or disfigurement should be disclosed unless there is some compelling reason not to do so. Minor complications that occur more often than 5% of the time should be explained. The more serious risks should be disclosed even if they are uncommon.

Cases in other jurisdictions have indicated that both commonly known and remote risks need not be disclosed. The difficulty is, of course, in the general nature of these exceptions.[26] The doctor relying on these exceptions takes the risk that a jury will disagree about what is "remote" or "common".

Two other exceptions to the need for informed consent should be mentioned: the patient's refusal and the "therapeutic privilege." Some patients may not want to know all the awful possibilities; they can refuse to receive the information or indicate that they wish to be treated regardless. It is prudent to document more carefully in these situations and to obtain a witness not just to the signing but also to the statement of the patient. Doctors will at times be concerned about the health effects of a thorough informed consent. A patient's condition may relatively contraindicate detailed information and cause the physician to wish to exercise a "therapeutic privilege" to withhold information. Although perhaps sound medically, such withholding is hazardous legally. The law requires full disclosure. A physician who wishes to withhold information because of the patient's condition should take all possible precautions.[27] Some authorities have suggested that a family member be involved in these situations and informed, but this response raises confidentiality issues.

Informed consent in medical practice is under increased scrutiny in an era of rampant consumerism. According to one sociologist medical patients "are more often bullied than informed into consent."[28] It is important to remember that an adult, competent patient has the right to refuse treatment or surgery even if that refusal is tantamount to suicide. There is something almost natural about a sick patient deferring to the wishes of his doctor.[29] Defensively, a doctor must make certain that the decision to agree or to decline treatment or surgery is the patient's not the doctor's. Pennsylvania's courts are straightforward about this: "Such informed consent is required of patients, absent an emergency, prior to a surgical operation."[30] The courts have, however, refused to extend the doctrine to cases involving drug administration.[31]

Consent by or for minors

Except for emergency treatment and first aid, minors cannot consent for their own care.

With a few exceptions, this is still true.[32] Ancient law regarded children as the property of their parents. Modern justifications for the policy include the presumed insufficient judgment of a child and the legal incapacity of children to enter contractual relations.

Under certain circumstances the law extends legal competency to minors. A person may consent to medical treatment or surgery although under 18 years of age and a minor if he or she is "emancipated," i.e., is married, has been pregnant, or is a high school graduate.[33] The statutes provide for other exceptions. A minor may consent to treatment of pregnancy, venereal disease, or any other reportable disease.[34] A minor parent also may consent to treatment of his or her own child.[35]

The most important exception to the rule against treatment of minors without consent is the emergency situation. Even without statutory grant, courts have recognized this exception.[36] Pennsylvania's legislature codified this rule to permit the physician to treat if in his judgment delay would endanger the life or health of the minor.[37]

The area of birth control services for minors is clearly a major concern to much of the public. The pro- and anti-abortion forces have focused on legislation in this area, and Pennsylvania has had its share of nationally prominent cases. A state statute requiring protection of a viable fetus and penalizing doctors who misjudged viability was struck down by the U.S. Supreme Court.[38] A law forbidding state funding of abortions except when the life or health of the mother was endangered was enjoined.[39] Especially applicable to minors was a provision requiring parental consent for abortion; it was also declared unconstitutional.[40]

If a minor is unable legally to consent to treatment or surgery, the consent of a parent or legal guardian is required. Even if a minor can legally consent, it is advisable to obtain the consent of a parent or legal guardian if the child's treatment would not thereby be jeopardized or if confidentiality would not be violated.

Parents are the natural custodians and guardians of their children. As such, a parent generally has authority to consent to the child's treatment or surgery. If the parents are divorced, the custody of a child may be placed with either or both parents. If custody is granted to one parent, that parent has total control of a child's health care unless the parents otherwise agree or the court granting the divorce otherwise directs.[41]

Shared custody is an order awarding shared legal and/or physical custody, which assures the child of frequent and continuing contact with both parents. If shared custody is granted, the parents are to agree or the court is to determine the rights and responsibilities of the parents for the physical care of the child, including health care.[42] Unfortunately, too many agreements and court determinations are vague or simply state that decisions will be made "jointly." If the parents are divorced, a doctor should ideally obtain the consent of both parents to a child's medical care unless the authority of one parent is clear or authorized by court order. The guardians' powers are broad. Although medical decisions are not specified in the statute, the legislature was at some pains to avoid limiting the guardian's authority.[43] Courts provide personal representatives with "letters of office" or papers to prove their authority. The doctor should request copies of letters of office, or the court's appointment order for the file and periodically confirm from time to time that the letters of office are still effective.

Although the parents' consent is generally required before treating minors, in some cases a parent may decline to allow the child to receive needed health care. Religious beliefs, for example, may interfere with what is considered proper diagnosis and treatment.[44] Jehovah's Witnesses prohibit the transfusion of blood,[45] and Christian Scientists rely on prayer as the only therapy for disease.

Courts have distinguished cases involving immediate need for life saving treatment and those without such immediacy.[46] In the latter, the courts are far less likely to override parental objections to treatment on philosophical or religious grounds.

Example

A 16-year-old boy had a curvature of the spine secondary to polio. He would need surgery if he were to have any chance of a normal life. His doctor wanted to operate, but not under the "no transfusions" restriction placed by the child's Jehovah's Witness mother. The Pennsylvania Supreme Court refused to substitute its judgment for the mother's, citing the lack of an immediate threat to the child's life.[47]

If the doctor believes that a parent or guardian is withholding needed and life-saving treatment, the doctor should contact the child welfare authorities. Under Pennsylvania law, a court can transfer temporary legal custody of a "dependent child" to a qualified individual.[48] A dependent child is one "without proper parental care or control . . . necessary for his . . . health."[49] This situation is a professional problem, charged with intense feelings and important but conflicting rights and interests.[50] But physicians not infrequently find themselves involved in these cases; they come with the turf.

Living will declarations

As medical technology has improved the ability of the health care system to keep alive the near-dead, public awareness and anxiety have grown about the system's ability to prolong life, perhaps against a patient's wishes. In an attempt to exert control in advance of a time when it may not be possible to do so, patients are executing so-called living wills. Many states have facilitated this effort by statutes; Pennsylvania has not.

Living wills dictate what life-sustaining measures may be utilized. The states with statutes lay out how and in what form the directive must be executed.[51] These laws generally are thought to give some comfort to the physicians who carry out these directives. They are enacted in hopes of encouraging physicians to follow the patient's wishes.

In jurisdictions without such statues, patients may still wish to identify ahead of time what treatments they do and do not want. Lawyers are advised, however, that they cannot assure a client in Pennsylvania that doctors relying on the directive will be protected from lawsuit or even criminal prosecution. Therefore the directive may not be followed.[52]

The situation is somewhat easier for the personal physician of the patient, who has had an opportunity to discuss the individual's wishes with him and knows the family's feelings. A hospital or doctor confronted with a written directive by the family of a new patient in a terminal state is not safe in following the directive. Without prior knowledge, heroic efforts should be maintained as long as medically indicated.[53] It is impossible to know immediately if this was the patient's signature, if he had changed his mind, or if he made it in anticipation of a different circumstance.

A form for living wills has been composed and suggested for use in Pennsylvania.[54] The proposed form attempts to make use of the notion of a durable power of attorney.[55] It also relies in part on the perception of a basic right, even in the absence of a statute, to have "living will" instructions carried out.[56]

LIVING WILL DECLARATION[57]

Instructions of (client's name) concerning life-sustaining procedures

(My "Living Will")

To my family, my next of kin, my physicians, any medical facility in whose care I happen to be, and whomever may be concerned with a decision to institute, continue, or withdraw life-sustaining procedures for me.

If at any time I should have an injury, disease or illness (whether physical or mental) which deprives me of the power to express decisions regarding my treatment, and which without life-sustaining procedures, would within reasonable medical judgment lead to my death, then I direct that there not be instituted or continued any life-sustaining procedure, except as hereinafter provided, involving mechanical or other artificial means to sustain, restore or supplant any vital function in order only to prolong my life artificially. In the event any such procedure or intervention has been commenced, I authorize its discontinuance and withdrawal.

"Life-sustaining procedure" as used herein shall not include: (a) the administration of medication or the performance of any medical procedure deemed necessary to alleviate pain; (b) procedures for

Continued

the administration of a food and water; (c) insertion of a cardiac pacemaker; (d) temporary cardiopulmonary resuscitation unless I am already in an otherwise terminal condition; and (e) receipt of an organ transplant only if there is a reasonable chance of restoring me to a comfortable and functional existence.

If I have been diagnosed as pregnant, this directive shall have no force or effect during the term of my pregnancy.

I intend that this directive remain effective until revoked by me by revocation endorsed hereon or by my destruction of this document. I further intend that this document be effective without having been made a part of my medical records or delivery to my physician or any similar restriction on effectiveness as may be provided in any applicable statute.

In the event any question arises as to whether a certain procedure or intervention should or should not be instituted or continued or withdrawn, and should I then be unable to or incompetent to make or express a decision, I designate ____________________ as my surrogate and ____________________ (the alternate surrogate) to make such decision for me.

I acknowledge that my attorney has informed me that at present the Commonwealth of Pennsylvania has no statute governing a document such as this and that I have been informed by my attorney that this document may not be legally binding or enforceable. Despite these advices, it is my desire that in the absence of my ability to give directions regarding use of such life-sustaining procedures, it is my intention that this directive shall be honored by my family and physicians and others responsible for my care. I further direct that anyone acting in good faith reliance on this instruction (my physicians, surrogate, family or next of kin) shall not be subject to either civil or criminal liability.

Signed this day of 19

____

(Name)

____

____

(Address)

Signed in the presence of the undersigned witnesses each of whom believes the declarer to be of sound mind at the time of signing.

____

____

From Aker, JB: 1985 Supplement to laws of wills in Pennsylvania, Philadelphia, 1985, George T Bisel Co.

Unauthorized postmortem procedures

***A physician may not perform postmortem procedures, including autopsies or organ harvesting for donations, without proper consent. As in most states, autopsy is governed by statute in Pennsylvania.*[58]**

Postmortem examinations are more common in Europe. In one country the law states that if the attending doctor is unsure of the cause of death, an unlimited autopsy may be performed without permission from the next of kin. This provides a wealth of data that is reflected in the studies published there. The balance between the society's need for information and individual and family rights to control the disposal and treatment of bodies is tipped toward the state there. Despite the intellectual attractiveness of such a system, most physicians would concede that such a system would not receive enthusiastic support in the United States. Some families have fierce objections to autopsy and organ donation for religious reasons.[59] Many people consider efforts to establish formal systems for organ harvesting as coercive and even ghoulish activities. In addition to the dead person's own wishes, the next of kin of a deceased person have an interest in the body.[60] Conflicts among those interests and with the state's interests not infrequently arise and create legal hazards for health care providers.

Pennsylvania employs a coroner system as opposed to a medical examiner system. The physician has a duty to notify the coroner in the event of a sudden death.[61] Burials and cremations are prohibited without proper certification.[62] The medical certificate can be supplied by the attending physician or dentist unless it has to be referred to the coroner.[63] Coroner referrals occur if:

- No physician or dentist was in attendance during the last illness of the deceased (only a physician in the event of fetal death), or
- The attending doctor cannot supply the necessary data, or
- The circumstances suggest the death was sudden, violent, or suspicious, or the result of other than natural causes.

The coroner is required to make an immediate investigation of these cases and supply the medical certificate.[64] Upon investigation, if the coroner is not satisfied that the death resulted from natural causes or suicide, he conducts an inquest, as part of which he may order an autopsy.[65] The family may object, but the coroner has statutory authority to have the postmortem examination performed.[66] The coroner is part of the Commonwealth's criminal investigative team.[67] There is, however, no due process right to an inquest in those who might be vindicated[68] by it or have their suspicions confirmed.[69]

Autopsy cases properly referred to the coroner are rarely a source of legal problems for physicians.[70] Otherwise, however, care must be exercised in obtaining consent for postmortem examination. Bodies unclaimed for 36 hours come under the state anatomical board's authority.[71] But these patients will almost always be coroner's cases. The physician wishing a postmortem examination will be dealing with family or someone else claiming the body. The law is specific regarding who may consent to the autopsy. Any of the following may authorize:

- The deceased (by writing signed during lifetime) AND the written consent of the surviving spouse, if any.
- The written authorization of someone the deceased empowered (again, in writing) to take charge of his body for burial AND the written consent of the surviving spouse, if any.
- Written authorization of the surviving spouse.
- If the surviving spouse is incompetent, unavailable, or doesn't claim the body (or if there is no surviving spouse), by written authorization of the following—in this order of precedence:
  a. Adult children
  b. Adult grandchildren
  c. Parents
  d. Siblings
  e. Nephews or nieces
  f. Grandparents
  g. Uncles or aunts
  h. Cousins
  i. Stepchildren
  j. Relatives of previously deceased spouse
- If none of the above are available to claim the body, whoever does claim the body.[72]

Note that the claimant must be willing to undertake the expense of burial to be authorized by the statute to give consent. Consent may be by telephone, but good practice dictates that a witness listen in.[73] Note also the order of precedence; this has proved important in cases in other jurisdictions.[74]

The value of routine autopsies has been questioned. In the past the educational value of the procedure was touted. Some teaching hospitals actually required all patients to sign an autopsy consent form as a condition for admission, even when a person was admitted for the simplest procedure. There is a medical-legal risk associated with postmortem examinations, especially insofar as consent is concerned.[75] The Joint Commission on Accreditation of Hospitals (JCAH) formerly specified a certain percentage of autopsies as a requirement for approval. This standard has been abandoned. However, on many occasions an unofficial autopsy is considered. Courageous physicians, even in today's malpractice climate, ask for postmortem examinations to discover if something more could have been done for the patient. Conversely, an autopsy can serve to exonerate a physician, depending on the true cause of death and condition.

If the patient dies and the doctor thinks an autopsy would be useful, the best thing to do is quietly sit down with the next of kin, explain the necessary details of the case, and then request permission for an autopsy. The doctor must explain why the examination is needed. Usually, no difficulty arises if the doctor had a trusting doctor-patient relationship with the patient and has rapport with the family. However, if the doctor appears arrogant, unfeeling, or not concerned enough to go to the hospital to officially pronounce death and console the family, he can expect a refusal and possibly a malpractice suit to boot. These tasks should not be delegated to the nursing staff. Proper concern must be given to attempting to reach the right family member, given the statutory order of preference, if they are not at the hospital.[76]

The topic of organ donations is of popular interest today. As in the case of autopsies, organ donations should not be made without proper consent. Sale or purchase (or transportation involving a purchase) of human organs and human nonregenerative tissues, pre- and postmortem, is prohibited.[77]

Pennsylvania, like all other states, has adopted the Uniform Anatomical Gift Act.[78] Under this law any competent adult or certain relatives and others may give all or any part of a person's body for education, research, therapy, or transplantation.[79] The people, in order, who may make anatomical gifts if the individual fails to make a gift are as follows:

- The spouse
- Adult sons or daughters
- Either parent
- Adult brothers or sisters
- A guardian of the person of the deceased at the time of death
- Any person authorized or under obligation to dispose of the body[80]

The law specifies the manner for making anatomical gifts. During his or her lifetime a person may make the gift by will or other signed document, such as organ donation card, witnessed by two people.[81] If a person fails to make a gift, relatives may make the gift by a signed document or by telegraphic, recorded telephonic, or other recorded message.[82] The Act requires that acute care hospitals request anatomical gifts, except when bodies or parts are not suitable for use by any medical criteria.[83]

Anatomical gifts are subject to revocation or amendment.[84] All that's needed is an oral statement to two persons or to an attending physician during a terminal illness. Additionally, if the hospital administration has actual notice of opposition and the deceased did not have a reliably executed donor card, the gift will not be requested.[85] While the family may not revoke a gift made by the deceased, common practice is to seek family permission for gifts anyway and honor the family's wishes if objections to the gifts arise. This practice may explain the legislature's enactment of a specific addition to the law, indicating that this precaution is not needed.[86]

Under the law, the time of a person's death must be determined by the person's attending doctor or, if no doctor was in attendance, by the doctor who certifies the death. However, in neither case may that doctor or his professional partners or associates participate in the removal or transplantation of an organ.[87]

A doctor who follows this law in good faith is not liable for any claims, civil or criminal.[88]

Essential in all postmortem cases is respect for and sensitivity to the deceased's family. In the stress of the emotion and grief, family members may be looking for someone to blame, someone at whom to lash out. Malpractice suits have germinated in the minds of family members at the time of interaction with the physician immediately after the death. It's important to let the caring concern exhibited toward the patient be reflected in dealing with the family.

Diagnosis

Malpractice cases in the past were overwhelmingly treatment problems. This changed gradually over a 10 to 20 year period. Now allegations of error or delay in diagnosis occur about as often as treatment claims. The change may be partially the result of increased sophistication of the plaintiffs' bar. Today's plantiff's lawyers work harder and understand more—the bad result's root cause is more likely to be discovered.

Misdiagnosis

A physician has an obligation to diagnose those conditions and ailments that a physician with the skill and knowledge of an appropriately comparable physician would diagnose under similar circumstances.

An increasingly common form of medical malpractice claim is misdiagnosis. Misdiagnosis may be claimed either because of failure to correctly diagnose a particular condition or because the condition simply was missed altogether. These claims are especially common in the area of cancer diagnosis. Misdiagnosis may also refer to a failure to recognize the severity of a problem.

Family practitioners, obstetricians, and emergency physicians are particularly vulnerable to accusations of this form of medical malpractice. Family practitioners see a wide variety of patients. Obstetricians are frequently accused of failing to recognize or foresee a complication and of not taking appropriate action. Emergency physicians, pressured to respond to an uncontrolled inflow of patients, are constantly in danger of making diagnostic errors.

Example

Gerard broke his arm in a football scrimmage at Bucknell. The two physicians who x-rayed and examined him that day applied a long-arm cast. But the arm failed to heal properly. Gerard then saw another physician closer to home. This doctor took more x-rays and splinted the arm.

Almost a year later, when the arm still hadn't healed, the patient saw Dr. Milane. Milane told Gerard that, given that kind of fracture, surgery should have been performed immediately after the injury. Dr. Milane did operate but Gerard was left with a partial loss of motion. He alleged that his injuries were the result of the misdiagnosis of his original Monteggia fracture.[89]

Delayed diagnosis

A physician has an obligation not to delay in making a definitive diagnosis.

The need for careful documentation and explanations to patients (defensive medicine) is never as great as when refraining from ordering some diagnostic modality. If a doctor's son injured his ankle and examination indicated a sprain, the doctor/father probably would not take an x-ray immediately. Even if a simple fracture is revealed, the delay in definitive diagnosis and treatment would really have no effect on the outcome. Nevertheless, if this protocol is followed with a hostile patient, an attorney could argue that the delay harmed the patient by resulting in pain, suffering, mental anguish, and even loss of earnings and employment during the delay. Unreliable patients can aggravate the results of a delay by not following instructions.

Delayed diagnosis claims are most often based on a doctor's failure to obtain tests or perform diagnostic procedures and less often on the lack of a proper examination. When doctors are sued, no one points out that they saved the insurer or patient some money. Evidence regarding the risk or cost versus benefit analysis can be introduced, but it holds little sway in the face of an injured patient.[90]

Example

The .44-caliber magnum pistol bullet entered the patient's leg just below the popliteal fossa. It came out the other side 4 inches lower. He was treated conservatively. After 3 weeks the patient had himself transferred to Reading Hospital. There, the leg was amputated 2 days later. The patient claimed that two different physicians at Reading told him the leg might have been salvageable had he been transferred there earlier.

The patient sued the first hospital and doctor, claiming that failure to perform an arteriogram earlier had deprived him of his leg. The jury was told they could award money to the patient if the delay was a substantial factor in or increased the risk of loss of the leg.[91]

Failure to refer

A doctor has a duty to advise a patient to consult a specialist or to refer the patient to a specialist if the doctor should realize that the nature of a patient's illness or condition requires the services of a specialist.

This is true not only of generalists but also of any practitioner confronted with a problem beyond his or her field and expertise.

In some cases, misdiagnosis can be avoided by use of a specialist. Certainly this claim is asserted by plaintiffs in "failure to refer" cases. Some hospital or medical staff bylaws actually require use of consultants in some cases.

If a diagnosis is not clear, or if a pathologic process doesn't progress as expected, a physician should consider referring the patient to another doctor or specialist for consultation. Even if a diagnosis is suspected, a consultant can serve to confirm it. The use of a consultant can be thought of as analogous to use of confirmatory lab work or procedure. And if medical malpractice is eventually claimed, the consultant can be a ready witness to support the doctor's position. This is a key point because with hindsight experts may review a chart and say what should have been done. The situation can appear quite different when it initially presents or at the time the consultant is used. A consultant provides a contemporaneous perspective and aids enormously in convincing a jury to judge the situation by how it appeared at the time and not judge the doctor's actions through retrospect.

Example

The patient was admitted with right hip and back pain with chills and fever. The physician explored the right retroperitoneum and drained an abscess. A month later, the same sequence recurred.

Following the second surgery, the patient went to a different hospital, and GI studies revealed regional ileitis. The involved bowel was excised, and a fistulous tract into the abscess area cleaned out. He successfully sued the first physician and hospital because he hadn't been referred to a gastroenterologist. His expert witnesses, Drs. Timmons and Brockmyer, testified that the first physician breached the standard of care by failing to obtain a G.I. work-up.[92]

Negligent referral

If a physician decides to refer a patient to another physician or another practitioner for care or treatment, the referring physician must use reasonable care in selecting and recommending the other physician.

To simply refer a patient when indicated is not enough. The referring doctor also must consider whether the other doctor is qualified and competent to care for or treat the patient. Friendships and business relationships are not the criteria; qualification and competency are. A doctor who negligently refers a patient may be liable for injuries done to the patient through the malpractice of the other doctor. Liability attaches not because the referring doctor is responsible for the other doctor's negligence; rather, liability is based on the referring doctor's own negligence in selecting the doctor to whom the patient was referred.

Treatment

Negligent treatment

A doctor is under the general obligation to exercise reasonable skill and judgment in the treatment and care of a patient.

What is reasonable is usually based on the standard of care that other doctors would exercise under the circumstances. The standard applies to both choice and performance of treatment.

This chapter covers specific forms of medical malpractice. It is important to keep in mind that medical malpractice may involve any conduct that falls below the requisite standard of care and thereby injures the patient.[93] Accusations of medical malpractice can arise from virtually any situation and any act or omission. Claims of malpractice by negligent treatment were once the predominant form of suits against doctors. Now diagnostic and other problems stimulate as many cases, but assertions of substandard treatment still occur in about half of the cases.

The fact of a bad result does not establish the fact of negligence.[94] Further, to establish malpractice the doctor's negligence must be a substantial factor in causing the injury, not just the natural process of the underlying disease or injury.[95] To recover, the patient must demonstrate that the doctor did not employ the skill and knowledge or exercise the care and judgment that an average, reasonable doctor practicing in the same or a similar community or hospital would have done in a similar case.[96]

Example

Thomas F. was admitted to the emergency department with severe abdominal pain. He was taken to surgery, and an *Escherichia coli* peritonitis lavaged, but the source wasn't found. The patient, after recovery, sued and claimed that surgery had not been needed, that medical therapy should have been used.

At trial, the physician and his experts testified that Thomas had been in shock and that emergency surgery had been required. The patient's expert said the lab slip interpreted by the defendant as "160" unit of amylase was actually "460." This witness testified that Thomas had had pancreatitis with a mild bacterial infection and that IV fluids and antibiotics were the recognized treatment. The jury awarded Thomas $75,000.

The physician defendant appealed. The superior court held that the medical expert shouldn't have been allowed to testify regarding the lab slip. He wasn't a handwriting expert. Further, the court said the trial judge committed an important error when he failed to instruct the jury on Pennsylvania's "two schools of thought" rule. The jury had weighed two different treatment options and had voted for the one they felt was preferable. This decision-making by the jury is not permitted, and the case was sent back for a new trial.[97]

The "two schools of thought" doctrine requires that, where medical authority is divided, a physician will not be liable if he followed a course of treatment supported by reputable, respectable, and reasonable medical experts.[98] The doctrine seems obvious common sense, necessary for the advancement of medicine and introduction of new treatments.[99] But it has been called the "bane of the plaintiff's medical malpractice bar."[100] While the doctrine is a concept already embodied in malpractice law, it's explicit statement for the jury makes it clear that there is not necessarily one single right way to treat a patient. That secondary message is the one which makes the instruction an important aid to defendant doctors. But the doctrine does not cover every situation where there is a difference of opinion.

Example

On Saturday night, Steven B. attended a wedding reception. Just as he started in on his roast beef sandwich and glass of beer, the thickly sliced meat lodged in his throat. Dr. Rex recommended esophagoscopy and after initially refusing, Steven agreed.

During the procedure, a screw on the grasping forceps broke. Enough meat was removed that the rest passed, but the forceps opened suddenly and touched the walls of the esophagus. Dr. Rex inspected and saw no damage, but by that night the patient was febrile and complained of abdominal cramps. Antibiotics were not started until the following morning, however. Multiple complications resulting in permanent disabilities followed.

At trial, Dr. Thompson appeared as the plaintiff's expert. He said on direct questioning that the standard of care required the administration of antibiotics immediately on suspicion of a perforated esophagus. On cross-examination, Dr. Thompson admitted that a "small respected body" of medical practitioners would have waited, but insisted that "the great majority" would not. After this testimony, the defendants asked the judge to throw the case out of court, because Dr. Thompson's own words brought Dr. Rex's choice under the "two schools of thought" doctrine. The trial judge agreed and on appeal, the superior court affirmed the decision.

But on the next appeal, the Pennsylvania Supreme Court reversed the lower court's decision. They limited the "two schools of thought" doctrine by explaining that more than a "small respected body" was required to support Dr. Rex's choice. They required that the treatment be advocated "by a considerable number" before the doctrine could apply. The Supreme Court ordered a new trial; this time the jury was allowed to decide whether or not Dr. Rex had been negligent.[101]

Delayed treatment

A physician has an obligation not to delay in providing appropriate treatment.

Closely related to claims of medical malpractice for delayed diagnosis are claims contending that treatment was negligently delayed. Physicians walk a fine line between overtreating and undertreating. When something goes wrong, the unhappy patient or family will be tempted to use any argument they can to recover damages. If the bad result is a complication of treatment, was the treatment too aggressive? If the concern is with a progressive or fatal disorder, was treatment delayed? It is difficult to defend a case with a bad result by asserting that at the time, waiting seemed wisest. The dead or injured patient's problem looms before the jury, reproaching the physician's choices in a grim, and sometimes overwhelming, way.

Example

Sharon was 15 when she saw her doctor for respiratory complaints. He diagnosed a viral infection and prescribed antihistamines and Tylenol. Three days later she was back with sore throat, cervical adenopathy, chest pains, and general malaise. The physician refused to prescribe an antibiotic despite requests, nor did he x-ray Sharon.

She worsened, and the family, dissatisfied with the doctor's services, did not follow his instructions to call. That night she began vomiting blood and the next morning was taken to an emergency room. An x-ray there showed a rapidly progressing, fulminating pneumonia. She died two days later of kidney and respiratory failure. The treating specialist said Sharon had died of a rare and rapidly progressive pulmonary disease.

Plaintiff's experts testified that earlier treatment would have given the patient a better chance of survival. The jury awarded $650,000.[102]

Refusal to treat

A doctor may not refuse to provide needed emergency treatment because of his patient's inability to pay.

Whether or not to undertake the treatment of a person is, at least initially, the doctor's decision. Generally, a doctor has no duty to enter into a doctor-patient relationship. While a doctor may decline to treat a person, once the physician-patient relationship is entered, all of the duties of the reasonable practitioner attach.

Unlike doctors, hospitals undertake a specific obligation when they offer or holdout emergency services. To satisfy this obligation, hospitals typically enter contractual relationships to provide emergency services. This may mean retaining an independent doctor or group to cover the emergency service (the "Alexandria plan"). Or a hospital may require members of its medical-dental staff to cover the emergency department (the "Pontiac plan"). Because of the contractual commitments or because of obligations as a member of the medical staff, a doctor may have a specific duty to provide emergency services when on call.

Guaranteed results and warranties

A doctor who guarantees or warrants a particular result may be liable if that result is not achieved, particularly if elective treatment is involved.

Most lawsuits brought against doctors are based on negligence. In essence, a doctor generally commits only to treat the patient with requisite skill and care. The doctor does not guarantee or warrant any particular result. Nevertheless, a doctor and patient may agree that a particular result will be achieved.

A doctor who guarantees or warrants a particular result is entering into an agreement or contract with a patient. A guarantee or warranty is simply a promise that the result will conform to the doctor's prediction. It can be oral and it may not require special consideration or payment. If the patient undergoes the procedure relying on that promise, the doctor can be sued for breach of the guarantee or warranty if the agreed-on result is not achieved *even if* the doctor is not negligent in treating the patient.

Contract suits are also brought under a different statute of limitations. A claim for damages in contract can be filed up to 6 years after the injury.[103] Therefore an individual thinking himself damaged, but deciding to sue after the 2-year period for personal injury has expired, may consider an attempt to prove violation of a contractual agreement. But a plaintiff can't avoid the 2-year limit by simply pleading a contract in a personal injury case.[104]

Courts traditionally have been hesitant to find that a doctor has made guarantees or warranties to a patient. They recognize that because medicine is an inexact science, a "cure" or a specific result is not within the physician's total control. Also, in making statements to a patient, a doctor is often simply giving information. The indications for a procedure or the therapeutic goals are not intended to be promised outcomes. However, physicians must be careful to avoid allowing the patient to assume that a result is guaranteed.

In other states, a number of well-meaning statements were considered guarantees of one sort or another. Some examples of these cases include:

- Statement that a proposed resection of an ulcer patient's stomach would take " . . . care of all your troubles . . . you can eat as you want to, you can drink as you want to. . . . You can throw your pillbox away, your Maalox you can throw away. . . .'"[105]

- Statement that an operation would make a hand 100% perfect.[106]
- Statement that removal of a growth under a certain procedure would effect a cure.[107]
- Statement that an operation could alleviate a partial loss of hearing without impairment of the existing ability to hear.[108]
- Statement that a prescribed radium treatment on swollen glands in a patient's neck would not leave a permanent scar.[109]
- Statement that a plastic surgical procedure would make a patient a model of harmonious perfection without pain or scarring.[110]
- Statement that an operation would leave only minor, hairline scarring.[111]
- Statement that plastic surgery on a patient's nose would enhance the patient's beauty and improve her appearance.[112]

The obvious examples above are not what usually gets medical practitioners into trouble. Patients can remember assumptions as promised outcomes. The general surgeon who fails to advise his cholecystectomy candidate that up to 20% of patients continue to have episodes of pain after gallbladder removal is taking a foolish risk. The patient may naturally assume that the surgeon is undertaking to permanently relieve the pain. When the pain doesn't abate, and after consultation with an attorney, that assumption can become a recollection that the surgeon promised a cure. Certainly, the patient would not have undergone the operation knowing it would be unsuccessful. Therefore the patient recalls relying on the surgeon's express or implied warranties in agreeing to have the operation. Even the limitations and disclaimers printed in the consent form may not be enough to protect the physician and convince the jury that no guarantee of results was involved.

Example

After Brenda's fourth child, she and Richard decided to have no more children. She underwent a tubal ligation that was uncomplicated. But about 1½ years later, Brenda was surprised to find herself pregnant again. She had an abortion, which was uncomplicated, and then had a second bilateral tubal ligation.

Brenda and Richard sued 4 years later. They claimed that the first surgeon had said the tubal ligation would prevent further pregnancies. The doctor and the hospital relied on the 2-year statute of limitations and the authorization to perform the surgery. That paper not only contained no such promise; in fact, it warned that success wasn't guaranteed AND released the doctor and hospital from responsibility in the event of failure.

The patient and her husband didn't deny signing the form. Brenda said that neither the meaning of the release nor the possibilities of failure of the surgery had been discussed with her. The trial court concluded that the release was not the entire agreement between the parties. Therefore evidence of the claimed verbal guarantee could be introduced in court. It was. The jury believed it and awarded $26,300.[113]

Physicians must go to the lengths necessary to avoid a claim of express or implied warranty. Justice Nix of Pennsylvania's Supreme Court said, "There is no question that a physician, as well as any other supplier of services, may expressly warrant a specific result."[114] Not only must the doctor be at pains to advise the patient that results are not guaranteed, but also documentation must be adequate to provide a defense when a contract claim is asserted.

In this state, most of these claims against health care providers appear in the context of failed sterilization. The same situations also are the basis for "wrongful life" claims.

Wrongful pregnancy, birth, or life

A physician can fail in his duty and be sued even when the result is generally thought desirable—the birth of a child.

The area of wrongful birth/wrongful life litigation is the most modern example of a new cause of action, a new form of malpractice.[115] Reported in only a handful of cases before 1980, these claims have dramatically increased in number, and they have confronted courts with difficult issues.

Wrongful pregnancy, birth, or life cases represent a significant change in judicial thinking. Traditional jurisprudence always considered children a blessing to the family, but modern law may hold the doctor responsible for damages equal to the cost of rearing an unwanted child to adulthood. These emotionally charged claims usually result from a failed sterilization or a failure to genetically diagnose or detect a defect in the fetus. The parents charge that if they had been adequately warned or the fetus tested, they would have had their unborn child aborted. Because the physician failed to warn them, the parents are demanding that the physician pay for the rearing of the child. Severe disabilities of the newborn often complicate these cases, and the parent's demand that the doctor pay the additional cost of a handicapped or institutionalized child.

These cases can be emotionally charged on both sides. Doctors who oppose abortion and who would not perform or recommend the procedure under any circumstances find it offensive to be required to "inform" parents about taking this step. After testifying that a pregnancy was unwanted, many parents request that the court file be sealed so the child will not learn what transpired at trial.

It is useful to distinguish among the various types of damages sought:

- ***Wrongful pregnancy.*** In a wrongful pregnancy action the alleged injury to the parents is the birth of an unplanned or unwanted but usually normal and healthy child resulting from the negligence of a doctor or other health care provider in performing an abortion or sterilization or in filling a prescription for contraceptives.[116] Wrongful pregnancy cases are sometimes referred to as claims for wrongful conception. Suit can be brought even if the pregnancy is terminated by abortion.[117]

- ***Wrongful birth.*** In a wrongful birth action the parents of the unwanted and unplanned child seek to recover for its existence.[118] They can claim these damages even if the child is healthy.
- ***Wrongful life.*** In a wrongful life action, unlike in wrongful pregnancy or wrongful birth action, parents bring suit on behalf of their child, not for their own injuries. In Pennsylvania, parents sue as natural guardians of their minor child. They claim that because of the doctor's negligence, the child's adult life will be burdened with an impaired existence occasioned by the child's abnormal or unusual health condition. An action for wrongful life centers on the argument that the child would have been better off not being born at all. But Pennsylvania's Supreme Court regards the issue of whether or not the child can sue as a separate issue from damages.[119]

If the child is defective or arguably suboptimal in any way, suit can be brought for the additional expenses involved. The parents can sue for the added expenses involved in caring for and raising such a child. The child, through the parents, can also sue. This claim, with its inherent implication that nonexistence is preferable, is most troubling for courts reviewing these cases.

Keeping the concepts of these actions separate and distinct is important because the doctor's liability varies depending on the type of case brought. These distinctions help explain why courts allow some jury awards and not others, and how the judges making these decisions can subdivide and analyze the differing claims involved.

In a wrongful pregnancy case, a patient or the patient's spouse usually may recover for the expenses of the unsuccessful operation; costs of any medical complications, disability, or disfigurement caused by the pregnancy; the costs of delivery; lost wages; and the expense of help required in the home because of the pregnancy.[120] If the claim is brought within 2 years and properly pleaded, personal injury damages, such as pain and suffering and loss of consortium, are possible.[121] In Pennsylvania, the parents may not recover for the future expenses of raising the child if the child is normal and healthy.[122] The Commonwealth's Supreme Court has quoted a 1957 County court decision:

> Many people would be willing to support this child were they given the right of custody and adoption, but according to plaintiff's statement, plaintiff does not want such. He wants to have the child and

> wants the doctor to support it. In our opinion, to allow such damages would be against public policy.[123]

But even this seemingly obvious position is not endowed with judicial unanimity. The Chief Justice of the State's highest court disagreed and found it inconsistent to allow compensation to the parents of a defective child, and not of a healthy one.

> (T)he . . . action is not an aspersion upon the value of the child's life. It is instead a recognition of the importance of the parent's fundamental right to control their own reproductivity. . . . It is not the relative health of the child but is instead the alleged negligence of the physician, that gives rise to all damages that are foreseeable.[124]

When the child is defective, the parents claim that the child would have been aborted had they known of the child's possible defects. They seek to recover from the doctor the extraordinary medical expenses of the child during his minority. Pennsylvania allows recovery of these expenses in suits by the parents.

Example

Donald was born with von Recklinghausen's neurofibromatosis. His parents learned that it was inherited. They remembered that Donald's father had been treated for skin spots. A physician had removed skin lesions and advised that they were caused by neurofibromatosis. When the child's mother became pregnant, the obstetrician had taken a medical history and learned that the father had a skin condition. The parents did not remember any further inquiries being made.

Donald's parents recalled that no one had ever warned them of the possibility of an inheritable disease. If they had been warned, they said, they would have had an abortion. They sued all three physicians for their expenses involved in caring for this sadly defective little boy.[125]

A wrongful life case effectively demands damages for extraordinary expenses associated with being born defective. Only in a very few jurisdictions are infants allowed to sue for wrongful life.[126] Pennsylvania is not one of these.[127]

Example

Phyllis and Howard decided to end their childbearing capacity. Phyllis went to Dr. Q for a bilateral tubal ligation. She and Howard said they were told the operation was a success. However, 3 years later, Phyllis was delivered of a son. The family sued Dr. Q on several bases, in part because the child had dextrocardia.

The parents sued for (1) Phyllis' lost earnings and earning capacity and (2) Howard's expenses in raising the child and expenses associated with the birth. The child sued for the damages he expected to suffer from being born with dextrocardia.

The defendant physician asked the court to throw out the suit, arguing that even if all allegations were proved, no legally allowable claim had been made. The court allowed the parent's second claim; those expenses could be the result of negligently performed sterilization. The parent's pain and suffering claim was rejected; the mental travail of Phyllis could not be distinguished from the suffering of parents of any diseased or injured child.

The child's own claim was disallowed as well. The court explained, "(T)here is no . . . fundamental right to be born as a whole, functional human being. Whether it is better to never have been born at all rather than to have been born with serious mental defects is a mystery more properly left to the philosophers and theologians, a mystery which would lead us into the field of metaphysics, beyond the realm of our understanding or ability to solve.[128]

Pennsylvania's Supreme Court has stated:

> (W)e hold that a child born deformed and diseased as the result of the failure of physicians to inform its parents of the possibility of a diseased birth may not recover in its own right for being born diseased.[129]

Wrongful life/wrongful birth claims are still relatively new forms of malpractice. Some limits have been drawn around the possibile extent of these suits, but the area is still in flux. In other states, for instance, suits have been brought by the siblings of an unexpected child because their slice of the family pie has been thinned.

Prescription and medication errors

A physician has an obligation to prescribe or administer appropriate and only appropriate medications in proper and only proper dosages. Further, a physician has an obligation to warn patients if the patient's mental or physical abilities will be affected by the medications, either alone or in combination with alcoholic beverages or other items the patient is likely to consume, or in certain reasonably predictable settings, such as driving.

One of the easier forms of medical malpractice to establish involves prescription or medication errors, because the standard of care is often easily established and a deviation clear-cut.

An example of medical malpractice in this area would be violation of one of the laws that govern the dispensing of drugs. A doctor should, accordingly, be well versed in the laws and regulations governing dispensing of drugs. Pennsylvania doctors are subject to the following laws and regulations.

- ***Federal Controlled Substances Act.*** Before prescribing or dispensing a narcotic, a doctor must have a Drug Enforcement Administration (DEA) registration number. To obtain a DEA number, a doctor must first have a permanent Pennsylvania medical license and a Pennsylvania Controlled Substances license.[130]
- ***Pennsylvania Medical Practice Act.*** A licensed doctor is entitled not only to practice medicine and surgery in all its branches but also to prescribe or dispense drugs or medicines. However, the act also provides that the drugs or medicines dispensed must be properly labeled.
- ***Pennsylvania Controlled Substances Act.*** The Controlled Substances Act covers not only narcotics but also many other substances considered to have an actual or related potential for abuse. Before dispensing substances covered by the act, a doctor must register with the Department of Registration and Education.

Another example of this form of medical malpractice occurs when a drug is administered contrary to the manufacturer's instructions. This may relate to such things as the way the drug is administered (for example, orally or by injection) or dosage. A drug manufacturer's explicit instructions on the proper manner of administering a drug and proper dosage and specific warnings of the hazards of proper administration establish the standard of care. FDA approved indications and contraindications also do this. The patient's attorney does not even have to offer expert testimony to show that the doctor deviated from the standard of care if these guidelines are violated.

The patient still must show that this violation of the standard of care caused injuries. The defendant can introduce other evidence and try to show that the dosage or administration was non-negligent. But the published standard gets the plaintiff over the most significant hurdle. Establishing that the doctor violated this standard effectively puts the ball in the defendant's court; plaintiffs must prove negligence by a preponderance of the evidence. Once the violation of standards is shown, the defendant must prove his actions reasonable—the burden of proof is shifted.

Still another example of this form of medical malpractice is based on misunderstood prescriptions. Prescriptions take two forms: verbal and written. Verbal prescriptions may be given over the telephone to a pharmacist or a hospital nurse or even as a hurried direction to a nurse. While verbal prescriptions cannot be entirely avoided, the safest way for a doctor to prescribe is by written prescription. Written prescriptions are normally made on a printed pad or in the record of a hospital patient. It is important to write prescriptions legibly. There is no excuse for the atrocious penmanship of many doctors. The illegibility can reach the level of endangering patients if it causes the pharmacist to dispense the wrong drug or dose. Too often, pharmacists and nurses struggle to guess the doctor's intent, instead of calling for clarification. Usually no remedial action is taken until the offender is zapped with a malpractice suit.

Example

Preston Pratt was rear-ended by Ms. Cheng in the summer of 1964. He was hospitalized for neck and back injuries for 8 days. His family physician sent him to an orthopedic group. His symptoms continued, and a myelogram was performed in December. One of the orthopedists operated on Mr. Pratt soon thereafter, doing a L3-L5 laminectomy and two discectomies.

A wound infection appeared and chloromycetin was begun on the sixth postoperative day. One of the orthopedic residents, in consultation with the treating physicians, changed to neomycin on the eighteenth postoperative day. The wound was irrigated with 5 grams of neomycin per day for 7 days. The wound was finally surgically opened and cleaned on the twenty-seventh postoperative day. For 2 more days, both sides of the wound were irrigated with neomycin.

Mr. Pratt developed renal failure, hearing loss, and paraparesis; he was not expected to survive. But by March he was discharged and eventually was able to ambulate with crutches, remaining deaf. He sued Ms. Cheng, the orthopedists, and the hospital.

During the 11-week trial, the orthopedic team attempted to defend their use of neomycin. The resident, on the witness stand, conceded the ototoxicity and nephrotoxicity of the drug but emphasized that Mr. Pratt's problem was life-threatening and another antibiotic had been ineffective. The defense conceded that the dosage of neomycin exceeded the PDR recommendations. However, they claimed these limits were inapplicable to irrigation, since this route of administration was not discussed in the PDR. Other experts testified regarding systemic absorption of neomycin when instilled into highly vascular granulation tissue and regarding the availability of alternative drugs.

The jury awarded $10,000 against Ms. Cheng and $1,000,000 against the health care providers.[131]

Abandonment

A physician does not have an obligation to accept a patient. However, once a physician accepts a patient, he must continue to care for him until (1) the patient discharges the physician or (2) the physician withdraws from the case after the patient is given a reasonable opportunity to find substitute care or has it already.[132]

In order for an obligation to care for a patient to arise, a doctor-patient relationship must be established.

A physician-patient relationship can be found by courts reviewing cases in retrospect and found in unexpected ways.[133] Usually these relationships are entered and the duties attached when the patient requests care or the physician is called in to assist and the patient has consented to this care. The relationship is like one formed with a contract. The physician gives professional assistance in return for money from the patient.

But physicians come into contact with people and directly or indirectly are involved with them in many ways other than the traditional setting. The doctor can render aid gratuitously or assist someone fairly casually in a social setting. The duty may attach with the call schedule. A doctor assisting another doctor, who is primarily responsible, may engage in a doctor-patient relationship. Predicting what limits the courts will set on implications of physician-patient relationships and attachments of duties is difficult. To be safe, one assumes the worst and is at pains to act reasonably in any situation where the relationship and the duties might be found.

One limit has been set in Pennsylvania. In the opinion on that case, the court said, "(The) (r)elationship customarily requires an immediate connection between the health care provider and the patient. . . ."[134]

Example

Dr. Linn wrote a diet book: *The Last Chance Diet.* Patricia Smith read the book, followed the diet, and died. Her husband sued the family doctor who supervised the diet, the manufacturer and distributor of the liquid protein used in the diet, and Dr. Linn and his publisher.

The court indicated that Mrs. Smith was not a patient of Dr. Linn's, merely a reader, and dismissed the suit against the author and publisher.[135]

Abandonment and attachment of the duties of the physican-patient relationship concern physicians and other health care professionals, especially in the "good samaritan" situation. Like most states, Pennsylvania has a statute purporting to protect those who render emergency aid gratuitously.

> Any physicians or any other practitioner of the healing arts or any registered nurse, licensed by any state, who happens by chance on the scene of an emergency . . . or who is called to the scene . . . by the police or other duly constituted officers . . . or who is present when an emergency occurs and who, in good faith, renders emergency care at the scene of the emergency shall not be liable . . . except (for) . . . any grossly negligent acts or omissions . . .[136]

Physicians should stop and help.[137] But to rely on the above statute to protect against lawsuit in that setting is unrealistic. Note the limitations to "scene of the emergency." Does the "scene" move with the patient once transport is initiated or does the physician confront the Hobson's choice of continuing to care for the victim and coming out from under the statute or discontinuing and being accused of abandonment?[138] A bigger perforation in the statute's protection is contained in the exclusion of "grossly negligent acts or omissions." "Grossly negligent" is clearly something worse than simple negligence, but it is all too easy to allege gross negligence. For this reason, if no other, the statute is a stumbling block for potential plaintiffs, but not an absolute block.[139] The best solution is to assure that liability insurance covers good samaritan situations.

Abandonment is at times confusing because the term is applied both to intentional breaking of the physician-patient relationship and to negligent failure to respond or continue care.[140] But the usual negligence analysis is employed: Did the patient have a reasonable opportunity to obtain another doctor? Did the physician, considering the nature of the problem and availability of alternatives, act reasonably?

A common circumstance in which abandonment is claimed follows an operation or procedure. The duty to continue treating a patient after surgery is not within a doctor's absolute discretion, but it is subject to the general standards of the medical profession.

Liability for others

Generally

A doctor, like anyone else, is legally responsible for his own acts. Under some circumstances, a doctor may be legally responsible for the acts of another person. This situation is referred to as vicarious liability.

A patient's attorney will typically name anyone even remotely potentially responsible for alleged malpractice. Among the reasons for this is that it provides more people with whom settlements can be reached—perhaps a "deep pocket." This can be particularly important if a person sued has no insurance coverage. There is also the hope that different defendants will point fingers at each other and make the plaintiff's case for him.

Partners and corporate shareholders

Doctors who practice medicine as a partnership are jointly and severally liable for the medical malpractice of each other. Doctors who are shareholders for a corporation, on the contrary, are not liable for each other's medical malpractice unless involved in the malpractice itself.

If several doctors associate together as co-owners of a medical practice, they have formed a partnership.[141] Many doctors do not realize that by doing so, they become legally liable for the acts of the other partners, including medical malpractice. Under Pennsylvania law, the partnership itself is liable for any injuries done by a partner to others in the course of the partnership's business (that is, the medical practice).[142] Each partner in turn is jointly and severally liable for the obligations of the partnership.[143]

Doctors can find themselves in partnership situations without an intention to enter a partnership or an agreement to form one. The law will find a partnership and hold the partners liable for each others' negligence if one physician has held himself out as part of a partnership and the other physician(s), knowing this, fails to correct the misunderstanding.[144] For example, if two physicians share office space with both names on the door, a patient might claim that he relied on the two doctors being in partnership.

Joint and several liability can be especially significant if concern exists about the competency of one of the partners or if the partners' vary in the extent of their assets or if the insurance policies are different. What joint and several liability means, in effect, is that a person who is injured by a partner can recover from the partner himself, the partnership, *and* the other partners. Thus a partner who had absolutely nothing to do with the malpractice may have to pay a judgment simply because of the legal relationship with the negligent doctor. A partner who pays a malpractice claim of another is technically entitled to be reimbursed what he pays in excess of his equal share, but this right is no better than the financial solvency of the negligent partner.

A partnership is continuing in nature. If the relationship between persons is not continuing in nature, it is a joint venture. A joint venture is similar to a partnership except that it is for a single project, usually temporary in nature. The term traditionally applies to a commercial or maritime enterprise with the more descriptive term of *joint adventure* (for example, an expedition to the New World.) With the distinction of scope and duration, the liabilities of joint venturers are the same as partners. Doctors may, but in the past infrequently did, engage in joint ventures with regard to their practices. Interest in these arrangements has heightened recently as a result of aggressive promotion by organizations and hospitals. For example, the partners in a CAT scanner purchase joint venture may not understand the extent of their liability.

General businesses have long avoided partnerships because of the existence of joint and several liability. Instead, those desiring to engage in business have done so under the legal form of a corporation. A corporation usually has the feature of limited liability. This means that although the corporation would be legally liable for the injuries caused by its employees and any employees causing injuries would be liable themselves, the other employees and any owners would not be.

Under Pennsylvania law, doctors may practice under the corporate form.[145] If this is done, a doctor would remain liable for his own malpractice and for the negligence of any person under his direct supervision and control.[146] However, a doctor would not be liable for the malpractice of a fellow doctor in the corporation if he (the first doctor) gave no medical service to the injured patient; did not sign any hospital records or medical reports on the patient; and did not exercise any supervision or control over the fellow doctor with regard to the patient's treatment. Incorporation may be advisable for many groups. Tax considerations may greatly affect this decision, but many adverse consequences can be avoided.

Because most doctors are insured, concerns about liability for a doctor-partner's malpractice were uncommon. With increasing awards soaring into the financial stratosphere, however, this may not always be the case. Thus planning for this potential liability is a must, given the possibility of failure of the cap fund.

Agents and employees

A doctor (or his partnership or corporation) is personally liable for the negligence of an agent or employee.

A doctor is liable not only for his or her own negligence but also for the negligence of employees.[147] This rule is formally known as the doctrine of *respondeat superior.* If a doctor practices as a partnership or corporation, the partnership or corporation would then be liable. However, as already discussed, the doctor may be liable for the partnership's obligations.

Liability for agents or employees is imposed regardless of whether the doctor is negligent, provided the malpractice alleged occurred within the scope of an agent or employee's employment. This is a form of vicarious liability. The employer is made to answer for the acts of agents or employees; the employee's negligence is imputed to the doctor. An employer, of course, may also be responsible for his or her own negligence, such as failing to provide a competent or qualified employee, or failing to review and supervise an employee's work. But vicarious liability is independent of any negligent acts or omissions in hiring or supervising.

Vicarious liability was first allowed before injured parties had means to discover if the hiring and supervision was negligent or not. It was a way to get at the employer and a way to find someone with money so a victorious plaintiff could collect. More theoretically, vicarious liability shifts the loss to the party better able to redistribute it or share out its costs.[148] With physicians confronting cost controls and other constraints, this argument loses some of its strength.

To avoid liability for an agent or employee, a doctor may retain the services of an independent contractor. The person retaining the services of an independent contractor will generally not be liable for the negligence of the independent contractor. But that independent status must be real. If the contracting physician has control over the individual, vicarious liability will attach.

A person working for a doctor usually is an employee. The doctor has the right to control and in fact does control the employee's actions. An independent contractor, as the name suggests, is independent and usually engaged in his or her own business. It is unlikely that a nurse would be treated as an independent contractor. But it is possible, depending largely on the specific terms of the services, that a physician would be treated as an independent contractor.

Doctors' classification of people as independent contractors will not always be upheld. Factors such as the control retained by the person retaining the services, the method of payment, and the appearance of who is providing the services will be critical in characterizing the relationship. If an effort is made to use the classification of independent contractor, the relationship should be clearly documented. This is particularly so if hospital-based doctors, such as radiologists or emergency physicians, are involved because in some states[149] a doctor's independent contractor status may be ignored if it appears that the doctor is an agent or employee of the hospital, even if technically he or she is not. This is known as apparent or ostensible agency.

The issue of whether or not one health care provider is the agent or employee of another can be critical when a malpractice claim is filed.

Example

Howard Gregory's index finger was crushed in a farming accident. He was taken to the emergency room where the physician on duty ordered a tetanus booster. The nurse on duty gave the injection, but 9 days later, Mr. Gregory died of tetanus.

The family sued. The case came up on appeal by the nurse, who claimed that she was immune from suit. She was an employee of the Commonwealth, acting within the scope of her employment, she argued. If found to be protected by sovereign immunity, she could not be sued![150]

The question of agency and vicarious liability is especially vexatious for hospitals. Assuring hospitals of reasonably predictable limits to their extended responsibility is difficult.

Example

The patient called his doctor in the early morning hours, complaining of symptoms which seemed to indicate a heart attack. The physician said he would be over shortly. However, the patient didn't wait—he had himself taken by ambulance to Riddle Memorial.

The family physician didn't have privileges at Riddle, but went to the emergency room. He and the resident on duty ran an ECG, which confirmed the MI. The family doctor had the patient transferred to a nearby hospital's coronary unit, where the doctor did have privileges. The resident did not sign any forms approving the transfer. The patient died enroute.

When all concerned were sued, Riddle Hospital argued that it shouldn't be held responsible. It claimed that the dead man had never really even been a patient in the hospital's emergency room. But the judge instructed the jury, "(T)he hospital must not act unreasonably in allowing the person to be removed from the premises. The law requires that such a patient be kept . . . if it is forseeable that his condition will be aggravated. . . ."[151]

Borrowed servants: The captain of the ship doctrine

A doctor may be held liable for the negligence of a hospital employee who is subject to the doctor's control and supervision.

The Restatement, an important and authoritative source for lawyers and judges, summarizes:

> A servant directed or permitted by his master to perform services for another may become the servant of such other in performing the services.

Thus even though the physician doesn't hire and cannot fire the hospital's personnel, he may be vicariously liable for their negligence. This can be so, even though the physician has no right to choose or reject an assigned employee!

Example

Dr. Pernell was the staff attending physician responsible for Mr. Vorston's care. The resident examined the patient and obtained permission from Dr. Pernell to operate. The resident assigned a medical student to do the admission history and physical.

The student failed to record Mr. Vorston's penicillin allergy. During surgery, the student tried to correct the error by asking the circulating nurse to note the allergy. After the operation, the resident ordered penicillin. It was given with disastrous consequences for Mr. Vorston.

The jury found for the patient. On appeal, the Court affirmed, saying the resident was vicariously liable for the student and Dr. Pernell for the resident.[152]

Pennsylvania has extended vicarious liability farther than other states, especially in the surgical setting.[153] Important in this extension was the charitable immunity doctrine. Until 1965, nonprofit hospitals were protected from suit.[154] Reaching out and touching the physician for the negligence of the hospital's own employees at least gave patients someone from whom they could collect their winnings. Pennsylvania courts allowed vicarious liability cases against physicians when an intern put too much silver nitrate in a newborn's eyes[155]; a nurse burned an infant's feet with a too-hot water bottle;[156] and a technician in the blood bank sent the wrong blood to the operating room.[157]

Vicarious liabilities for employees, ostensible agents, and borrowed servants are all justified, at least in part, by the physician's actual control or right to control. When liability is extended to professional peers, the doctrine used to justify that extension has fewer control features—the captain of the ship doctrine.

This jaunty nautical expression was used in 1949 by Pennsylvania's Supreme Court to describe the relationship between the surgeon and others in the operating room.[158] Initially applied in a borrowed servant situation, it has been used since in situations where the negligent act was by a professional capable of independent judgment and peer status.

Example

Dr. Kaplan had not yet come into the operating room when the regional block anesthesia was begun. The anesthesiology resident injected the sodium pentothol into Mr. Rockwell's artery. Two hours later, at the conclusion of the surgery, Dr. Kaplan was advised. He immediately attempted to save Mr. Rockwell's arm, but it had to be amputated a few days later.

The court allowed a jury to award damages against both the chief of anesthesiology, who was present, AND against Dr. Kaplan as "captain of the ship."[159]

There have been cases cutting off the extension of vicarious liability and more may appear because of the end of charitable immunity.[160] Vicarious liability was not allowed in cases in which an intern caused injury while removing sutures, outside the surgeon's presence;[161] routine nursing care in the hospital was said to be substandard;[162] the accused physician was not present and did not advise an amniocentesis that ended in death.[163] Control continues to be discussed in these cases. Where there is any right to control or direct (or perhaps even opportunity), the possibility of vicarious liability exists.

Joint and successive tortfeasors

Where two or more doctors (or others) are responsible for an injury to a patient, they can both be liable as joint tortfeasors.

Patient's attorneys typically file "shotgun" suits; they sue anyone who ever arguably came near an allegedly injured patient. If two different parties committed different acts of negligence, they are successive or concurrent tortfeasors. But if they jointly and inseparably caused the injuries, they are joint tortfeasors. The distinction can be critically important in some cases.

Separate tortfeasors are entitled to have their share of the damages apportioned based on the degree to which the negligence of each caused the injury.[164] True joint tortfeasors are entitled to contribution from each other depending on each's proportion of causative negligence.[165] A successful plaintiff may recover the whole award from any one or more of the joint tortfeasors.[166] Then the joint tortfeasor who had to pay tries to get the proportionate shares from the other joint tortfeasors.

Pennsylvania's legislature has adopted the theory of comparative negligence among those responsible for a tort, including the person bringing suit.[167] Pennsylvania's courts have applied this statute to joint tortfeasors.[168] Under comparative negligence, liability for damages is apportioned among parties, on the basis of fault, by the judge or jury deciding the case. If the injured person contributed to the injures to the extent of, say, 20 percent, damages are reduced by that amount. The relative fault of each defendant, (for example, doctor, hospital, nurse) is similarly determined. Before the theory of comparative negligence was established, a patient who was contributorily negligent (who had contributed to his own injuries) might not be able to recover damages at all, even if his fault were a very small part of the problem. Contributory negligence includes such things as a patient's failure to follow instructions or disclose information about his or her condition. Thus comparative negligence reduces the amount recovered by patients in some cases, but allows at least some recovery in others.

The question of whether or not a physician defendant is a joint tortfeasor is important when one of the defendants has settled and gotten out of the case. Generally, plaintiffs will execute a release for the settling party. This release can also let off joint tortfeasors.[169] But the intent of the parties to the release determines its effect, and suit can still be brought if there has not been full compensation.[170]

Example

Loretta Lauer was walking along a road when William Strauck drove by in his loaded truck. A roll of chainlink fencing fell off the truck and severely injured Ms. Lauer. She was taken to Muhlenberg Medical Center but soon died.

The estate sued Mr. Strauck and his loader as well as the hospital and physicians who had cared for Ms. Lauer, claiming negligent care. The loader and driver were able to be relieved for $100,000, but their release specified that the doctors and hospital were not being let go.

The health care providers wanted to keep the fence company in the case and appealed. The appeal was rejected. Not only were the physicians and hospital not entitled to contribution for any judgment against them, the superior court did not require apportionment from the driver and loader either. Those originally responsible for Ms. Lauer's injuries did not even have to appear at trial.[171]

Disclosure of records or information

Generally

Ethical obligations require doctors to protect confidential relationships existing with patients. These obligations include preventing the disclosure of records or information.

For physicians the confidential relationship with patients is founded in The Hippocratic Oath, the American Medical Association's (AMA's) *Principles of Medical Ethics,* and the *Current Opinions of the Judicial Council of the American Medical Association.* These ethical considerations, according to one other state's court, "underscore the highly confidential nature of the physician-patient relationship and, perhaps more importantly, affirmatively advertise to the public that a patient can properly expect his physician to protect those medical confidences which are disclosed during the physician-patient relationship."[172]

The Hippocratic Oath was first conceived during the fifth century B.C. and, as such, is one of the oldest statements of ethics governing the medical profession. The oath states in part:

> What I may see or hear in the course of the treatment or even outside the treatment in regard to the life of men, which on no account one must spread abroad, I will keep to myself, holding such things shameful to be spoken about.[173]

The confidentiality of the physician-patient relationship is rooted deep in the history of the medical profession and remains a consistent expectation among patients.

The AMA's *Principles of Medical Ethics* reflects the Hippocratic Oath in Principle IV by stating that:

> A physician shall respect the rights of patients, of colleagues, and of other health professionals, and shall safeguard patient confidences within the constraints of the law.

The Current Opinions of the Judicial Council of the AMA provide additional guidance. Section 5.05 of the Current Opinions, for example, provides:

> The information disclosed to a physician during the course of the relationship between physician and patient is confidential to the greatest possible degree.... The physician should not reveal confi-

dential communications or information without the express consent of the patient unless required to do so by law.

Section 5.07 of the Current Opinions states:

> Both the protection of confidentiality and the appropriate release of information in records is the rightful expectation of the patient. A physician should respect the patient's expectations of confidentiality concerning medical records that involve the patient's care and treatment.

Other health care providers similarly are subject to ethical standards requiring the confidentiality of their relationships with patients. In addition, the law recognizes various rights limiting disclosure of patient records or information.

Sometimes, doctors misunderstand the nature of the restrictions and release information about patients. The confidentiality is not a right or even a privilege held by physicians. The privilege is held by the patient and is for his benefit.[174]

Invasion of privacy

A patient has a right to reasonable visual and auditory privacy.

Before 1890, no English or American court had ever recognized what we now call the right of privacy. In that year the *Harvard Law Review* included a now-famous article by Samuel D. Warren and Louis D. Brandeis that proposed the right.[175] The law now distinguishes four forms of invasion of privacy: (1) unreasonable intrusion upon the seclusion of another; (2) appropriation of the other's name or likeness; (3) unreasonable publicity given to the other's private life; and (4) publicity that unreasonably places the other in a false light before the public. The right of privacy, particularly as it prohibits the public disclosure of private facts, is significant in health care.

A patient has a right of privacy. If a doctor communicates information about the patient, especially if it relates to the patient's medical condition or the doctor's diagnosis or treatment, this would be an invasion of privacy. The information need not be false, as in a defamation case. If the communication to a third person was unauthorized, suit can be maintained.[176]

The JCAH *Accreditation Manual for Hospitals* specifically recognizes a patient's right to privacy in the hospital setting. It provides that patients have a right:

> To be interviewed and examined in surroundings designed to assure reasonable visual and auditory privacy. This includes the right to have a person of one's sex present during certain parts of a physical examination, treatment, or procedure performed by a health professional of the opposite sex and the right not to remain disrobed any

longer than is required for accomplishing the medical purpose for which the patient was asked to disrobe.[177]

Health care practitioners, especially in teaching centers, commonly use photographs. Caution and proprieties must be observed in obtaining consent prior to photographing patients, no matter how worthy the purpose. Defending the photography of an unconscious patient on the basis that the pictures have not been improperly used will not be sufficient—lawsuit and recovery are possible.[178]

In general, the doctors can avoid these problems by being scrupulously respectful of the patient's right to privacy.

Divulgence of confidential information

A doctor may not, with certain exceptions, disclose any information acquired while attending a patient.

Example

At about 8:30 PM one July evening in Philadelphia, the Alexander family was driving north on Broad Street. While at a traffic light, they were rear-ended.

Mrs. Alexander was in traction for 22 days and out of work for 16 months because of a whiplash injury. In the course of treatment, Dr. Muntagh, a neurosurgeon, stated that he felt a marked hysterical element was present because the patient was emotionally unstable.

Later another physician, Dr. Ezickson, contacted Dr. Muntagh requesting a report from the neurosurgeon and paying him $50 for it. The defense counsel employed Dr. Ezickson for this purpose.

When the Alexanders sued the other driver, the wife was awarded only $200 for pain and suffering. The plaintiffs asked for a new trial based on the alleged inadequacy of this award.

In the course of affirming the lower court's decision to grant a new trial, the superior court took the unusual step of commenting on the report obtained by Dr. Ezickson: "We are of the opinion that members of a profession, especially the medical profession, stand in a confidential or fiduciary capacity as to their patients. They owe their patients . . . a duty to aid the patient in litigation, to render reports when necessary and to attend court when needed. That further includes a duty to refuse affirmative assistance to the patient's antagonist in litigation. THE DOCTOR, OF COURSE, OWES A DUTY TO CONSCIENCE TO SPEAK THE TRUTH; HE NEED, HOWEVER, SPEAK ONLY AT THE PROPER TIME. Dr. Ezickson's role in inducing Dr. Muntagh's breach of his confidential relationship to his own patient is to be and is condemned (emphasis added).[179]

Unauthorized disclosures are an invasion of the patient's privacy. The physician can be sued for making them and for the damages resulting from

REPORTABLE DISEASES IN PENNSYLVANIA[184]

Amebiasis
Animal bite
Anthrax
Botulism
Brucellosis
Cancer
Cholera
Diphtheria
Encephalitis
Food poisoning
Giardiasis
Gonococcal infections
Guillain-Barre syndrome
Hepatitis, viral, including type A and type B
Malaria
Measles
Meningitis—all types
Meningococcal disease
Mumps
Pertussis (whooping cough)
Plague
Poliomyelitis
Psittacosis (ornithosis)
Rabies
Reye's syndrome
Rickettsial diseases, including Rocky Mountain spotted fever
Rubella (German measles) and congenital rubella syndrome
Salmonellosis
Shigellosis
Smallpox
Syphilis—all stages
Tetanus
Toxoplasmosis
Trichinosis
Tuberculosis—all forms
Typhoid
Yellow fever

them.[180] The biggest problem areas are unauthorized disclosures to employees, spouses, insurers, and antagonists in litigation.[181]

The rationale behind the policy of confidentiality is the same as that behind other such relationships. Be it doctor-patient, attorney-client, or priest-penitant, society has an interest in encouraging these relationships and in encouraging the participants to be forthright and open. Sometimes this interest clashes with other interests, such as the need for control of communicable disease. But concern for the confidentiality of the relationship, though it may be overridden by other policy needs, is still present.[182]

By the presumption of confidentiality is perforated in numerous areas. The sources of the most holes through which information is to flow are statutory and regulative. Like other states, Pennsylvania's legislature has enacted a reporting statute.[183] The box below lists the reportable diseases issued by regulation, promulgated by the State Department of Health:

Multiple other statutes impact on reporting and suspend physician-patient confidentiality for that report:

- Any wound from a deadly weapon must be reported immediately by telephone AND in writing to the police.[185]
- If a physician is appointed by the court to examine a person for alleged incompetency, he will submit a report to the court and to the parties to the hearing.[186]
- When a waterway patrolman appears with a suspected drunken boater in tow, no physician, nurse or technician may administratively refuse to perform a breath or blood test. The test results are admissible in court.[187]
- Similarly so with drunken automobile drivers.[188]
- Abused children.[189]

As can be imagined, the area of child abuse and neglect is the source of much difficulty and litigation.[190] Like other states, Pennsylvania's statute refers to reports made in "good faith;" those making good faith reports of child abuse and neglect are immune from civil liability.[191] However, this does not mean they are immune from having suits brought against them:

Example

A high school guidance counsellor was worried about a tenth grade boy. Beyond the common fears of his age group about being a homosexual and difficulties with his strict, religious parents, the child seemed to have an inability to function in reality. The counselor met with the parents and urged professional help, but they refused.

The counselor referred the problem to the county children's resources social worker. This individual then filed with the court under the Abused and Neglected Child Act to request that the child be adjudged dependent and undergo psychiatric evaluation. The petition to the court necessarily involved an assertion that the boy was neglected and lacked needed medical attention.

The court held a hearing and denied the social worker's petition. The parents then sued the counsellor and the social worker.

The court dismissed the suit based on the immunity provided in the statute requiring reporting of abused children. The judge explained that the reporting individual need not have made an absolute diagnosis of abuse or neglect—"reason to believe" was enough.[192]

If disclosure is required, the laws sometimes provide that a doctor may not be sued for making a required report, but this is not always the case. Other required disclosures carry with them a general understanding that the physician should not be sued for acting in good faith to carry out a statutory duty. The physician is best advised to consult a lawyer when problems arise, such as the patient's objection. The physician should inform the patient what the law requires the physician to do and, throughout the process, be conscious of the duty to protect the patient's confidentiality as much as possible.

Defamation

If a doctor is otherwise entitled to disclose information about a patient, he has an obligation to refrain from making untrue statements that injure the patient's reputation.

Defamation is made up of the twin torts of libel and slander. Libel is defamation by written or printed words, pictures, or a form other than spoken words or gestures. Slander is defamation by oral utterances. In either case, defamation generally involves making an untrue statment that tends to injure a person's reputation in the popular sense: to diminish the esteem, respect, good will or confidence in which a person is held, or to excite adverse, derogatory, or unpleasant feelings or opinions against the person.[193]

If a defamatory statement is involved, courts first consider the type of defamation. The most serious type, so-called per se defamation, involves the imputation of crime, a loathsome disease, a maiden's unchastity, or defamations affecting a person in his business, trade, profession, office or calling. Per se defamation is considered so serious that the person doesn't even have to prove specific consequential injury; damages will be awarded. In all other cases, in order to recover, the defamed person must prove some special damage.

Under some circumstances a statement may be made even if defamatory. For example, on the floor of the U.S. Senate, a senator can say virtually anything he or she wants in connection with the business at hand, even if false. A senator is absolutely privileged in that setting. Similarly, attorneys usually enjoy an absolute privilege for any written or oral statements made in court, regardless of whether the statements are false or maliciously made.

Besides absolute privilege, courts recognize a qualified privilege. If a doctor makes a statement in connection with his practice, it may be protected by a qualified privilege. To be protected the statement must be made in good faith to serve a legitimate purpose, such as obtaining payment from the patient's health insurance carrier, and limited in its scope to that purpose.[194] Good faith also implies that the statement be made at a proper time, in a proper manner and only to proper parties. If a qualified privilege applies, a communication can be the basis for a lawsuit only if that privilege has been abused. This is the importance of privilege in defamation cases. In addition to truth, which must be proved by the defendant, privilege is a defense.[195] To sue for a privileged communication requires proof of actual malice, such as actual knowledge that the statement is false or making the statement without reasonable grounds for believing it is true.[196]

Anyone can be accused of defamation. However, doctors are particularly vulnerable because they are frequently asked for information about a patient that is often of an extremely personal nature. Statements may necessarily fall into the per se categories of defamation involving disease, chastity and work ability. Thus, even if a statement must be made in connection with a doctor's practice, care must be taken.

Failure to protect

Failure to protect against suicide

If a doctor considers a patient a potential suicide risk, the doctor may be under an obligation to take reasonable steps to prevent the patient from harming himself.

When a person commits suicide, the distressed relatives often seek to blame someone. If the person was under a professional's care, that professional is a likely target. If a reasonably skillful physician would consider a patient a suicide risk, a doctor is under an obligation to take reasonable steps to prevent the patient from harming himself.[197]

Failure to protect victims

If a doctor determines that a patient presents a serious danger to another, the doctor may have an obligation to use reasonable care to protect the potential victim.

Psychiatrists often deal with patients who present a danger to others. Although Pennsylvania's courts have not reported confronting the issue, it has been found elsewhere that when a doctor or other professional determines, or under the standards of the profession should determine, that a patient presents a serious danger of violence to another, he incurs an obligation to use reasonable care to protect the intended victim against the danger. The discharge of this duty may require the doctor to take various steps, depending upon the nature of the case. Thus this duty may require the doctor to warn the intended victim or others likely to apprise the victim of the danger, to notify the police, or to take whatever other steps are reasonably necessary under the circumstances.

Example

Prosenjit Poddar was being treated by Dr. Lawrence Moore, a psychologist. During the course of his treatment, Poddar confided an intention to kill an unnamed girl, readily identifiable as Tatiana Tarasoff, when she returned to California after spending the summer in Brazil. Dr. Moore, in consultation with others, decided that Poddar should be committed for observation in a mental hospital. He also requested the assistance of the police department in securing Poddar's confinement.

When the police officers took Poddar into custody, they were satisfied that he was rational and so released him on his promise to stay away from Tatiana. Dr. Moore's supervisor then directed that no further action be taken to confine Poddar for evaluation.

Poddar then persuaded Tatiana's brother to share an apartment with him near Tatiana's residence. Shortly after her return from Brazil, Poddar, as he had stated he would do, went to her residence and killed her.

The California Supreme Court held that a therapist has a duty to warn a patient's intended victim or others likely to apprise the victim of the threatened danger.[198]

The possibility of liability to nonpatients is of great concern to physicians because it is open-ended. Traditional concepts of foreseeability don't offer much in the way of a reliable limitation. In a Florida case, a family member of a patient sued a physician. The family member contracted tuberculosis and alleged it was because the doctor had failed to diagnose TB in his patient.[199] But in a federal case applying Pennsylvania law, the court refused to extend the duty to a third party:

Example

Mrs. Soto became unconscious at home and was taken to the hospital and admitted. The admitting diagnosis was drug overdose. She signed out a few days later. Less than a month following, Mr. Soto passed out at home and died. His death was caused by carbon monoxide poisoning, and Mrs. Soto discovered a defective gas heater in their home.

Mrs. Soto sued the gas company, the landlord, and the doctors who had treated her. She never had an opportunity to try and prove the physicians were negligent—the case against them was thrown out. The court said they'd owed no duty to the dead man because no communicable disease was involved. While not accepting Tarasoff as controlling, the court explained that this case was different because Mrs. Soto hadn't caused her husband's death.[200]

Failure to warn

Physicians have an obligation to inform patients about their condition or treatment. This includes warning them about activities made more dangerous by the condition or treatment.

This is well understood by physicians when prescribing drugs that, for example, make it unsafe to drive. The doctor risks liability to those injured by his sleepy patient as well.[201] But problems can arise when the doctor allows the patient to return to routine activity that might be dangerous because of the nature of the disease itself.

Example

Mr. Berry was admitted June 8, complaining of chest pain, nausea and shortness of breath. He was found to have congestive heart failure, diabetes mellitus, and chronic lung disease. When he was discharged on June 15, he was advised to stop smoking, stop drinking, and lose some of his 275 pounds.

Mr. Berry was also told by the doctor that he could return to work June 23 and that he should obtain a private physician. On June 23, Mr. Berry returned to work and suffered a devastating heart attack.

The widow brought suit against the doctor and won. She claimed that Mr. Berry should have been warned away from work a longer time.[202]

Negligently performed physician examination

A doctor retained by a third party, such as a prospective employer, to perform a physical examination must do so in accordance with the appropriate standard of care.

Most doctors perform physical examinations of individuals for third parties, such as prospective employers. These exams are potential problem areas legally and must be treated seriously. However, a doctor may be liable to the person for whom the examination is done if it is performed in a negligent fashion and the doctor fails to accurately disclose disabilities that should have been disclosed.[203]

If doctors perform physicals for a third party, they should make very clear to the person examined that a doctor-patient relationship is not being established and that they are not undertaking the care or treatment of the person examined. Confirmation of this in writing may be appropriate. Courts in the United States have been divided on the issue of whether or not there is a duty to the person examined. Pennsylvania is currently in the category of not finding a duty owed.

Example

Dorian Craddock hurt his back at work. After almost 6 months of disability and compensation, the worker's compensation carrier arranged for an examination by a physician hired by the insuror. The doctor believed Mr. Craddock fully recovered.

The benefits were terminated and, over his own protests, Mr. Craddock returned to work. He alleged that after a brief period, he suffered a severe aggravation of his back injury. He sued the physician.

The court said no trial was needed and dismissed the suit. The physician owed no duty to Mr. Craddock and as such, even if all the allegations were proved true, he couldn't sue that doctor for malpractice.[204]

Other forms of medical malpractice

Misrepresentations and nondisclosure

Although a doctor has no obligation to disclose or remedy the effects of prior acts of malpractice, he or she may not intentionally misrepresent or fraudulently conceal the malpractice.

Attorneys have admonished doctors to "come clean" when they commit malpractice.[205] This cleansing ritual is a clear way to invite a malpractice suit or to lose one if it is filed. A doctor actually has no obligation to disclose his or her malpractice if no harm results. However, a doctor who intentionally misrepresents or fraudulently conceals the malpractice may be liable to a patient. Additionally, fraudulent concealment of malpractice may extend the statute of limitations and give the doctor's malpractice carrier grounds to deny coverage.

Obviously, concealment of a fact of potential importance to the patient's health is intolerable, even if it was negligently caused.[206] If any doubt exists as to the potential health impact, the situation must be revealed. Attempts at cover-up or active misrepresentation can make an otherwise close case indefensible and escalate damages awarded by an outraged jury.

Infliction of emotional distress

A doctor may be liable for emotional distress caused to others by intentional or negligent acts under limited circumstances.

A developing area of the law deals with the circumstances under which a person may recover for mental disturbances caused by another. Claims of this sort are categorized generally as those for infliction of emotional distress.

Infliction of emotional distress may either be intentional or negligent. Pennsylvania recognizes both forms.[207]

Intentional infliction of emotional distress allows a person to recover for mental disturbances resulting from some intentional and outrageous conduct. The conduct must have been intentional and must have been atrocious. The conduct complained of must be so outrageous, so atrocious, and so utterly intolerable that a person of ordinary sensibilities could not be reasonably expected to endure it.[208] The claim may be made by the person against whom outrageous conduct is directed as well as third parties, typically those who are not only present at the time but whom the perpetrator knows to be present. Relatives of crime victims often have a claim for intentional infliction of emotional distress.

Unlike intentional infliction of emotional distress, which results from some intentional act, negligent infliction of emotional distress results from some negligent act. Witnesses to an accident or injury make most claims. Some states will deny a claim for negligently caused emotional distress brought by a bystander unless it is accompanied by a contemporaneous physical injury to or impact on the person making the claim, but Pennsylvania has expanded the rule to allow suits by those very nearby. Instead of the "impact rule," Pennsylvania has adopted the "zone-of-physical-danger rule."[209] Under this rule the person making the claim must be in such proximity as to create physical danger and, because of another's negligence, have reasonable fear for his own safety. This rule does not require that the bystander actually suffer a physical impact or injury at the time of the negligent act, but it does hold that the bystander must have been close enough to the accident in which the direct victim was physically injured that a high risk of physical impact on the bystander existed. The bystander must show some physical injury or illness resulting from the emotional distress caused by the negligence. The emotional injury alone is not enough.[210]

Claims against doctors for negligent infliction of emotional distress will probably increase as the law in this area develops. With the present open policy of many delivery rooms, it is entirely possible that claims may be made if a family member witnesses some act of medical malpractice.

Example

After the delivery of their stillborn child, the Boarts sued the obstetrician and the hospital. After the defendant's initial pleading, the plaintiff's changed their claims to one for negligent infliction of emotional distress.

The case was dismissed without trial. The court said first that the change in claim wouldn't be allowed. Two years had passed and the change wasn't an amendment but a new issue. Second, there wasn't an arguable claim for emotional distress anyway, because no physical manifestation of the injury was claimed.[211]

If the plaintiff alleges physical injury from the emotional distress or if intentional infliction is claimed, he may get a chance to prove his case before a jury.

Example

Tom and Joe's fisticuffs resulted in Tom undergoing surgery for a fractured jaw. Tom died during surgery and Joe was arrested.

Joe sued, claiming both negligent and intentional infliction of emotional distress. He claimed the doctors had prepared records indicating that the fight was the sole cause of Tom's death, but that their malpractice had actually been the cause.

Because Joe's complaint claimed no physical harm, the negligent infliction count was dismissed. But Joe won an opportunity to try and prove that the physicians had acted intentionally and outrageously.[212]

False imprisonment and wrongful commitment

A doctor may not restrain or confine a patient without the patient's consent except as permitted by law.

False imprisonment, sometimes called false arrest, involves restraining or confining a person without his consent and contrary to law. Imprisonment in this sense does not require stone walls, iron bars, or the like.[213] Rather, the prohibition against false imprisonment protects a person's freedom of movement.

Few doctors are ever accused of false imprisonment. While a patient may be physically restrained, such as with a Posey belt, the patient nevertheless has sought treatment from the doctor that may have involved the use of physical restraints. The patient could, however, choose to decline further treatment and leave. The current greater risk is premature discharge.[214]

The most likely instance in which a doctor could face a possible claim of false imprisonment occurs when a patient wishes to refuse further treatment that the doctor believes is indicated. As discussed in connection with patient consent, a competent patient is generally free to accept or refuse treatment. If an adult is involved, documenting the refusal of treatment and the capacity to knowingly refuse is important. If a minor is involved, however, the consent comes from the parents. Simple refusal to discharge is not false imprisonment; some element of actual or treatment force is necessary.[215]

Like other so-called "intentional torts," multiple different claims can arise out of one incident. For example, the physican can be accused of negligence in diagnosing the need for restraints and an intentional wrong in ordering their application. The "intent" involved does not refer to a plan or desire to harm someone or violate their rights. Rather the issue is the intent to bring about the result (i.e., restraint) or a knowledge that restraint is the likely result (i.e., "lacking a ward to keep one patient from leaving and thereby confining others").[216]

Litigation has been initiated in Pennsylvania by commited persons or following attempts to commit a person.[217] Caution is needed in these situations, as the abuse potential is great. The physican need not police the motives of those bringing a patient for evaluation for possible commitment, but an objective analysis of the totality of the history and the examination is necessary before depriving an individual of his freedom.[218] A statute exists purporting to make immune from liability physicians who participate in the commitment process, but only to the extent that no willful misconduct or gross negligence is involved.[219] The statute only protects regarding the decision to commit, not regarding care rendered after the decision is made.[220]

Sexual misconduct

A physician has a duty to refrain from conduct, including sexual activities, detrimental to a patient's well-being.

A doctor who engages in criminal sexual misconduct may be prosecuted under the criminal law.

In other states, some question may arise regarding consensual sexual contact between the health professional and the patient.[221] It is doubtful that this issue would arise in Pennsylvania. Especially in the case of psychotherapists and patients, the validity of the patient's consent to sexual activity is questionable.[222] Because of the professional relationship, the court may view the patient's will to refuse as overcome by the therapist or in some other way lacking free choice.

Example

Gail G. came to Dr. McCabe as a patient in 1968. Using both verbal and drug psychotherapy, Dr. McCabe treated her for 6 months before they began to have sexual relations.

The affair lasted six years, the last 2 of which they lived together. Then one morning, he beat her. Gail sued for medical malpractice, claiming as injuries:

Left frontal skull fracture
Cerebral concussion
Headaches
Blurred vision
Intravaginal trauma
Parametritis
Multiple contusions
Abrasions and bites
Scarring

Shock
Mental anxiety
Embarrassment
Injury to her nerves and nervous system
Pain and mental suffering
Lost earnings and earning capacity
Special damages

The jury awarded her $665,000, including $300,000 in punitive damages.[223]

Future forms of medical malpractice

The situations giving rise to professional liability and theories of recovery are not stagnant concepts. Customary and accepted medicine today may be malpractice tomorrow. But why?

The courts decide whether a doctor can be sued for doing or not doing something. Very simply, a judge is convinced that under these circumstances, redress should be available if a patient is injured as a result of the actions or inactions of a doctor.

Many factors are considered in deciding whether redress should be available. The broad factors considered in making this determination include:

- The extent to which the doctor could or should have anticipated that his actions or inactions would result in the patient's injury. Courts refer to this as the extent injury was "foreseeable."
- The magnitude of the burden of guarding against the injury and the consequences of placing that burden upon the doctor.
- The desirablity in terms of public policy of imposing a duty on the doctor to guard against the risk that is involved.
- Concerns about who should bear the costs of an injury—the injured person or someone else.

As applied to medical malpractice, these broad factors are flanked by an ever-widening view that injuries should be compensible regardless of fault. The public increasingly expects perfect results. But the eventual result of the mortal condition is death and few will naturally have perfect health until that inescapable end.

What will be the novel forms of medical malpractice in the future? Lawyer Melvin M. Belli, the "King of Torts," suggests a number of areas ripe for litigation, including:

- ***Preferred provider organizations.*** Belli considers this system a prime target for liability claims. For example, when a provider contract is terminated and a patient still requires care, the doctor could be considered to have abandoned the patient. Similarly, a provider contract may discourage referrals to other providers even though the doctor's standard of care may dictate otherwise. Belli also points out that a doctor's own insurance may not cover liability arising from provider contracts.[224]

- ***Diagnosis related groups.*** Under the DRG and similar cost-containment systems, patients can be ousted from the hospital after the allotted treatment time is up. If the DRGs don't fit, tests ordered won't be paid for. According to Belli, a doctor has a duty to provide not only care consistent with community standards but also all the care that's medically necessary. Therefore if a doctor goes along with terminating treatment for financial reasons when the standard of care would dictate that treatment is needed, the doctor could be liable to the patient.[225]
- ***"Do not resuscitate" orders.*** Belli points out that "do not resuscitate" orders are a likely source of problems. Standards are limited, and doctors are reluctant to document these decisions. Belli believes documentation, including informed statements from family members, is essential to avoid problems in this area.[226]
- ***Continuing education.*** Medical science develops rapidly, with alternative treatments becoming available all the time. Belli considers a doctor's failure to be knowledgeable of alternative treatments a significant source of liability. It is thus important for doctors to keep up on developments.[227]
- ***Consultations and referrals.*** As medicine becomes more specialized, the need increases to better determine when consultations and referrals are required. Belli states that a doctor's hesitancy to seek consultations or make referrals boils down to "economics and ego." Very simply, either the doctor is trying to hold down the patient's costs and keep the patient or the doctor believes he can handle the case. According to Belli, neither will be placed above good patient care when a medical malpractice claim is made.[228] This will also be a problem for HMOs and other cost-containing organizations.
- ***Birth injuries.*** Belli sees prenatal care and delivery as a particularly risky danger area in the medical-legal limelight. Physicians are being sued at greater rates, and the awards are well into the millions. He expects this trend to continue.[229]

Another developing area is known as strict liability in tort. Under this theory a person is automatically liable even though not actually negligent. Strict liability is often imposed on manufacturers of defective products. This means that if the product sold caused the injury, the manufacturer and/or seller must pay for the injury, even if they were perfectly careful. In Pennsylvania, the seller of a defective product can be liable, even if he exercised all possible care in preparation and sale of that product.[230] The reasoning so far has been applied to hospitals in this state.[231] One case eliminated the strict need for the provider of the product to be engaged in the business of selling it. But it has been effectively mooted by the passage of a statute making blood products a service, not a product.[232] However, the reasoning of that case should be applied to physicians.[233]

Perhaps an even greater threat to doctors is liability to nonpatients.[234] Thus a doctor is forced to worry not only about claims from his own patient but also about the possibility of a claim from someone who might be injured by the patient.

Endnotes

1. The seminal and summary statement on the subject is that of Justice Cardozo: "Every human being of adult years and sound mind has a right to determine what shall be done with his own body . . ." Schalendorff v. Society of New York Hospital, 211 N.Y. 125, 129-30, 105 N.E. 92, 93 (1914).
2. From Cooper v. Roberts, 220 Pa.Sup. 260, 386 A.2d 647 (1971). The lower court stated the rule followed in most of the states. Pennsylvania's version of the minority rule was codified by the legislature in 40 Pa.S.A. subsection 1301.103 (1987 Purdon), but the statute was declared unconstitutional insofar as it applies to primary and mandatory jurisdiction of the panels. Mattas v. Thompson, 491 Pa. 385, 421 A.2d 190 (1980).
3. Verbal consent can be just as effective and acceptable as written consent, if the requirements for valid consent are met. Statutes or regulations or local rules may specify written consent requirements, however. For example, a hospital's medical staff may require written consents for certain procedures.
4. The patient's informed permission should not be confused with the writing itself. Too many health care providers think of "a consent" as but another dreary routine bit of paperwork. "Consent is a process, not a form." Rozovsky, Consent to Treatment: A Practical Guide, Boston, 1984, Little, Brown & Co., p. 3.
5. A patient may, of course, change his mind. We have moved forward from the pre-anesthetic era when patients requiring amputation were asked but once. The eighteenth century English surgeon, chosen for his speed, entered holding the saw behind his back. "Will you have it off?" he'd ask, and the patient giving consent was not heeded if he raised objections thereafter.
6. Smith v. Yohe, 412 Pa. 94, 107-8, 194 A.2d 167, 174 (1963).
7. Gray v. Grunnagle, 423 Pa., 144, 166, 223 A.2d 663, 674 (1966).
8. In the case cited *Id.*, the admitting orthopedist obtained consent but the operating neurosurgeon did not.
9. For example Meretsky v. Ellenby, 370 So. 2d 1222, 1224 (1979).
10. Dunham v. Wright, 423 F.2d 940, 947 (1970).
11. Satz v. Perlmutter, 379 So.2d 359 (Fla. 1980).
12. *See generally* Bleiler, E.: How your patient's religion can affect his treatment, Medical Economics, May 28, 1984. This article briefly discusses the beliefs of various religions.
13. Jehovah's Witnesses believe that the bible forbids consuming blood. *See, e.g.,* Acts 15:20, 28, 29; 21:25. Neither transfusion nor transplants are acceptable. *See* Watch Tower Bible and Tract Society of Pennsylvania: Jehovah's Witnesses and the question of blood, New York, 1977, Watchtower Bible and Tract Society of New York, Inc. and International Bible Students Association.
14. Richardson, Doctors, Lawyers, and the Courts, W. H. Anderson (1965), p. 259, citing In re Queens, 167 Pa. Super. 10, 74 A.2d 705 (1950). Comment, an Assessment of the Pennsylvania Estate Guardianship Incompetency Standard, **124** U. Pa. L. Rev. 1048 (1976)
15. 20 Pa. C.S.A. subsection 5511 (Purdon 1975).
16. From Matter of Terwilliger, 304 Pa. Super. 553, 450 A.2d 376 (1982). See also Solnick, Proxy Consent for Incompetent Non-terminally Ill Adult Patients; **6** J. Leg. Med. 1 (1985).

17. 20 Pa. C.S.A. Section 5602 (Purdon 1987).
18. 20 Pa. C.S.A. Section 5604 (Purdon 1987).
19. Application of President and Directors of Georgetown College, Inc., 331 F.2d 100, 1008 (D.C.CA), cert. den. 377 U.S. 978 (1964). These cases suggest that when life-saving treatment is refused, dependence should be considered as well as mental capacity.
20. For example, 35 Pa.C.S.A. Section 521.8 (Purdon 1959) provides that persons arrested for sex crimes can be compelled to submit to examination for venereal disease.
21. 40 Pa.C.S.A. Section 1301.103 (Purdon 1987).
22. Keeton, W.: Prosser and Keeton on the Law of Torts (ed. 5) at 190, St. Paul, Minn., 1984, West Publishing Co.
23. Rozovsky, supra, n.4 at 6-8.
24. Cooper v. Roberts, 220 Pa. Super. 260, 286 A.2d 647, 651 (1971). The court left the door open to require expert testimony where technical expertise is needed to determine what should have been disclosed. *Id.* The majority of states require the expert's testimony. Rozovsky, supra. n.4, at 78-79.
25. Rogers v. Lu, 335 Pa. Super. 595, 485 A.2d 54 (1984).
26. Rozovsky, supra, n.4, at 66-7.
27. A detailed note in the record is mandatory. Consultation should be considered. Consideration should also be given to asking the patient if he wishes to be informed and telling him that there is an obligation to inform absent patient refusal.
28. *See* Riskin, L.: Informed consent: Looking for the action, University of Illinois Law Forum **1975:** 580, 1975.
29. *Id.*
30. Malloy v. Shanahan, 280 Pa. Super. 440, 421 A.2d 802, 804 (1980).
31. *Id.*
32. Rozovsky, supra, n. 4 at 237-9.
33. 35 Pa.C.S.A. Section 10101 (Purdon 1976).
34. 35 Pa.C.S.A. Section 10103 (Purdon 1976).
35. 35 Pa.C.S.A. Section 10102 (Purdon 1976).
36. Rozovsky, supra, n.4 at 239-40.
37. 356 Pa.C.S.A. Section 10104 (Purdon 1976).
38. 35 Pa.C.S.A. Section 6603 (Purdon 1976), in Colautti v. Franklin, 439 U.S. 379 (1979). See also, Note, United States Supreme Court Abortion Decision Clarifies Concept of Fetal Viability and Scope of Physician's Discretion in Determining When Viability Is Reached, **52** Temple L.Q. 1240 (1979).
39. Roe v. Casey, 623 F.2d 899 (4CA 1980), addressing 35 Pa.C.S.A. Section 6607 (Purdon 1976).
40. Planned Parenthood Association v. Fitzpatrick, 401 F. Supp. 554, 561 (E.D. Pa. 1975).
41. By statute, "legal custody" includes the legal right to make medical decisions. 23 Pa.C.S.A. Section 5302 (Purdon 1987).
42. *Id.*
43. 20 Pa.C.S.A. Section 5144, 3332 and Official Comment (1949) (Purdon 1987).
44. *See generally* Bleiler, E.: How your patient's religion can affect his treatment, Medical Economics, May 28, 1984. This article briefly discusses the beliefs of various religions.
45. *See* Watch Tower Bible and Tract Society of Pennsylvania: Jehovah's Witnesses and the question of blood, New York, Watchtower Bible and Tract Society of New York, Inc., and International Bible Students Association, 1977.
46. Rozovsky, supra, n.4 at 314-3221.
47. In re Green, 448 Pa. 338, 292 A.2d 387 (1972); overruling 220 Pa. Super. 191, 286 A.2d 681 (1971).
48. 42 Pa.S.C.A. Section 6341 (Purdon 1982).
49. 42 Pa.S.C.A. Section 6302 (Purdon 1982).
50. *See generally* 24 POF2d 169, Circumstances Warranting Court-Ordered Medical Treatment of Minors. Also, Note, Compulsory Medical Treatment of Children: Rights in Conflict. **35** U. Pitt. L. Rev. 369 (1973).
51. For example, see Cal. Health. and Safety Code Section 7185 et seq (West 1976).
52. Aker, Law of Wills in Pennsylvania, Section 21.6. Bisel, 1985.
53. Rozovsky, supra, n.4 at 483.

54. Aker, supra, n.52 at Section 22.44.
55. See discussion above and fn. 18.
56. Report of the President's Commission for the Study of Ethical Problems in Medicine and Biomedical and Behavioral Research, Deciding to Forego Life-Sustaining Treatment. (1983).
57. Aker, supra, n.52, reprinted by permission.
58. Rozovsky, supra, n.4 at 620. In Pennsylvania the statute is 35 Pa.C.S.A. Section 1111, et seq. (Purdon 1977).
59. *See* Snyder v. Holy Cross Hosp., 30 Md. App. 317, 352 A.2d 334 (1976).
60. *In re* Kopechne, 47 D. & C. 2d 579, 586 (1969). Despite nationwide interest, Mary Jo's parents were able to block her disinternment.
61. Frick v. McClelland, 122 A.2d 43, 46 (1956).
62. 35 Pa.C.S.A. Sect. 450.504 and 1121 (Purdon 1977).
63. 35 Pa.C.S.A. Sect. 450.502 (Purdon 1977).
64. *Id.*, at Sect. 450.503.
65. 35 Pa.C.S.A. Sect 1238 (Purdon 1956).
66. Absent bad faith or arbitrary or capricious acts, this authority of the coroner cannot be challenged. Frick, supra, n.61, at 45.
67. Commonwealth v. Anderson, 253 Pa.448, 194 A.2d, 365, (1978).
68. Commonwealth ex rel. Fox v. Maroney, 417 Pa.308 207 A.2d 810 (1965).
69. *In re* Kopechne, supra, n.60.
70. Frick, supra, n.61, at 46. In addition to the case against the coroner, the widow's suit against the physician requesting the coroner to order an autopsy was dismissed.
71. 35 Pa.C.S.A. Sect. 1114 (Purdon 1977).
72. *Id.*, at Sect. 1111.
73. *Id.*, at Sect. 1112.
74. Annot, Liability for performing an autopsy, 83 ALR 2d 955, 964 (1962).
75. *Id.*
76. 35 Pa.C.S.A. Sect. 1111. Except for the spouse, unwillingness to claim the body themselves does not remove other family members from the preference sequence.
77. 35 Pa.C.S.A. Sect. 10025 (Purdon 1984).
78. 20 Pa.C.S.A. Sect. 8604, et seq. (Purdon 1972). Uniform laws covering various subjects are proposed by "commmissioners" and can be adopted with or without variation by the states. Pennsylvania's statute varied little from that proposed by the commissioners. Uniform Anatomical Gift Act (U.L.A. 1972)
79. 20 Pa.C.S.A. Sect 8602 (Purdon 1972). The age specified had been 21, now is 18.
80. *Id.*, at (b).
81. 20 Pa.C.S.A. Sect. 8604. Pennsylvania added the requirement that a gift of the whole body must be in writing at least 15 days prior to death. This could create problems for physicians regarding the validity of undated documents.
82. 20 Pa.C.S.A. Sect. 8604(e) (Purdon 1972).
83. 20 Pa.C.S.A. Sect. 8608 (Purdon 1986).
84. 20 Pa.C.S.A. Sect. 8606 (Purdon 1972).
85. 20 Pa.C.S.A. Sect. 8608 (Purdon 1986).
86. 20 Pa.C.S.A. Sect. 8604(d.1) (Purdon 1986).
87. 20 Pa.C.S.A. Sect. 8607 (Purdon 1972).
88. *Id.*
89. Adapted from Capone v. Donovan, 480 A.2d 1249 (Pa. Super. 1984). The hometown doctor settled for $25,000, but the suit was allowed to proceed against the other two physicians.
90. The proper measure would be a comparison of the overall risk and cost of doing the test or procedure on all patients in that situation. For example, CAT scans for simple headaches. But in court, the lawyer will make comparison of the cost or risk of the test or procedure not done with the damage to that particular patient. The retrospectoscope is a cruel instrument.
91. The jury didn't. The case was decided in favor of the physician in part because the patient's credibility (regarding the statements made to him in Reading) was questioned. Taken from Brozana v. Flanigan, 454 A.2d 1125 (Pa. Super. 1983).

92. Denardo v. Carnerval, 444 A.2d 135 (Pa. Super. 1982).
93. These general concepts are discussed in Chapter 2.
94. Pratt v. Stein, 444 A.2d 674, 689 (Pa. Super 1982).
95. Brozana v. Flanigan, 454 A.2d 1125, 1127-8 (Pa. Super. 1983).
96. Pratt, supra. n.94, at 689, fn. 23
97. From Furey v. Thomas Jefferson University Hospital, 472 A.2d 1083 (Pa. Super 1984). Also important was the trial judge's reading the slip himself as "460" within the jury's hearing. Generally, experts are asked about the basis for their opinion at deposition. Differences in opinion about the facts of the case are brought out at that time.
98. *Id.* at 1089.
99. Fala, The Law of Medical Malpractice in Pennsylvania, **36** U. Pitt. L. Rev. 203, 216 (1974).
100. McBride, Tort Law, **56** Pa. B.A.Q. 24, 35 (1985).
101. From Branner v. Lankenau Hospital, 417 A.2d 196 (PA 1980). This sort of appellate decision dosen't mean that the doctor loses. It simply means that the judge can't take the decision away from the jury on the basis of the appealed issue.
102. From Clark v. Hoerner, 525, A.2d 377 (Pa. Super. 1987). The appeals court reversed and ordered a new trial because of the appearance of a surprise witness. Dr. William Atkinson, Chief of Pulmonary Medicine at the University of Pennsylvania's Presbyterian Hospital, came in on the eighth day of trial to testify that the cause of death was a bacterial infection and that a CXR was required on the second visit. The superior court said this was unfair, that trial by ambush was not to be countenanced. *Id.,* at 384.
103. 42 Pa.C.S.A. Sect. 5527 (2).
104. Murray v. University of Pennsylvania Hosp., 490 A.2d 839, 841 (Pa. Super. 1985) and cases cited therein.
105. Guilmet v. Campbell, 385 Mich. 57, 188 N.W.2d 601 (1971).
106. Hawkins v. McGee, 84 N.H. 114, 146 A. 641 (1929).
107. Robins v. Finestone, 308 N.Y. 543, 127 N.E.2d 330 (1955).
108. Noel v. Proud, 189 Kan. 6, 367 P.2d 61 (1961).
109. Crawford v. Duncan, 61 Cal. App. 647, 215 P. 573 (1923).
110. Bailey v. Harmon, 74 Colo. 390, 222 P. 393 (1924).
111. Composano v. Claiborn, 2 Conn. Cir. 135, 196 A.2d 129 (1963).
112. Sullivan v. O'Connor, 363 Mass. 579, 296 N.E.2d 183 (1973).
113. From Murray v. Univ. of Pennsylvania Hosp., 490 A.2d 839 (Pa. Super. 1985). Part of defendants' problem was their failure at trial to object to jury instructions which allowed the jury to award pain and suffering damages. These damages are part of personal injury awards, not contract.
114. Mason v. Western Pennsylvania Hosp., 453 A.2d 974, 979 (PA. 1982), Nix, J. Concurring and dissenting. See also Annot. 43 A.L.R.3d 1221, Contract to Effect Specific Medical Result.
115. **53** Temple L.Q. 176.
116. Murray, supra, n.113.
117. Murray, supra, n.113.
118. Speck v. Finegold, 439 A.2d 110, 118 (Pa. 1981).
119. *Id.*
120. Murray, supra, n.113.
121. Mason, supra, n.114, at 976. But not so when the suit is in contract, as for a breach of express or implied warranty. See above, section on Guaranteed Results and Warranties.
122. Mason, supra, n.114, at 976. Most of the states who have considered this issue agree. *Id.*
123. Mason, supra, n.114, at 976, quoting Shaheen v. Knight, **11** D. & C. 2d 41, 46 (1957).
124. *Id.,* at 976-7, C.J. O'Brien, concurring and dissenting, quoting Cockrum v. Baumgartner, 425 N.E. 2d 968, 970 (Ill. App. 1981).
125. From Ellis v. Sherman, 478 A.2d 1339 (Pa. Super. 1982), affirmed on other grounds, 515 A.2d 1327 (Pa. 1986).

126. Schedder, Woman's Reproductive Rights, Is there a Conflict with a Child's Right to Be Born Free From Defects? 7 J. Leg. Med. 358, 9 (1986).
127. Speck, supra, n.118.
128. Adapted from Stribling v. deQuernedo, 432 A.2d 239 (Pa. Super. 1980), citing and quoting Speck, supra, n.118.
129. Ellis v. Sherman, 515 A.2d 1327 (Pa. 1986). Health professional readers should understand what it means to disallow a claim as a matter of law. Physicians and other providers, beset by litigation and insurance premium supernovas, often are indignant that more cases are not thrown out by the judge. But to do so denies the plaintiff their right to trial by jury. Consider the importance of this right and appreciate why claims are decided by judges so infrequently.
130. Information regarding the law can be obtained from the U.S. Department of Justice, Registration Section, P.O. Box 28083, Central Station, Drug Enforcement Administration, Washington, D.C. 20005, or by telephoning its Chicago office at (312) 353-7889. The Drug Enforcement Administration publishes an "Outline of the Controlled Substance Act of 1970—A Manual for the Medical Practitioner," which should be reviewed by every practitioner.
131. Adapted from Pratt v. Stein, 444 A.2d 674 (Pa. Super. 1982). The long delay between trial (1966) and initial argument on appeal (1980) was not explained by the court. Other issues at trial included whether or not the surgery was indicated, whether or not surgery should have been first attempted on the cervical spine, concerns about cultures and responses to them, and the delay before opening and debriding the infected operative site.
132. See generally **3** Am. Jur. POF 2d 117.
133. See Chapter 2 above, section on Duty.
134. Smith v. Linn, 414 A.2d 1106, 1107 (Pa. Cmmwlth. 1980).
135. *Id.* The decision applied the now defunct arbitration statute, but it is still a great source of comfort to this author.
136. 42 Pa.C.S.A. Section 8331 (Purdon 1982). The Veterinary good samaritan statute is at 42 Pa.C.S.A. Section 8331.1 (Purdon 1980).
137. For support and a discussion of the affirmative duty in civil law countries, see Note, The Duty to Rescue the Good Samaritan, **71** Dick. L. Rev. 75 (1966).
138. Note, Good Samaritan Legislation: An Analysis and a Proposal, **38** Temple L. Q. 418, 424-7 (1965).
139. Chayet, Legal Implications of Emergency Care, Boston, 1969, McGraw-Hill Book Co. p. 25.
140. King, The Law of Medical Malpractice, 2nd Ed., St. Paul, Minn., 1986, West Publishing Co. p. 26.
141. In Pennsylvania, the definition is simple. A partnership is an association of two or more persons to carry on, as co-owners, a business for profit. 59 Pa.C.S.A. Section 311(a) (Purdon 1987).
142. 59 Pa.C.S.A. Section 325 (Purdon 1987).
143. 59 Pa.C.S.A. Section 327 (Purdon 1987).
144. 59 Pa.C.S.A. Section 328 (Purdon 1987). Establishing the non-partnership arrangement formally and clarifying that it is not a partnership in correspondence, etc., can help.
145. 15 Pa.C.S.A. Section 2901 et seq. (Purdon 1987). Like other states, Pennsylvania has a separate set of laws allowing smaller organizations to obtain the benefits of doing business in the corporate form.
146. 15 Pa.C.S.A. Section 2913 (Purdon 1987).
147. See generally annotation: **85** A.L.R. 2d 881.
148. King, supra, n.140, at 233.
149. Stanhope v. Los Angeles Law of Chiropractic, 54 Cal. App. 2d 141, 128 P.2d 705 (1942); Williams v. St. Claire Medical Center, 657 S.W.2d 590 (Ky. Ct. App. 1983); Hannola v. City of Lakewood, 68 Ohio App. 2d 61, 426 N.E.2d 1187 (1980; Smith v. St. Francis Hospital, 676 P.2d 279 (Okl. App. Ct. 1983); Themins v. Emanuel Lutheran Charity Bd., 54 Or. App. 901, 637 P.2d 155 (1981); Adamski v. Tacoma General Hospital, 20 Wash. App. 98, 579 P.2d 970 (1978).
150. From Gregory v. Martyak, 408 A.2d 188 (Pa. Cmmwlth. 1979). Sovereign immunity is

an ancient concept which comes to us today from the politics of olde England. As the crown's authority became less absolute, the monarchy clung to some privileges more tenaciously than others. One principle adhered to was that the king could not be sued. "The king can do no wrong," it was said, and this mantle of immunity fell onto the shoulders of the government acting for the monarch. In America, sovereign immunity was held by state and federal governments for many years. But in this century, many of the states and U.S. Congress have passed laws giving up this protection, or some part of it. See 42 Pa.C.S.A. Sections 1722(a)(1), 5524(2), and 8301.

151. Adapted from Riddle Memoral Hospital v. Doahn, 475 A.2d 1314 (PA 1984). Despite this instruction, the jury found for both Riddle and the doctor. But it could have gone the other way. By allowing the jury to decide, the court was saying, in effect, that Riddle could be held responsible.
152. Adapted from Yorston v. Pennell, 153 A.2d 255 (Pa. 1959).
153. Fala, supra, n.99, at 238-9.
154. The doctrine ws abolished that year in the case of Flagiello v. Pennsylvania Hospital, 208 A.2d 193 (PA 1965).
155. McConnell v. Williams, 65 A.2d 243 (PA 1949).
156. Benedict v. Bandi, 122 A.2d 209 (PA 1956).
157. Mazer v. Lipschutz, 327 F.2d 42 (3CA 1963). This was a federal case applying Pennsylvania law. In addition to the technician's error, the anesthesiologist misinterpreted the blood label.
158. McConnell, supra, n.155, at 246.
159. Rockwell v. Kaplan, 173 A.2d 54 (PA 1961). The case against the anesthesiologist was Rockwell v. Stone, 173 A.2d 48 (PA 1961).
160. More cases will come up, too, because of the increasing tendency to "shotgun" and name all health care providers involved in any way, when the suits are filed.
161. Shull v. Schwartz, 173 A.2d 402 (PA 1950).
162. Powell v. Resser, 122 A.2d 209 (PA 1956).
163. Karas v. Jackson, 582 F. Supp. 43 (E.D. PA 1983).
164. Embrey v. Borough of West Mifflin, 390 A.2d 765 (Pa. Super. 1978).
165. 42 Pa.C.S.A. Section 7102(b) (Purdon 1982).
166. *Id.* Physicians fear, not unreasonably, that they will be the preferred target when they are the losers along with non-physicians in a personal injury lawsuit. This sort of liability, where one defendant can be required to pay for all, is termed "joint and several liability." It is a major focus of tort reform efforts.
167. 42 Pa.C.S.A. Section 7102 (Purdon 1982).
168. Harka v. Nabati, 487 A.2d 432 (Pa. Super. 1985).
169. See Annotations: Release of One Responsible for Injury as Affecting Liability of Physician or Surgeon for Negligent Treatment of Injury, **39** A.L.R. 3d 260 (1971).
170. Lasprogata v. Qualls, 397 A.2d 803 (Pa. Super. 1979).
171. From Harka, supra, n.168.
172. Petrillo v. Syntex Laboratories, Inc., 148 Ill. App. 3d 581, 499 N.E.2d 952, 102 Ill. Dec. 172 (1986).
173. From the translation by Ludwig Edelstim in Lyons and Petrucelli, Medicine—A Pictoral History, New York, 1978, Harry Abrams. p. 214-215.
174. Ladd, Privileges, Law & Soc. Order 555, 580-83.
175. Warren, S. & Brandeis, L.: The right to privacy, **4** Harv. L. Rev. 193, 1890.
176. Note, Tortous Invasion of Privacy, **4** Wm. Mitchell R. 163 (1975).
177. JCAH Accreditation Manual for Hospitals at xii (1986).
178. Clayman v. Bernstein, **38** Pa. D. & C. 543 (1940).
179. Alexander v. Knight, 177 A.2d 142, 146 (Pa. Super. 1962). The information could still have reached the jury without the forbidden report. By putting her condition at issue, Mrs. Alexander could not block testimony in court about that condition.
180. See Annotation: Physician's Tort Liability for Unauthorized Disclosure of Confidential Information About Patients, **48** A.L.R. 4th 668 (1986).
181. *Id.*, at 697-9.
182. See Annotation: Physician-Patient Privilege as Extending to Patient's Medical or Hospital Records, **10** A.L.R. 4th 552 (1981).

183. 35 Pa.C.S.A. Section 521.4. The report may go to the local health board, or to the state if required by regulation.
184. 28 Pa. Code Section 27.2 (1983). As of 1987, there is no more recent update of the list. As of this writing, AIDS is not listed.
185. 18 Pa.C.S.A. Section 5106 (Purdon 1983). "Deadly weapon" is defined in 18 Pa.C.S.A. Section 2301 as a firearm, loaded or unloaded, or any device which, when used as intended, is calculated or likely to produce serious bodily injury.
186. 20 Pa.C.S.A. Section 5511(c) (Purdon 1975).
187. 30 Pa.C.S.A. Section 5125(f) (Purdon 1975).
188. 75 Pa.C.S.A. Section 3755 (Purdon 1987). "Administrative refusal" is not defined.
189. 11 Pa.C.S.A. Section 2204 (Purdon 1987).
190. See Annotation: Validity, construction, and application of statute limiting physician-patient privilege in judicial proceedings relating to child abuse and neglect, **44** A.L.R. 4th 649 (1986).
191. 11 Pa.C.S.A. Section 2211 (Purdon 1987).
192. Roman v. Appleby, 558 F. Supp. 449 (E.D. Pa. 1983).
193. Keeton, W.: Prosser and Keeton on the Law of Torts (ed. 5) at 773, St. Paul, Minn., 1984, West Publishing Co.
194. Montgomery v. City of Philadelphia, 140 A.2d 100 (Pa. 1958).
195. Coralu v. Curtis Pub. Co., 273 A.2d 899 (Pa. 1971).
196. Montgomery, supra, n.199, at 102-3.
197. See Annotation: Liability of doctor, psychiatrist, or psychologist for failure to take steps to prevent patient's suicide, **17** A.L.R. 4th 1128 (1982).
198. Adapted from Tarasoff v. Regents of the Univ. of Cal., 17 Cal. 3d 425, 551 P.2d 334, 131 Cal. Rptr. 14 (1976).
199. Hofmann v. Blackmon, 241 So. 2d 752 (Dist. Ct. App. Fla. 1970).
200. Adapted from Soto v. Frankford, 478 F. Supp. 1134 (E.D. Pa. 1979).
201. Kaiser v. Suburban Transportation System, 398 P.2d 14 (Wa. 1965).
202. From Berry v. Friday, 472 A.2d 191 (Pa. Super. 1984).
203. *See* Annot., **24** A.L.R. 4th 1311 (1983), Physician's negligence in conducting or reporting physical examination as rendering him liable to third person relying thereon.
204. Craddock v. Gross, 504 A.2d 1300 (Pa.Super. 1986). This ruling may be held limited to worker's compensation cases at some point in the future, so caution is warranted. It was possibly significant that, in this case, the plaintiff's attorney was present and affirmed that Dr. Gross offered no advice, diagnosis, treatment or prescriptions at the time of the examination. *Id.*, at 1300.
205. Vogel and Delgado, To Tell The Truth: Physicians' Duty to Disclose Medical Mistakes, **28** U.C.L.A. L. Rev. 53 (1980).
206. LeBlanc and King, Tort Liability for Nondisclosure: The Physician's Legal Obligations to Disclose Patient Illness and Injury, **89** Dick. L. Rev. 1 (1984).
207. Intentional: Hooten v. Pennsylvania College of Optometry, 601 F. Supp 1151 (E.D. Pa. 1984). Negligent: Crivellano v. Pennsylvania Power and Light Co., 491 A.2d 207 (Pa. Super. 1985).
208. Restatement Torts 2d, Section 46(1) (1965). "Generally, the case is one in which the recitation of the facts to an average member of the community would arouse his resentment against the doctor and lead him to exclaim 'outrageous!' "
209. Sinn v. Burd, 404 A.2d 672, 675-6 (PA 1979).
210. Lazor v. Milne, 499 A.2d 369 (Pa. Super. 1985).
211. Adapted from Boarts v. McCord, 511 A.2d 204 (Pa. Super 1986).
212. From Banyas v. Lower Bucks Hospital, 437 A.2d 1236 (Pa. Super. 1981).
213. Keeton, W.: Prosser and Keeton on the law of torts (ed. 5) at 47, St. Paul, Minn., 1984, West Publishing Co.
214. *See below* for discussion of future forms of medical malpractice.
215. Crinellaro v. Pa. Power and Light Co., **24** D. & C. 3rd 590 (Pa. Comm. Pl. 1982).
216. Restatement, Second, Torts Section 35(1)(a), Comment d. (1965).
217. Note, Standards for Involuntary Civil Committment in Pennsylvania, **38** U. Pitt. L. Rev. 535 (1977).
218. Myers, Involuntary Civil Committment of the Mentally Ill: A Symptom in Need of

Change, **29** Will. L. Rev. 367 (1984). This excellent article reviews the history of involuntary commitment and discusses the failures of the deinstitutionalization movement of the last two decades.

219. 50 Pa.C.S.A. Section 7114 (Purdon 1987). This makes it more difficult for patients to prove their case but they can get a chance to win the jury's hearts and minds if the claim alleges these forms of worsened or aggravated negligence.
220. *Id.*, Notes of Decisions, citing Venesky v. Community Medical Center, **30** D. & C. 3rd 96 (1984).
221. Martino v. Family Service Agency of Adams County, 112 Ill. App. 3d 593, 445 N.E. 2d 6, 67 Ill. Dec. 714 (1983). Horak v. Biris, 130 Ill. App. 3d 140, 474 N.E. 2d 13, 85 Ill. Dec. 599 (1985).
222. King, supra, n.140, at 181.
223. Adapted from Aetna Life and Cas. Co. v. McCabe, 556 F. Supp. 1342 (ED PA 1983). The case came upon appeal by the insurance company, claiming it didn't have to cover the award. This is also why Gail sued for medical malpractice—she could win more money if insurance coverage was available. The punitive damages had to come from McCabe's own pocket, as a matter of policy in Pennsylvania, but the insuror had to pay the rest. Aetna had not notified the doctor that they might deny coverage until after they'd undertaken and started the defense effort.
224. Belli, M.: Belli for your malpractice defense at 202, Oradell, N.J., 1986, Medical Economics Books.
225. *Id.* at 203.
226. *Id.* at 204.
227. *Id.* at 205.
228. *Id.* at 206.
229. *Id.* at 210.
230. Berkelide v. Brantly Helicoptor Corp., 281 A.2d 707 (Pa. Super. 1971).
231. Gruble v. Albert Einstein Med. Center, 387 A.2d 480 (Pa. Super. 1978).
232. 35 Pa.C.S.A. Section 10021 (Purdon 1977).
233. Hoffman v. Misericordia Hospital, 267 A.2d 867 (Pa. 1970).
234. Discussed above with "Failure to protect."

PRELIMINARIES TO MEDICAL MALPRACTICE LITIGATION

In the enemy camp

4

Synopsis

A doctor may expect a medical malpractice suit because of a less-than-perfect result or an obviously dissatisfied patient. He may also encounter individuals who try to get out of paying their bills by threatening suit. Sometimes, a patient with an obviously hostile attitude may simply desire to "stick it to the doctor" for some real or imagined slight. But frequently a doctor's first inkling that he is being sued occurs when the local sheriff or deputy clumps into the office during business hours in full uniform and armed with a .357 Magnum, handcuffs, and a club! In a loud voice, audible to the entire waiting room, he announces that he has papers to serve in a lawsuit. Panic and dismay reign as the doctor is presented with the patient's complaint.

Before a patient's complaint is served on the doctor, an attorney for the patient should have already devoted considerable work and thought to the case. Doctors should thus step into the enemy camp and know the preliminaries to filing a medical malpractice case.

Attorney contact and contract

No doubt cases occur in which attorneys go to patients and offer to sue doctors (these attorneys are known as ambulance chasers) and hospital employees tip off attorneys about good prospects (such employees are known as "runners").[1] But most suits for medical malpractice start with a disgruntled patient who goes to an attorney's office to inquire about the possibility of suing or demanding to sue. Patients seek out an attorney for various reasons, but some common ones are:

- ***The result was considered unsatisfactory.*** The patient may make this determination himself, but very often relatives and friends of the patient make it. This is the most straightforward reason to consider suit, but almost always some personal interaction enables or augments this factor. Unexpected bad results trigger suits, anticipated and discussed problems do not.
- ***The patient is being pressed for a bill.*** In many cases, a complaint of medical malpractice is raised when a doctor is trying to collect the fee. The patient cries medical malpractice to get out of paying. Some

patients are angry or distressed about the result, and the bill or collection effort catalyzes that feeling into a suit.

- ***Another doctor, a nurse, or another professional implies or states that medical malpractice has occurred.*** Perhaps a nurse or other professional, particularly in hospitals, makes some comment to a patient. Sadly, a comment by a subsequent treating doctor often prompts the initial visit to an attorney. Young doctors trying to expand their practice or generate patient confidence by noting that "modern procedures" were not followed previously sometimes make these unfortunate comments. Also, the second professional can generate the reactions of voice tone and body language: "He did that to you?!?" Although the subsequent treating doctor is rarely willing to testify that the previous doctor was negligent, a professional expert witness may. Had the subsequent doctor contacted the original doctor, he or she might have received an entirely different story from that told by the patient.
- ***A health and accident insurance agent may suggest there has been medical malpractice.*** Health and accident insurance carriers are trying to control expenditures, as all insurors. To do so, or for some other reason, a carrier may advise a patient that particular surgery was unnecessary. More commonly, insurors notify that they won't pay the full amount of the bill and they make some negative aspersion on the charge: ". . . exceeds the reasonable fee for what was done." A patient who may have been quite satisfied with treatment is thus signaled to pursue a malpractice claim.
- ***The idea of pursuing a medical malpractice claim is initiated by the attorney in connection with another case.*** A patient may, for example, have been involved in an automobile accident. The patient actually contacts the attorney to pursue a claim against the person who caused that accident. The attorney then becomes convinced that while the accident may have initially caused the patient's injuries, the doctor negligently treated those injuries. Or the attorney sees the possibility of a higher fee in a malpractice suit.
- ***Perception of economically motivated or inhumane treatment.*** In their grief and pain, families of sick, injured, or dead patients may focus on what they believe to be an unfeeling doctor. He then becomes the target and repository of all those negative feelings.
- ***Desire to protect other potential victims of that malpractice.*** Although this reason is probably stated more often than it is present, attorneys do get mileage out of arguing to wavering clients that they have a social responsibility to pursue the case.
- ***Newspaper reports, or other media.*** After a paper has printed a story of a million-dollar malpractice claim, or worse yet, a settlement or judgment of a large amount, the number of patients visiting lawyers goes up.

- ***Attorney ads.*** Not all parts of Pennsylvania confront this phenomenon yet, but many urban areas are plagued by media advertising by attorneys, with many ads focusing on personal injuries. These ads encourage people who might have felt intimidated or hesitant to take their concerns to a lawyer for discussion.
- ***$$$.*** Money is what almost all malpractice cases are about. How many people can resist the chance to turn misfortune into big bucks, without any expense to themselves and only a limited time investment?

LEGAL ALERT

Be especially cautious in serious injury cases in which a patient has no insurance and the patient's own negligence caused the injuries, or when there is no one else to sue. These are just the kinds of cases in which the patient or his attorney will try to find a medical malpractice claim. Automobile and boating accidents and those involving alcohol or drugs are typical problem situations.

Keeping this alert in mind is important when making reports of the patient's injuries. The physician may think that he is helping the patient make a case against the person who caused the accident when in fact the doctor is building a case against himself.

When contacted, the attorney will usually listen and make notes regarding the patient's complaint against the doctor. If the attorney decides that it is at least worth investigating, he or she may enter into a contract with the patient. Some attorneys wait to enter into a contract until after they have investigated and agreed to take the case. More often attorneys contract with the patient immediately, but retain the prerogative to decline the case after investigation.

Medical malpractice cases are commonly handled by attorneys on a contingent fee basis. Although attorneys sometimes appear to be excessively compensated in contingency fee cases, the theory allowing the arrangement is that it makes courts accessible to those who cannot otherwise afford an attorney. It also takes into account that, because the risk of losing such cases is high, the attorney should be appropriately compensated for taking that risk.[2] Since the 1850s the contingent fee has been a unique luxury enjoyed almost exclusively by U.S. attorneys. England, France, and most other countries consider it illegal and unethical.[3]

A contingent fee arrangement is one in which the amount of the attorney's compensation is wholly or partly contingent upon the successful accomplishment (by settlement or litigation) of the case being handled. The fee arrangement must be put in writing and executed in duplicate.[4] By statutory rule, it is open to inspection by the court and Bar Association.[5]

Concerns about contingency fee abuse focus on the patient/client, not the doctor/defendant.

Using a formula has become the most common way of determining a contingency fee. Thus, for example, the attorney would traditionally receive a third to half of the recovery. In 1984, the Pennsylvania Supreme Court ruled unconstitutional the statute putting a ceiling on attorney fees in medical malpractice cases.[6] That statute had limited contingency fees to 30% of the first $100,000, 25% of the second $100,000, and 20% thereafter.[7] It was described by the court as a violation of the separation of powers.[8]

The Pennsylvania state legislature has also acted to protect injured patients from attempts to take advantage of their vulnerable state initially after their injury. For the first 15 days after an injury, those who might be sued for the injury and attorneys seeking a contingency fee agreement are prohibited from negotiating with the patient.[9] The patient can avoid this restriction by giving a written statement 5 days in advance of the agreement or release being signed.[10]

Referral of case

Many doctors would be surprised to learn that the attorney with whom they chatted at the country club or racket club one week might be the same person who initiates or encourages a medical malpractice suit the next. Attorneys manage the feat of staying friends with local doctors yet participating in a lucrative malpractice suit by referring prospective suits to another attorney, often in a more remote city. If they keep the case, they will argue the justness of their client's claim at every instance, implying that they will only take outrageous negligence cases. Or they will stand on the patient's right to sue and be forthright about their own involvement.

Fee-splitting arrangements between lawyers are not illegal or even unethical, unlike such agreements between doctors. There are restrictions, however. The client must consent, if the second attorney is not part of the first's firm, and the total fee must be "reasonable".[11] In one case, where lawyers sued each other over the fee, one tried to defend on the basis that the fee-splitting agreement had been unethical.[12] The court held the verbal contract still enforceable.[13]

Besides referring malpractice cases to avoid bitterness from local doctors, attorneys may refer cases because they do not feel familiar with the area of law. As medical malpractice litigation becomes even more specialized, referrals for this reason become even more likely. Some threats to involve a big name plaintiff's attorney are not serious and are used to encourage settlement negotiations. But many of the names that strike terror into the hearts and wallets of insurors and professionals alike have large referral practices.

Obtaining and reviewing records

Hospital records

After the initial interview the attorney goes for the records. Because most medical malpractice suits originate in hospitals, the attorney will normally obtain those first.[14] The lawyer will not be allowed access to review committee records.[15] However, by-laws, policies and procedures, etc. may be obtained by motion to produce documents.

The Department of Health publishes regulations governing hospital records that are part of that agency's statutory authority.[17] Within these regulations is a requirement that patients or their designees have access to their medical records, although continuous or immediate access is not required.[18] In 1980, the University of Pennsylvania's Health Law Project surveyed hospitals in the state and found that most administrators would release records to the patient if that patient's physician did not object.[19]

LEGAL ALERT

A request for hospital records may signal a likely medical malpractice claim. Therefore, all hospital medical-dental staffs should set up an early warning system that includes a rule requiring the medical records department to notify immediately attending physicians, surgeons, or dentists that a request has been received from an attorney, insurance company or anyone else, including the patient, for copies of the records.[20]

Under no circumstances should a hospital allow anyone to simply walk into the record room and be given immediate access to the records.[21] Have a policy requiring that the request be in writing and accompanied by an authorizing document, which should be confirmed and responded to only after a reasonable period of time. A reasonable fee may be charged for photocopying. Another precaution is to make certain that the hospital never gives out the original of any patient record, x-ray, or the like. Patients and their attorneys have been known to conveniently lose, remove, or alter unfavorable records. Only copies should be released unless a subpoena or court order requires that the originals be produced. Even then, the hospital's attorney should be consulted to make certain that this is actually required. If the originals must be produced, make copies to retain and obtain a receipt for every item taken. Be leery of a request for too many records. Consideration must be given to the confidentiality of patients who are named in, for example, operating room logs, but who are not parties to the suit.[22]

Physician records

A request to examine the physician's records often follows an attorney's request for the hospital's records. The same precautions for hospital records apply to the physician's records. A basic principle here is that while the paper, the physical record, belongs to the doctor, the patient has a right to the information thereon. Confidentiality, the privilege against disclosure, can only be raised by the patient, not the physician who is the custodian of the records.[23] Therefore, confidentiality cannot bar the patient's own access to the records.

Alteration or correction of records

If a doctor knows that records are to be copied, he or she should review them before they are inspected or copied. Faced with a deluge of papers, every doctor signs hospital or medical records that may contain inaccuracies because of garbled dictation or typing errors or signs records without reading them.

If the doctor discovers errors upon reviewing the records, the problem can be handled in two ways:

- The doctor can say nothing until the patient or the patient's attorney brings up the matter. The attorney may never notice it. If the doctor chooses this course, he or she should nevertheless prepare a written explanation and keep it handy.
- A carefully drafted, written explanation can be prepared, made part of the record, and possibly sent along with the records to the attorney.

In either case the explanation can follow this format:

On this day ___(date)___, I reviewed the attached records and found that the following errors exist: ________________________

____.

In my opinion, this error occurred because: ____________________

____.

I make the following correction or clarification: __________________

____.

____

Signature

A physician who admits an error must be very, very careful in drafting this explanation. An attorney may twist things around and use this against the physician. The attorney may try to imply that the physician generally does sloppy work and that is the reason the doctor is in the courtroom. The safer course is to send records as they are with supplementary letters of explanation on request if the matter is not a potential malpractice case.

LEGAL ALERT

One thing the physician must not do is change the records! No surer way of losing a suit exists than attempting to change the records to conceal an error. Never change a record to cover up something. This applies even when the error is discovered before any suggestion of suit arises. Scratching out a word or portions of the record looks bad whenever it is done. Even drawing a line through a statement leaves doubt as to when a change was made, regardless of initialing or dating. If an error exists, attach an explanatory document or say nothing.

Some authors suggest that lining out without obliterating is acceptable, as long as the date and person making the change are indicated.[24] This technique is best limited to contemporary corrections made when the document is created.

Attorney's evaluation of case

Has the doctor breached the standard of care?

The patient's attorney next determines if the patient's story and the medical records demonstrate a good case. In Chapter 2 we discussed the elements of a medical malpractice case (that is, duty, breach, damages, and causation). However, the most critical question considered in most cases is whether the doctor breached the standard of care.

If the spectre of an attorney, as a nonmedical person, deciding on the correctness or lack of medical care seems ludicrous, don't laugh! With our legal standard of "reasonableness" applying to so many legal matters, attorneys are constantly judging the relative merits of others' behavior. This is one reason why some lawyers are arrogant. Whether it is builders, government officials, entertainers, or any professional, the attorney sees problem situations. Without even having been in the shoes of the reviewed individual, the lawyer must decide whether or not the individual acted reasonably.

Once a doctor accepts a patient, he has the obligation to use a reasonable amount of care and skill in treating the patient. This doesn't mean that the doctor possess the highest order of qualification, but rather that standard or degree of skill and care that is ordinarily possessed by members of his profession. This standard of care is determined under the so-called locality rule by what a reasonably competent doctor practicing in the same or a similar community would do under the circumstances.[25]

Can we find an expert witness who will say the standard of care was breached?

The standards of care that doctors are expected to meet must normally be determined by an expert witness.[26] An expert witness is a person who possesses special skill or knowledge beyond that of the average layman. An expert can render opinions founded on this skill or knowledge to aid the judge or jury in deciding a case. In medical malpractice cases this effectively means that if a doctor is to be found guilty of malpractice, another doctor must agree.[27] Thus the attorney will have to determine whether an agreeable expert witness can be found.

At one time attorneys complained that it was nearly impossible to get one doctor to testify against another. They referred to this as a "conspiracy of silence." Now, however, even Melvin M. Belli has acknowledged that the conspiracy of silence has broken down, and more and more topflight specialists are making themselves available as expert witnesses.[28]

Experts are readily available. They come in all shapes, sizes, credentials, and most importantly, integrity. Attorneys who handle medical malpractice cases usually have their own favorite medical consultants. Some firms even have a stable of these experts. They not only evaluate the case from a medical-legal standpoint, they frequently serve as expert witnesses as the case develops. Attorneys also regularly receive advertisements from experts. The ABA Journal, the magazine of the American Bar Association, actually has a classified advertisement section dedicated to "Litigation Support, Medical." Excerpts from one issue give some idea of just how available experts are:

- Anesthesiologists; medical malpractice evaluation/testimony. . . .
- Emergency room medical specialist, consultation/testimony. . . .
- 2,500 Board-Certified Medical Experts for medical and hospital malpractice, personal injury and product liability cases. Case review, written reports and expert testimony. 14,000 cases for 5,000 attorney clients in eleven years. Free educational books and seminars; free telephone preliminary case evaluation. Call one of our medical directors to discuss your cases. . . .
- Dental malpractice. Consultation/testimony. Staff covering all dental specialties. . . .
- Infectious disease specialists; medical malpractice evaluation/testimony. . . .
- Neurosurgeon/neurologist. Consultation/testimony. . . .
- Experienced M.D., J.D., professor of urology. Co-counsel or expert witness. . . .
- Medical malpractice consultant. Gastroenterology, board certified, outstanding credentials, expert public speaker. . . .

If this seems like a healthy list, take a look at *Trial,* the magazine of the Association of Trial Lawyers of America, which is written primarily for the plaintiff's attorney. One firm advertised in *Barrister,* another legal publication, in full page ads, "Hire a Doctor Who Knows How to Operate in Court."

Further, many well-meaning colleagues, particularly young and inexperienced doctors, have unrealistic expectations of therapeutic outcomes, and a smooth-talking attorney can trap them into making a statement or writing a letter that could establish a standard of care that few, if any, experienced practitioners routinely practice. They unwittingly become the expert witnesses. Physicians who do not understand the difference between "Standard of Care" and optimum or "ideal care" also make useful plaintiffs' witnesses.[30]

The court determines whether or not a proposed expert witness qualifies as an expert and may exclude the person's opinion.[31] But the standard applied is liberal: "A witness should be qualified as an expert if he or she has any reasonable pretension to specialized knowledge on the subject under investigation."[32]

Before filing a suit against a doctor, the patient's attorney usually will have hired experts or have had another practitioner in the area read the record and give an opinion on the merits of the case (that is, whether the standard of care was breached). These consultants are then frequently used as expert witnesses against the doctor. If a statutory deadline is near, attorneys will file just to preserve the case.

Although a patient's lawyer should have an expert's opinion in hand and a willing witness lined up before suit is filed, this is not always the case. Unfortunately, countersuits against attorneys for unreasonably filing meritless claims have been notoriously unsuccessful.[33] The tort of abuse of process in Pennsylvania is only available where suits are filed with an ulterior motive, as a perversion of the process, not a stretching of its limits.[34] The distinct tort of malicious *use* of process is also unhelpful in frivolous malpractice cases. Lack of probable cause is an element of this tort.[35] But the courts have made it clear that they will insist on the old English rule of a requirement of an arrest or seizure of property as part of the claim in a malicious use of process suit.[36]

If we can't get a hired expert, can we use the doctor sued as our expert witness?

Believe it or not, a patient's attorney might expect the physician to hang himself at trial. And in some cases the attorney can accomplish this.

With careful questioning a patient's attorney can get the doctor sued to testify on the standard of care. This is nearly unavoidable, although usually the doctor's own lawyer attempts to elucidate this testimony. If the physician/defendant is not careful, his own words may state a standard that the plaintiff will argue was not met.

Often, when multiple health care provider defendants are involved, plaintiffs hope that one will break ranks and testify against the other. This may seem to be a desirable tactic to an innocent doctor named as a codefendant with a negligent one, but jurors will sometimes respond to multiple cross-accusations by finding everyone negligent and escalating the award.

If we can't get an expert, is this a case in which an expert isn't needed?

An attorney usually wants and, indeed, needs an expert at trial to establish the standard of care and the doctor's breach of that standard. Patients' attorneys moan and groan and try to evade the expert testimony requirement by claiming that there is a "conspiracy" or "veil of silence" and that doctors coerce each other out of testifying. Under some circumstances, courts listen and will allow cases to go forward without an expert. And so, if expert testimony is not available or an expert is hesitant to testify, the attorney will search for an alternative method to establish medical malpractice.

One method to establish medical malpractice without expert testimony is to use circumstantial evidence. The most common type of circumstantial evidence is that which is given the name of *res ipsa loquitur*. This Latin phrase, which means nothing more than "the thing speaks for itself," is the offspring of a casual word of a famous English jurist. During an argument with another attorney in a case in 1863, in which a barrel of flour rolled out of a warehouse window and fell on a passing pedestrian, it was said that the warehouseman's negligence was obvious.[37] In its inception the principle was nothing more than a reasonable conclusion, from the circumstances of an unusual accident, that the person sued was probably negligent.[38] From the circumstances a judge or jury could infer or assume that someone was negligent. When properly invoked, the doctrine effectively operates to require a person sued to present facts showing that he or she was not negligent.[39]

In 1981, Pennsylvania's Supreme Court changed the law. Up until that time, the doctrine of res ipsa loquitur could not be used in medical malpractice suits in the state—the plaintiff had to have an expert witness.[40] The pre-1981 court opinions were emphatic, at times, in insisting on this necessity.[41] But then Mrs. Jones' case came before the Court:

Example

In 1972, Mary Belle Jones had a D & C, laparoscopy, and laparotomy at Harrisburg Polyclinic Hospital. The surgery proceeded without complication, but when she woke up, Mrs. Jones had a suprascapular nerve palsy.

She settled with the hospital, the resident and the nurse-anesthetist for $25,000. At trial, no expert established negligence for Mrs. Jones. Who could say what had happened in the operating room? The jury, which wasn't told of the settlement, returned a verdict of $56,000 against the surgeon, the nurse-anesthetist, and the hospital. Defendants appealed confidently, because Pennsylvania law required an expert.

The state Supreme Court affirmed the lower court's decision. "We are satisfied that expert testimony should no longer be a *per se* requirement in proof of negligence in all cases of alleged medical malpractice."[42]

In fairness, it should be explained that the court did not boldly reverse itself without warning. In earlier cases, res ipsa loquitor was made to apply in other types of cases.[43] Earlier cases had suggested that expert testimony was not needed where "the negligent act or commission was obvious and no special knowledge was required to discuss it."[44]

The court adopted the formulation of res ipsa loquitur from the Restatement of Torts.[45] By this formulation:

- ***The patient must show that he or she was injured in an occurrence that ordinarily would not have happened in the absence of negligence.*** This element may be shown by expert testimony or, in an appropriate situation, may be within the common knowledge of laymen. For exmple, a doctor reluctant to testify against another is often more willing to say that a particular injury would not ordinarily occur if proper care is exercised than to say that a fellow doctor was negligent. Proof of an unusual or unexpected medical result that simply should not have occurred unless there was substandard medical care will also suffice to allow application of the doctrine.
- ***The plaintiff/patient must eliminate other causes, including the plaintiff's own conduct.*** Insofar as other parties are concerned, plaintiff satisfies this element by naming everyone involved as defendants.
- ***The patient must show that the negligent act or omission was within the scope of the defendant's duty to the patient.*** Given health care providers' broad duty to care and, when the patient is helpless, to protect, this element is easily shown in the operating room application of res ipsa loquitor.

An example of the application of res ipsa loquitur would be a case involving sponges or instruments left in the abdomen after surgery. It is said that the doctrine best applies in "black box" situations—the patient went in all right and came out damaged and no one knows what happened. Part of the justification for use of the doctrine is that only the medical personnel in the "black box" with the patient know what happened—and they aren't talking. Some jurisdictions require that the defendant(s) must have had exclusive control of the plaintiff when the injury occurred, but shared control is enough in Pennsylvania.[46]

If an expert witness is not available and the res ipsa loquitur doctrine does not apply, the patient's attorneys will attempt to find a written procedure, explicit instructions from a drug manufacturer, or some other resource to establish the standard of care. In some cases the resources tend to establish the standard of care themselves; in other cases they are used in conjunction with expert testimony. Examples of these resources include:

- *Physician's Desk Reference* (PDR)
- U.S. Food and Drug Administration (FDA) releases
- Manufacturers' recommendations
- Hospital or clinic bylaws, rules, or regulations

- Standards or guidelines adopted by organizations to which a doctor might belong
- Books and journals in the field[47]

Of these resources the *Physician's Desk Reference* is particularly significant because it is available to every attorney and layman. It is important to identify exactly what this publication is. The *Physician's Desk Reference* is simply a compilation of the package inserts, prepared by the drug manufacturers' attorneys, listing every possible reaction. The purpose is not only to comply with FDA regulations but primarily to protect the drug company from legal attacks resulting from adverse reactions. The responsibility, then, is laid on the prescribing doctor with: "The advantage must be weighed against . . ." or similar words. Every physician has had the experience of a detail man coming in and orally giving information about a product that is entirely different from what appears on the insert. Furthermore, if the medical doctor followed every precaution and did every test the insert mandates, the cost to the patient would be prohibitive. However, if the manufacturer's instructions are not followed and something goes wrong, the doctor is in peril.[48] The same is true of FDA releases and equipment manufacturers' instructions.

Every organization likes to establish standards or rules of one sort or another. They give the organization status and suggest that all of its staff or members are 24-karat gold. This is a most dangerous trap and a common one in the era of competition for patients and health care dollars.

A prime example is the bylaws, rules, and regulations of a hospital medical-dental staff. A temptation exists to codify a Utopian set of rules that defy strict compliance. However, attorneys are quick to take advantage of this. In the landmark Illinois case *Darling v. Charleston Community Memorial Hospital,*[51] the Illinois Supreme Court ruled that a hospital's standard of care was to be determined not only by reference to the standard of practice of other hospitals in the community but also by reference to the hospital's own bylaws and other written standards of practice. Goals and ideals should never be allowed to become the standard of care, i.e., the minimum acceptable standard by which the institution and its professionals will be judged.

LEGAL ALERT

Doctors should insist that a disclaimer be included in the bylaws, rules, and regulations of the hospital:

The medical-dental staff will adopt such rules and regulations as necessary for the proper conduct of its work. Such rules and regulations will be in conformity with these bylaws but are to be regarded as guidelines and not as absolutes. As general procedures, they will not necessarily be appropriate in all circumstances and are not designed to interfere with the sound exercise of medical judgment of staff members. They are specifically not designed as defining a standard of care under tort or other law.

If the hospital's attorney objects to such a disclaimer, the doctors should remember whose side the attorney is on, and the staff should get its own attorney.

A doctor who is a member of any organization or board should read any so-called standards very, very carefully. If they cannot be rewritten, he must be prepared to testify that these are ideals and that total attainment is elusive and impossible. The physician can point out that the medical profession would like everyone to be in perpetual good health and live forever. Furthermore, most medical care continues to improve because doctors continue to strive for goals that seem impossible. But the frustrated, besieged physician perceives that the public's minimum expectation is perfect health forever.

LEGAL ALERT

Doctors should avoid including direct or indirect references to the standards of any organization or board in the hospital or staff bylaws, rules, or regulations. A direct reference may specifically require that an organization or board's standards be followed irrespective of control or change in those standards. An indirect reference may require membership. When standards are referenced, they are seldom entirely followed and only help support malpractice claims. They include many requirements that, if studied in detail, might be inapplicable to a locality. Also, changes are sometimes made without the staff realizing they have been made. If standards are to be established, be sure they are spelled out precisely in the hospital or staff bylaws, rules, or regulations.

As should be apparent, it is vital that the physician constantly keep in mind the extent and content of the material that the patient's attorney is digesting and preparing to use in the lawsuit. The physician must be prepared and know this material backward, forward, and upside down to avoid being trapped.

Has the statute of limitations run on the case?

Every state has statutes that limit the time within which a lawsuit can be filed. These are known as statutes of limitations. An attorney evaluating a case will determine whether the statute of limitations has elapsed, or "run," as attorneys call it.

In Pennsylvania, the statute of limitations for all personal injury cases, including malpractice, reads in applicable part:

> The following actions must be commenced within two years . . . (2)An action to recover damages for injuries to the person or for the death of an individual caused by the wrongful act or neglect . . . or negligence of another.[52]

The older name for statutes limiting the time during which legal action must be initiated was statutes of repose. The rationale for the limit is suggested by the older name. Unacceptable instability in normal dealing would result from open-ended ability to sue. Further, with the passage of time, memories fade and the difficulties increase of producing an accurate, valid result. Insurance companies could not predict their range of liabilities. Defendants put on notice within a reasonable period of time can investigate and prepare.[53]

The discerning reader will have asked "Two years from what?" The time that the statute's time period begins to run is critical in malpractice cases. The older rule still followed in some states is that the time runs from the moment of the wrongful or negligent act.[54] Pennsylvania has, since 1895, accepted the "discovery" rule.[55] By this rule, the statute of limitations does not begin to run until the patient could have discovered the doctor's legal responsibility for the patient's injuries.[56] The possibility of discovery is not a matter of passivity; the patient must have been unable—in the exercise of reasonable diligence—to learn of the negligent cause.[57] Otherwise the statute begins to run.

Example

Kenneth was born in 1965 after a very difficult pregnancy. It was a frank breech, and forceps were applied. Kenneth's development made it clear that he would be permanently disabled. Mentally and physically retarded, he remained unable to walk or talk.

At a family reunion in 1977, Kenneth's mother heard of a lawsuit over a similarly defective child. She went to an attorney, obtained the hospital record, and sued the obstetrician 14 years after the birth. The trial court threw out the case, stating that the 2-year statute of limitations had run and that Kenneth's mother had not acted diligently to investigate the cause of her son's problems.

The appellate court carefully reviewed whether or not Kenneth's mother had acted reasonably in not making further investigations. The court concluded that a jury could decide that the mother had been reasonable and that therefore the case should go to trial.[58]

The statue of limitations will start when the negligence is known or knowable. Whether the plaintiff acted reasonably is determined by three phases of knowledge, each of which must have been known or knowable before the 2-year period starts to run: (1) Knowledge of the injury; (2) knowledge of the operative course of the injury; and (3) knowledge of the causal connection between the injury and the conduct.[59]

The example of Kenneth above also involved minority. In many states, the statute is tolled, which means it doesn't run during the period of infancy of the injured person. There, an individual might have 20 years to bring suit for a birth injury—18 years plus the statute of limitations. Pennsylvania does not toll for minority.[60] The statute limits suit by or on behalf of minors as it does adults.

The several basic exceptions to the general statute of limitations are:

- ***Concealment.*** If a doctor conceals medical malpractice or the patient is lulled or misled by the defendant, the statute of limitations doesn't apply. The doctor is "estopped" from relying on the statute of limitations.[61]
- ***Suits for pure contract damages.*** The longer 6-year statute for contract damages applies only to suits for costs of completing or remedying performance and the like. Personal injury damages are barred after 2 years, even if the patient claims it is a contract case.
- ***Joinder of additional defendants.*** The court may allow a defendant to bring in another party after the original statute has expired.[63] Thus a hospital might decide that a physician was at fault in a case where the hospital is being sued and bring in that doctor as another defendant. It is not clear how late this can be done, but the courts have said that the statute is to be applied liberally.[64] In one case, where a hospital initially hesitated to join a doctor as an additional defendant because he was a high-ranking member of its staff, the hospital was disallowed from joining him after the statute had run.[65]

Other states may toll the statute in situations where Pennsylvania does not. For example, other disabilities in addition to minority do not toll the statute.[66] Further, the natural and inherent extension of the time for filing suits provided by the discovery rule is not available in wrongful death cases.[67]

LEGAL ALERT

Because many medical malpractice suits are motivated by a patient who can't or won't pay a bill, it's a good idea to review cases before pressing the patient for payment. If any possible claim of malpractice exists, services can be billed, but any collection efforts, particularly filing suit, should be undertaken with caution. This caution is still important, even after the statute of limitations has expired. Remember the discovery rule!

If the doctor has any inkling that he or she might be sued (for

example, the early warning system at the hospital informs the doctor that an attorney has requested records), the doctor should check the statute of limitations. If the doctor-patient relationship is not in effect, consideration should be given to never seeing this patient again. The patient's attorney may have learned that the statute of limitations expired and may have suggested that the patient see the physician again for the same ailment in an effort to keep the case alive. If the patient can claim that he was lulled into not investigating a possible act of malpractice by the doctor in an ongoing relationship, he may be able to argue an "estoppel" theory, i.e. to stop the doctor from defending on the basis of the statute of limitations.[68] If the patient is dissatisfied and changes doctors, the statute can begin to run at that time.[69]

Do I really want to take this case?

An attorney concludes the review by deciding whether he or she wants to take the case. In reality, this decision usually boils down to whether or not money can be made in the case. To more accurately "value" a case, the attorney may well subscribe to a number of books or services that provide information on awards or settlements in other cases.[70]

Attorneys look for two basic categories of money—lots and easy. If "lots" of money or damages is at stake, an attorney would usually take the case even if liability is marginal. On the other hand, if "lots" of money isn't involved, an attorney may be unwilling to take the case (if he or she has anything else to do) unless "easy" money is involved. Such a case may have a clear liability but limited damages. Insurance companies have done a great disservice to doctors by eagerly settling claims for nuisance value. The companies know that even a bogus case would cost thousands of dollars to defend, so they settle them for the defense costs. Consequently, doctors shopping for malpractice insurance should attempt to obtain a policy that gives the insured a veto over any proposed settlement. These have become increasingly hard to obtain because of the converse problem—doctors who stubbornly refuse to settle valid claims despite the probability of big damage awards which the insuror must then pay.

The best reputation an insurance company or doctor can have with attorneys is the assurance that the attorney who sues them will have to earn every cent he or she gets. This reputation will not and should not prevent the truly meritorious cases from being filed, but it will prevent many nuisance cases.

In more recent years, the decision whether to take a case has also involved the attorney's own evaluation of the client. Just as doctors should carefully pick their patients, so attorneys are now being warned to carefully pick their clients. A client who has a borderline case at best and wants to sue the doctor might well want to sue the attorney next!

Settlement efforts before filing suit

Once an attorney decides to take a medical malpractice case, he or she seldom files suit as the opening volley against the doctor unless the statute of limitations is about to run. Instead, the attorney will often write the doctor, explain that the client plans to sue and request the doctor to have his or her insurance carrier contact the attorney in an effort to settle the case. To make these letters especially effective and intimidating, an attorney may include the draft of the written complaint he or she plans to file. A complaint with its stilted language can be impressive when the doctor first sees it.[71]

The obvious purpose of these letters, as they state, is to initiate settlement negotiations with the doctor's insurance carrier. In many, many cases the attorney would rather get some quick settlement than drag the matter into court. After all, the attorneys' contingent fee rewards an attorney who can settle the claim before doing the work of filing suit. These demand letters also serve the subtle role of smoking out iron-clad defenses and possible admissions from the doctor.

More dangerous are attorneys who investigate before giving notice of intent. Cases have been lost—before they were filed—by physicians who unwittingly revealed information or made an admission to a potential opponent. Doctors are, on the whole, a cooperative lot. They prefer to be helpful and nonconfrontational. These same characteristics have caused tragic results for incautious physicians contacted by patient's lawyers.

Although candid statements may be used against a doctor, settlement offers may not. For example, an attorney may not, at trial, state that an offer to settle was made and that this was tantamount to an admission of liability. Even so, the doctor is best advised to let his or her attorney handle any communication with the patient or the patient's attorney.

Receiving a letter from an attorney sets up an important opportunity for nipping a suit in the bud. A doctor must be certain to take advantage of it if the circumstances fit.[72] A large percentage of cases which have merit are settled at this stage. Also, a few cases that have no merit can be avoided if the patient's attorney can be shown that it is not worth his while to pursue the case.

Filing suit

Generally

If settlement efforts have failed and the patient wants to pursue the case, the attorney will next file suit. This is the last step before the more open forms of warfare begin.

The American legal system

For a society to function smoothly, it must not only establish rules of conduct but also a mechanism for settling disputes. Although some physicians may consider dueling a preferred alternative method of dispute settlement when compared with medical malpractice lawsuits, society does not. Neither does it allow vendetta, feud, or any of the other more violent means of dispute settlement employed over the centuries. In this sense, the state is indifferent to whether or not the results are fair or even whether the results encourage beneficial practices, as long as the citizenry resorts to the courts.

In Pennsylvania the sources of the rules of conduct are the U.S. and Pennsylvania constitutions; federal and state statutes, rules, and regulations; and finally, court decisions. These rules of conduct are called laws. The people, or voters, adopt constitutions. Congress and the Pennsylvania legislature adopt statutes and authorize various agencies to adopt regulations, and in the process of interpreting and applying these laws, judges render the decisions of the courts.

The United States has two separate court systems for tort suits—federal and state. Medical malpractice cases against Pennsylvania doctors are most often filed in state court.

Whether a court will, or for that matter can, hear a particular case depends on whether the court has the legal authority to do so. This is called jurisdiction. The jurisdiction of federal and state courts differ in some respects.

The primary purpose and, therefore, jurisdiction of the federal courts is to interpret and apply federal law. For example, if a doctor has a dispute with the U.S. Department of Justice because it failed to issue a narcotics license, the federal courts would hear that dispute because federal law is involved. If a case has nothing to do with federal law, however, the federal courts won't get involved. Medical malpractice cases rarely involve federal law, except for those against military personnel or federal employees, and so are not filed in the federal courts for this reason.

However, in one area the federal courts do have jurisdiction to hear cases that do not involve federal law. When the United States was founded, the individual states were more independent than now. Citizens from one state who were sued in another state thought they would not be treated fairly in the other state. And so the U.S. Constitution allowed federal courts to consider cases involving citizens of different states even if federal law was not involved.[73] This is called diversity jurisdiction because it requires diversity of residence. If a doctor treats a patient from another state, the doctor could be sued in federal court. However, this situation remains less frequent than the usual case involving state residents.

The Pennsylvania judicial system

Most medical malpractice cases in Pennsylvania are brought in the state court. The Commonwealth's court system is composed of three tiers. The initial level of this system is the Court of Common Pleas.[74] This is the trial court of general jurisdiction.[75] It also hears appeals from such lower courts as traffic or municipal court. This means that most cases begin there. Thus, if a doctor is sued for medical malpractice, he or she will be sued in the Court of Common Pleas.

The Courts of Common Pleas are divided into 60 "districts." Each county is a district unto itself, except for 14 of the less populous counties, which are doubled up 2 to a district and Philadelphia County, which is part of a district with the city.[76] The number of judges for each varies with the district, from 1 to 85.[77] The districts are established primarily for administrative purposes.

Each county is assigned to a district. Except for certain administrative needs, such as sharing judges, the Court of Common Pleas of each district is completely separate from the court of every other district. Some Common Pleas Courts have subdivisions, each with its own administrating head judge.[78] Like other judges, those serving on the Court of Common Pleas are elected.[79] Vacancies are filled by gubernatorial appointment until the next municipal election.[80] The judges serve 10 years.[81] There is a nine-member review board, composed of five judges, two lawyers, and two nonlawyers, all of whom are appointed by the governor. This board can suspend, discipline, or forcibly retire sitting judges.[82]

Above the Court of Common Pleas on the judicial ladder are the Superior and Commonwealth Courts. Commonwealth Court hears appeals and has original jurisdiction over cases in which the state or a state agency is a party.[83] Therefore it would rarely be involved with a medical malpractice claim, considering the retention of sovereign immunity.

The Superior Court hears the appeals from medical malpractice suits in the Courts of Common Pleas. Superior Court sits in regular session in Harrisburg, Philadelphia, and Pittsburgh, and can decide to sit elsewhere.[84] It is composed of 15 judges.[85] Like other appellate courts, it doesn't decide on issues not raised at trial and will not overturn a trial judge's decision unless there has been an error of law or an abuse of discretion. This basically means that the judge and jury can call the facts as they see them and only legal technical errors will be reversed.

The Supreme Court of Pennsylvania is the Commonwealth's highest court. It is composed of the chief justice and six associate justices.[86] The Court does not try factual situations but only hears appeals. Parties are not entitled to appeal to the Supreme Court from the Superior Court. Final orders of the Superior Court will be heard only if any two justices of the Supreme Court wish.[87] However, the Supreme Court may, on its own or on a request, reach down into any lower court and assume jurisdiction of any pending matter, if it involves "immediate public importance."[88]

From the Pennsylvania Supreme Court, assuming it even hears the case, no automatic right to appeal to the U.S. Supreme Court exists. The U.S. Supreme Court, like Pennsylvania's highest court, hears only those cases it desires to review. Further, it will only consider those cases that involve some issue under the U.S. Constitution.

Of these courts, the Court of Common Pleas has the greatest practical significance in medical malpractice litigation. The Common Pleas judge may exercise broad discretion in handling or deciding cases. The Superior Court will not reverse a Common Pleas decision simply because its justices have a difference of opinion, but only where the judge clearly made a mistake. The Pennsylvania Supreme Court considers few and the U.S. Supreme Court virtually no medical malpractice cases (except those under federal law, such as the Federal Tort Claims Act). When a person claims he'll take a case to the Supreme Court, the person usually doesn't know what he's talking about![89] The medical malpractice battle is usually fought and won or lost in the Common Pleas Court, at the trial level.

No matter in which court the doctor ends up, the doctor will be surrounded by attorneys bowing to judges. The judge is perhaps the most dangerous participant. Behind the illusion of impartiality sits an attorney wearing a robe. Doctors expect a natural conservatism in judges to be of assistance, but judges also feel a duty to protect the powerless. Too often, an injured patient seems worthy of this protection.

Where suit is filed: venue

As much as attorneys might like to, they can't sue the doctor in whatever Common Pleas Court they choose. Instead, although each Common Pleas Court has the same legal power, or jurisdiction, as any other to hear a case, a suit against the doctor must be filed in a prescribed court. The term *venue* refers to the proper court where suit must be filed.

The proper venue in a personal injury lawsuit is the county of residence of any person sued or, alternatively, the county in which the matter involved took place.[90] If a corporation or a partnership is sued, it may be sued wherever it regularly does business or where the act or omission occurred.[91] Therefore if a doctor, hospital, and all others involved in a case are from the same county, they must be sued in that county. If they are from different counties, they can be sued in any of the counties where one of them does business or resides.

Some counties are more disposed to making big awards in cases than others. So attorneys will try to shop around—forum shopping they call it—to pick the best possible court. The courts where a suit may be filed will, of course, depend on where venue is proper.

In part, to assure the largest selection of counties in which to bring suit, the attorney will seek to join multiple defendants from many counties. For example, if a patient is transferred to a regional health center or sent to another doctor for consultation in a different county, that is another county in which suit can be brought if the hospital or doctor can be tied into the case. Similarly, if a drug manufacturer can be added to the suit, the possible counties from which to choose may be broadened considerably.

After the suit is filed, the doctor's attorney will determine whether venue is proper. If venue is improper, or defendants have been improperly joined to establish venue in a particular county, the doctor's attorney will ask to have the case transferred to another county, such as the one where the doctor lives. It can only be moved to another county where proper venue was available originally. Change can also be requested for the convenience of the parties, but this includes all the parties, not just the defendant.[92]

Preparing and filing the complaint

While determining where to sue, the patient's attorney will prepare a complaint against the doctor and others to be sued. As the name suggests, a complaint sets forth the patient's "complaint," or claims against those sued.[93] The complaint is then filed with the Court of Common Pleas selected by the attorney, so long as the venue is proper.

Pursuing the case

When suit is filed, the patient's attorney should usually have done the following:

- Heard and apparently accepted the patient's (or the family's) story
- Reviewed the hospital and medical records
- Had the records reviewed by another doctor or comparable consultant
- Determined that the statute of limitations has not run on the case

Endnotes

1. Stimulating groundless litigation is an offense known as barratry, but advertising or promoting the availability of services is permitted.
2. Rickette v. Solomon, 187 A.2d 910 (Pa. 1963).
3. **71** A.B.A. Journal at 38 (December, 1985) (comments of Grant P. DuBois).
4. Carol v. Perbumitten, 41 D. & C. 702 (Pa. Comm. Pl. 1941).
5. 42 Pa. R.C.P. Rule 202 (Purdon 1975).
6. Heller v. Frankston, 475 A.2d 1291 (Pa. 1984).
7. 40 Pa. C.S.A. §1301.604 (Purdon 1987).
8. Heller, supra n.6.
9. 42 Pa. C.S.A. §7101 (Purdon 1982).
10. 42 Pa. C.S.A. §7101b (Purdon 1982).
11. DR 2-107, Code of Professional Responsibility.
12. Foote v. Shapiro, 6 D. & C.3rd 574 (Pa. Comm. Pleas 1977).
13. *Id.* (The author is at a loss to discern which statement of the two preceding footnotes 12 and 13 is more deserving of an exclamation point noting amazement).
14. **22** Am. Jur. POF 2d 1: Hospital records: medical malpractice—use of hospital records.
15. Holliday v. Klimoski, 75 D. & C.2d 408 (Pa. Comm. Pl. 1976).
16. 42 Pa. R.C.P. 4009 (1).
17. Hospital Association of Pennsylvania v. MacLeod, 410 A.2d 731, 735 (Pa. 1980). There are, in fact, so many hospital regulations that it is surprising that every malpractice suit against a hospital doesn't include at least one allegation of a violation of a regulation. 28 Pa. Code §101 et seq.
18. 28 Pa. Code §115.29 (1986).
19. Gottschalk and Stellman, Hospital Regs. on Medical Records: Progress in Patient's Right to Know, vol **III** #25 Pa. L. J. 2 (June 23, 1980).
20. Durkin and Korsak, A Risk Management Primer for Medical Record Practitioners, Medical Record News, June 1980, p. 285.

21. Patient's attorneys sometimes attempt to do this and try to badger hospital employees until the records are released. No legal requirement exists for immediate access for nonmedical reasons, so don't let this happen.
22. Faltin v. Marbach, 68 D. & C.2d 97, 98 (Pa. Comm. Pl. 1974). Application for and review of staff applications of defendant physicians are discoverable. Fowler v. Piris, 34 D. & C. 3d 530 (Pa. Comm. Pl. 1981).
23. Moore v. Whitman, 75 D. & C.2d 412 (Pa. Comm. Pl. 1976). Therefore, patient requests are paramount.
24. Richards and Rathburn, Medical Risk Management, 112, Rockville, Md, 1983, Aspen.
25. Standard of care is discussed further in Chapter 2.
26. Dorman v. Johnston, 218 A.2d 808 (Pa. 1966).
27. This topic is discussed further in Chapter 2. But also see the exception discussed under res ipsa loquitur below.
28. Belli, M.: Belli for your malpractice defense, at 8 and 207, Oradell, N.J., 1986, Medical Economics Company.
29. A.B.A. Journal at 133 (May 1, 1987). These are common to any issue of the Journal.
30. This is addressed above in Chapter 2, under "Standard of Care."
31. Donaldson v. Maffucci, 156 A.2d 835 (Pa. 1960).
32. Taylor v. Spencer Hospital, 292 A.2d 449 (Pa. Super. 1972).
33. Annotation, Medical Malpractice Countersuits, **84** A.L.R. 3d 555 (1978).
34. Psinakis v. Psinakis, 221 F.2d 418, 423-4 (3 Cal. 1955).
35. Shaffer v. Stewart, 473 A.2d 1017 (Pa. Super. 1984).
36. Garcia v. Wall & Ochs, Inc., 389 A.2d 607, 608 (Pa. Super. 1978). Perhaps this countersuit should still be considered where the proceedings included a forced placement of a bond or some other arguable "seizure" of property.
37. Keeton, Prosser and Keeton on the Law of Torts, (ed. 5) at 243, St. Paul, Minn., 1984, West Publishing Co.
38. *Id.*
39. In other words, it is not conclusive, it simply "shifts" the burden of proof to the defendant.
40. Chandler v. Cook, 265 A.2d 794 (Pa. 1970).
41. Scacchi v. Montgomery, 75 A.2d 535 (Pa 1950).
42. From Jones v. Harrisburg Polyclinic Hospital, 437 A.2d 1134 (Pa. 1981).
43. Gilbert v. Korvette's, 327 A.2d 94 (Pa. 1975).
44. Hodgson v. Bigelow, 7 A.2d 338 (Pa. 1939).
45. Restatement Torts, Second §328 D.
46. Jones, supra n. 42, at 1140.
47. Treatises and journal articles have to be authenticated by an expert and relied on in his opinion before those learned works can go out to the jury. 32 C.J.S. §573-575. Evansvik v. Univ. of Pittsburgh W. Psych. I. & C., 338 A.2d 636 (Pa. Super. 1975). But witnesses can be cross-examined on literature that they have not cited or relied upon. Cummings v. Borough of Nazareth, 242 A.2d 460 (Pa. 1968).
48. If a claim is made, it is important to keep in mind that it is not illegal or necessarily wrong to prescribe a marketed drug for an unapproved indication. The Food and Drug Administration's Bulletin of October 1972 notes that: "The labeling is not intended either to preclude the physician from using his best judgment in the interest of the patient, or to impose liability if he does not follow the package insert." Establishment of a violation of F.D.A. standards shifts the burden to defendant to prove he did no wrong.
49. Reference deleted.
50. Reference deleted.
51. 211 N.E.2d 253 (Ill. 1965).
52. 42 Pa. C.S.A. §5524 (Purdon 1987). A review of attorney considerations is found in Cuker, The Statute of Limitations in Medical Malpractice Cases: A Guide, **51** Pa. B.A.Q. 132 (1980).
53. King, The Law of Medical Malpractice, 2nd Ed. 267, St. Paul, Minn., 1986, West Publishing Co. Purpose is to expedite litigation and discourage stale claims. Moore v. McComsey, 459 A.2d 841 (Pa. Super. 1983).

54. Annotation: When Statute of Limitations Commences to Run Against Malpractice Action Based on Leaving Foreign Substance in Patient's Body, **70** A.L.R.3d 7 (1976).
55. Lewey v. Fricke Coke Co., 31 A.261, 264 (Pa. 1895).
56. Gruble v. Albert Einstein Med. Center, 387 A.2d 480 (Pa. Super. 1978).
57. Keating v. Zerrel, 421 A.2d 1181, 1183 (Pa. Super. 1980).
58. Adapted from Petri v. Smith, 453 A.2d 342 (Pa. Super. 1982). This was the kind of case that makes insurance companies shudder. Regardless of the fairness or lack of it, the jury will now have to sit and listen to testimony about stale facts. Meanwhile sitting (if he can) before them will be a horribly deformed human being. The overwhelming sympathy that this evokes is very difficult to defeat except on a technical point of law, such as one the defendants lost in this case.
59. Stein v. The Washington Hospital, 448 A.2d 558 (Pa. Super. 1982).
60. De Santis v. Yaw, 434 A.2d 1273 (Pa. Super. 1981).
61. Walters v. Ditzler, 227 A.2d 833 (Pa. 1967).
62. Murray v. University of Pennsylvania Hosp., 490 A.2d 839 (Pa. Super 1985).
63. 42 Pa. R.C.P. §2252 (Purdon 1987).
64. Rogan v. Stein, 331 A.2d 724, 730 (Pa. Super. 1974).
65. Moyer v. Lado, 12 D.&C. 3d 635 (Pa. Comm. Pl. 1977).
66. Hippersteel v. W.C.A.B., 457 A.2d 137 (Pa. Commonwealth 1983), dicta.
67. Note, Discovery Rule not Extended to Wrongful Death and Survival Actions, **55** Temple L. Q. 625 (1982).
68. This is Pennsylvania's version of the "continuing treatment" issue, as it is referred to in other jurisdictions.
69. Held v. Neft, 507 A.2d 839 (Pa. Super. 1986).
70. *See* Chapter 8, regarding these and other library resources.
71. Personal reactions to a claim are discussed in Chapter 5.
72. In Chapter 5 we discuss various initial reactions to filing suit. These also apply to receiving letters from attorneys and should be reviewed.
73. U.S. Const. Art III, sec. 2. *See also* U.S.C. §1331.
74. Pa. Constitution Art. V., §.
75. 42 Pa. C.S.A. §931 (Purdon 1981).
76. 42 Pa. C.S.A. §901 (Purdon 1987).
77. 42 Pa. C.S.A. §90.1 (1) (Purdon 1987).
78. 42 Pa. C.S.A. §951 and 953 (Purdon 1987).
79. Pa. Constitution Art. V., §13 (Purdon 1969).
80. *Id.,* (b) (Purdon 1987).
81. Pa. Constitution Art. V., §15 (Purdon 1969).
82. Pa. Constitution Art. V., §18 (Purdon 1969).
83. General State Authority v. Pacific Indem. Co., 354 A.2d 56 (Pa. Commonwealth 1976).
84. 42 Pa. C.S.A. §543 (Purdon 1981).
85. 42 Pa. C.S.A. §541 (Purdon 1981).
86. 42 Pa. C.S.A. §501 (Purdon 1981).
87. 42 Pa. C.S.A. §724 (Purdon 1981).
88. 42 Pa. C.S.A. §726 (Purdon 1981).
89. One exception would be in New York, where the equivalent of the Pennsylvania Superior Court is known as the New York Supreme Court.
90. 42 Pa. R.C.P. Rule 1006 (Purdon 1986). Residence is encompassed by the propriety of service of process these. Rule 233.
91. 42 Pa. R.C.P. Rules 2179 and 2130 (Purdon 1975).
92. 42 Pa. R.C.P. Rule 1006 (b) (Purdon 1986).
93. The complaint is discussed in greater detail in Chapter 5.

YOU ARE SUED FOR MEDICAL MALPRACTICE

The battle begins

5

Synopsis

Almost inevitably the day will come when the doctor is sued for medical malpractice. It's a day he or she will never forget. An important professional battle begins.[1]

Service of summons: the first blow

Personal reactions

Although a doctor may anticipate that a medical malpractice suit is being filed, no feeling compares with being served with a summons. The summons is the formal legal document that tells the doctor that he has been sued.

After receiving and reading the summons, most doctors are numb and in shock. Many are so angry that rational thought requires effort. To make matters worse, service of the summons is often preceded or followed by a notice in the local newspaper. Although a doctor might try to take the attitude "I'm not worried—the insurance company will take care of it," physicians all react as if they have been diagnosed with a fatal disease. And no wonder—since working toward securing admission to medical school the physician has believed himself to be a healer and a helper. Now, in derrogation of everything his professional life is about, the doctor stands accused of actually *causing* injury or harm.

The doctor may go through the motions of continuing the practice that day but usually is barely able to function. Many sleepless nights follow. The doctor is filled with fear of financial ruin and professional ridicule. He immediately becomes bitter and defensive, regarding every patient as a potential litigant. Even if exonerated, the doctor will bear permanent psychic scars.[2]

The series of emotional states that a doctor goes through after being sued for medical malpractice is aptly described as a variation of the grief reaction:

- Shock and disbelief
- Fear of impending doom
- Anger, particularly toward the legal system, its practitioners, and the former patient (and possibly other patients).
- Resolve to fight
- Attempt to carry on
- Desire to retaliate (for example, sue for malicious prosecution)

It's important to let the first three stages pass quickly and move into a resolve to fight. The patient's attorney is counting on the shock effect to panic the doctor into a quick settlement, particularly if a claim is frivolous. Doctors shouldn't succumb to this ploy. This is a time for hard, cold logic, not "gut" reactions.

The doctor's personal attorney can be very helpful in learning more of the background of the patient's attorney. For example, we are all creatures of habit and tend to repeat our behavior; thus reviewing the tests that a teacher gave in the past will give a very accurate idea of what will be asked in the future and how it will be asked. Similarly, a thorough study of the opposing attorney's background and habits will serve the doctor well in defending against the suit. That attorney, not his or her client, will be controlling the course of the litigation.

Attorneys, like doctors, talk to one another. They know which attorneys hit the bottle, chase around, have family problems (spouse, kids on drugs, etc.), or are emotionally unstable or financially stressed. They know what schools their colleagues attended, their track records, how many times they took to pass the bar examination, whether they really wanted to be a doctor and just couldn't make it, and other significant facts. Has the lawyer changed firms and what are his work ethics? Doctors should ask that their personal attorneys report this information to them because it may be vital in understanding the opponent's motives and helping predict how the suit will progress.

More important is the attorney's history with this kind of case. Is medical malpractice a specialty of the lawyer? Does he run a "settlement" practice, rarely going to trial or referring the case at that point? Does he tend to take weak cases or does he do his homework early on? Is the named attorney the one actually working on the case, or does he turn cases over to a junior associate in the firm?

Books are available that contain biographies of attorneys, such as the *Martindale-Hubbel Law Directory*.[3] Some of these also rate attorneys on the basis of legal ethics and ability. Interestingly, one critic of this directory is Melvin M. Belli. Although the book lists most attorneys in the United States, it doesn't list Belli, by his express order.[4] The doctor might find it worthwhile to review what the directory says about the patient's attorney.

The doctor may also discover that the patient's attorney has been involved in a number of similar malpractice cases. If any of these cases were appealed, a transcript of each case will exist. Reviewing a case to see just how the attorney asked questions might be helpful. Alternatively or additionally, the doctor can attend a trial involving the patient's lawyer.

These techniques are not unfamiliar to a doctor who uses them every day in taking a patient's history. The doctor should be prepared to use every advantage because the opponent will! The insurance attorney, whom the doctor may never have seen and hopefully will never see again, will probably be reluctant to reveal or gather this kind of information, but the physician's personal attorney usually will be willing to do it. In a time when insurance availability is low and the sellers' market noncompetitive, it becomes more difficult to insist that the insurer-appointed attorney take these extra steps. One physician described dealing with the insurance lawyer: "Now I know how the family feels when the surgeon comes out and says 'There's been a little complication,' spends 2 minutes and disappears. I feel like my terribly important case is being handled as if it were routine and in a casual way."

Who is suing

Most often the person who sues will be the doctor's own patient. This is not always the case, however.

If a minor is involved and no legal guardian has been appointed for the child, a parent or other adult can sue for the minor as his "guardian ad litem", or "next friend." The idea is to "cure" the infancy and protect the minor.[5] A next friend is simply a person who brings a suit on behalf of a minor without being formally appointed the child's legal guardian. If a legal guardian has been appointed to manage the child's estate, then the legal guardian would bring suit on the child's behalf. Although a parent automatically has custody of a child, the parent is not automatically in charge of the child's estate or money.[6,7] Alternatively, the orphans court may appoint a guardian ad litem on request of anyone with an interest in the litigation.[8]

Under older law, if the patient died because of medical malpractice or before a claim was resolved, the right to sue was terminated. Thus it was legally better to negligently kill rather than maim someone. (This is an example of legal thinking.) This situation changed with the adoption of a wrongful death statute. Under this law, the legal representative (for example, executor or administrator) of a deceased's estate may file suit on behalf of the deceased's next of kin, or the kin can sue on their own behalf.[9] Such suits on their own behalf seek to recover the pecuniary or money losses resulting from the death, such as lost support.

Under some circumstances those indirectly injured as a result of medical malpractice may bring their own action against a doctor. For example, if a wife is unable or unwilling to have sex because of some medical malpractice, the husband may be able to sue for loss of consortium, the conjugal fellowship of husband and wife.[10] A person injured by a patient may similarly have a claim against a doctor if the doctor's negligence contributed to the injury.[11]

The interest of the person who brings a suit and the asserted reason the doctor has been sued are normally described at the beginning of the complaint.

What is a summons?

A summons is a formal notice from the clerk of the court advising a doctor that a suit has been filed. The sheriff of the county in which the doctor resides, or a sheriff's deputy, usually serves the summons, although private individuals are sometimes used to serve it. The summons server is merely a messenger. The doctor should avoid venting spleen on the process server, especially since the comments can be used against the doctor in court. Attached to the summons is a copy of the complaint prepared by the patient's attorney.

For those who have never seen one, a summons is an ominous document, couched in legal jargon. The essential part of it reads something like this:

Commonwealth of Pennsylvania

County of ________________________________

In the Court of Common Pleas,

County of ________________________________

Civil Action # ____________________

Ima Patient, Plaintiff

v.

Your Name Here, ____________________________ MD, Defendant

To: ____________________________ M.D.

You are hereby notified that (Name(s) of Plaintiff(s), the plaintiff(s), has, (have) commenced an action in (Form of Action, like "Assumpsit" or "Tresspass") against you which you are required to defend or a default judgment may be entered against you.

Date ________________ (Name of Court Clerk)

By (Deputy)[12]

NOTICE TO DEFEND

You have been sued in court. If you wish to defend against the claims set forth in the following pages, you must take action within twenty (20) days after this complaint and notice are served, by entering a written appearance personally or by attorney and filing in writing with the court your defense or objections to the claims set forth against you. You are warned that if you fail to do so the case may proceed without you and a judgment may be entered against you by the court without further notice for any money claimed in the complaint or for any other claim or relief requested by the plaintiff. You may lose money or property or other rights important to you.

YOU SHOULD TAKE THIS PAPER TO YOUR LAWYER AT ONCE. IF YOU DO NOT HAVE A LAWYER OR CANNOT AFFORD ONE, GO TO OR TELEPHONE THE OFFICE SET FORTH BELOW TO FIND OUT WHERE YOU CAN GET LEGAL HELP.

____

Name

____

Address

____

Telephone Number

What this all means is that the doctor is advised that he or she is being sued. The doctor can respond if he or she chooses within 20 days.[13] If the doctor doesn't, the court may assume the complaint is true and grant the patient the relief sought.

Although attorneys find it incomprehensible, doctors have been known to sit on these complaints and not act. The reasons given later vary: "I thought it must have been a mistake," "The insurance company was served notice too, wasn't it?" "I've just been too busy to do anything about it." "That problem occurred when I was in residency." "I didn't accept the paper from the sheriff." The unstated reason may be a psychological reaction formation; thoughts too horrible to be accepted can be suppressed from consciousness. But the threat of a default judgment is real—if the physician doesn't act within the allowed time, he can lose the case and have to pay all the demanded money without any trial. Insurance contracts usually require prompt notification of the company. It is possible that an insurer could try and deny coverage to a physician who ignores a summons and complaint.

Two examples from Pennsylvania case law should highlight what can happen if the physician doesn't respond in a timely manner:

Example

The sheriff appeared at the nursing home one morning looking for Doctor C. The sheriff knew that Dr. C. had regular hours there on Thursday mornings. Dr. C. read the paper the sheriff handed him but gave it back and refused to accept it. The sheriff left it with a nurse.

After 20 days had elapsed, the plaintiff's lawyer gleefully moved for a default judgment against Dr. C., and it was granted. Notice of this judgment got a response, and Dr. C. petitioned to have the case reopened so he could try to defend himself. The reviewing court refused and affirmed the default judgment.[14]

The court will reopen the case if a justifiable reason is presented, but the excuse must be plausible.

Example

The summons came to the office by certified mail. Dr. J. immediately forwarded it to the insurance company along with a copy of the medical records. He claimed later that he did not know that the company had moved. When the undelivered envelope was returned to Dr. J.'s office later, his office staff filed it in the patient's folder without telling him.

After initially granting a default judgment, the case was reopened when Dr. J. explained what had happened.[15]

If the service is made, then the response is required. An instantaneous contact between the physician and the insurance company and with his attorney must follow.

The complaint

Attached to the summons is a copy of the written complaint the patient is making against the doctor. The complaint tells the doctor what the patient claims the doctor did or failed to do. In it the patient (or whoever is bringing the suit) will be designated the "plaintiff." The name, address, and telephone number of the attorney who represents the plaintiff is provided on the summons and at the end of the complaint. The doctor and everyone else sued is designated as "defendant." The complaint charges one or more of the forms of medical malpractice discussed in Chapter 3. If more than one form of malpractice is claimed, the complaint will set forth each form in separate counts.

At the end of the complaint (or each count), the legal relief sought by the patient is stated. This is known as the prayer for relief. A claim for money damages in the prayer for relief is referred to as the *ad damnum.* In contrast to the hopes and expectations of many doctors, the phrase is not Latin for the judgment Radamanthus will pronounce on the souls of all plaintiffs' lawyers. Patients attorneys can make ridiculous money demands (for example, for $25 million). These demands are intended to intimidate the doctor, prejudice the doctor's position in the community, and generate publicity to pressure the doctor to settle. To the lawyer, outrageous demands are justified—he can only retreat from that figure. He cannot get more than that amount. Additionally, if the physician fails to respond, a bigger default judgment results. The complaint must contain a demand for the relief sought.[16] Anytime it is not included, the complaint is deficient.

Doctors are immediately appalled by the arrogant and accusatory language in the complaint. Attorneys rationalize it as merely "lawyer talk." Sometimes, it's picked up and quoted in the news media. It is especially unfortunate that, even if the doctor is ultimately vindicated, the damage to his or her reputation, much less practice, is not compensable and is only incompletely reversible.

A patient in a medical malpractice case can request the claim be heard by a jury. If the patient desires a trial by jury, the complaint or a separate document will demand a jury trial.[17] It is very rare for an attorney to recommend a trial by the judge only, a "bench" trial, to a malpractice plaintiff. It is generally accepted that juries award more money and that they are more easily swayed by feelings than judges. If the patient does not demand a jury trial, the physician defendant may do so.

Involving your personal attorney

Doctors who are sued commonly are told to immediately contact the insurance carrier and let it handle matters. But we suggest that a doctor instead consider contacting his personal attorney and allowing the attorney to contact the insurance carrier. This presupposes that the physician has an ongoing relationship with a lawyer. If the physician does not, then the possibility of malpractice litigation is good reason to develop such a relationship.

Insurance companies are businesses. They are not especially interested in the impact of a case on the doctor personally or the medical profession in general, except insofar as it affects their bottom line. They are interested in limiting their losses arising from any claim. Insurance companies consider overall risk management and cost. Macroeconomics is the watch word. Accordingly, insurance companies will often settle frivolous cases that probably should be fought; they sometimes fight meritorious cases that probably should be settled. Such abuses have been curbed somewhat by the tort of "bad faith." In essence, if the doctor's carrier refuses an opportunity to settle a meritorious claim within policy limits and judgment is rendered in excess of the policy limits, the insurer may be forced to pay the excess.

Although the doctor's personal attorney will not change the perspective of the insurance carrier, he or she will be able to get the defense off on the right foot and make certain the insurance company is sensitive to the doctor's concerns, both initially and as the case develops. The physician's own lawyer can be helpful in recommending a choice of defense attorneys from the company's list or in passing on the attorney the company offers. The personal attorney also can serve as a valuable liaison between the doctor, the carrier, and the carrier's attorney. The doctor who has a personal attorney involved is more likely to get the best possible treatment, more frequent and detailed reports of litigation progress, and better representation by the carrier and his attorney.

Although conflicts do not often arise between a doctor sued for medical malpractice and his carrier, they do happen. The doctor's personal attorney will help guard the doctor's interests if this happens. Doctors shouldn't forget that while the carrier is obligated to defend them, it not only selects but also pays the attorney. The attorney will often be the one the carrier uses regularly for defense work. The hourly rate charged the company is less than the attorney's usual fee and may even be below average. Thus the attorney actually represents both the doctor and the carrier. Ethics require that the attorney's undivided fidelity be to the client doctor.[18] In theory an attorney can represent both the doctor and the carrier with the consent of both.[19] But the economic pressure is not inconsequential on a professional whose life's work is rationalizing and excusing.

If the attorney selected by the company is less than the best available, the physician should raise cain! The policy may not entitle the insured to choice of attorney, but the physician need not passively accept someone weak or unacceptable.

The insurance carrier's attorney may also tend to report major litigation developments to the company only and seek directives from a claims supervisor without notifying the doctor. Even if the available coverage is definitely sufficient to pay the claim, doctors should insist that they and their personal attorneys have access to such information. The claims supervisor's attitude may be to exclude the doctor and his personal attorney from important discussions since the insurer will bear the loss. But both the carrier's financial reserves and the risk manager's living come from the policy holder's premiums. The doctor should not be overlooked and should receive copies of all reports regarding the case.

The physician can rely on what common ground is shared with the insurer. A positive approach, firmly insistent on the doctor's position but with respect for the company's responsibilities is most likely to succeed. One of the reasons insurers do not offer contracts giving physicians veto powers over settlements is past experience with such contracts. The companies perceived some physicians as unreasonably intransigent, pig-headed, and insisting on trial where a favorable settlement was offered. Doctors cannot change the realities of a case and cannot expect to have sole control, uninfluenced by the insurance company. But physicians can and should be aggressively and actively involved in the defense. Often, the best way to accomplish this is by involving a personal attorney.

Shut up!

There is no nice way to put it. When doctors are sued for malpractice, they should shut their mouths about the case except to their personal attorney, insurance carrier, and the attorney the carrier selects to defend them.

When notified of a claim some doctors are foolish enough to contact the patient or the patient's attorney to explain the care rendered or the reason for a particular complication. This doesn't do a bit of good. What it does is give the patient's attorney more ammunition, such as any admissions, to use against the doctor.

One trap of which many physicians are ignorant is the potentially differing interests of other health care providers involved in the care of the patient. Yes, a unified defense is far better than finger-pointing among defendants. Hang together or hang separately! But admissions made to other providers can come back to haunt the doctor later if that other provider claims against or demands indemnity from the doctor. Hospital risk managers, for example, requesting a taped interview should be politely told no and the defense attorney advised of this development.

It is important to realize that in Pennsylvania, unlike in most other states, signed reports or communications from a doctor to his attorney are not confidential. Most importantly, this means that such reports are not privileged from disclosure. The patient's attorney can force this information to be given to him, and it can be used against the doctor. Likewise, in Pennsylvania a report or communication by an insured doctor to his liability carrier is not confidential, nor are the insurance investigator's notes protected.[20] To maintain the privilege the information cannot be shared with others, however well intentioned. Don't do it.

Contacting your insurance carrier

Reviewing your coverage

When a doctor is sued for medical malpractice, he or she should review the insurance coverage. This may well be the first time a doctor really reads the insurance policy, being concerned previously with only the costs and limits of coverage. That was a mistake. Before taking out a policy, long before ever actually being sued, a doctor should have gone over the coverage and understood it well or involved his personal attorney in explaining the policy.

The two basic types of medical malpractice policies are:

- ***Occurrence policies,*** which provide coverage for malpractice committed during the policy term. A doctor who has an occurrence policy will be covered for malpractice that occurs during a year that the policy is in force, regardless of what year a lawsuit is filed. These are less frequently available because insurers claim to have lost money on these contracts in recent years.
- ***Claims-made policies,*** which provide coverage for claims that are first made during the time the policy is in force. These policies differ in what event triggers the coverage: complaint, claim, or suit being filed. Claims-made policies are sometimes referred to as discovery policies. The doctor who has a claims-made policy is covered only if the policy is effective in the year the malpractice claim is made or suit is filed and if the negligence occurred during this time or within an earlier time specified in the policy (for example, since the first date that the continuous claims-made coverage became effective with the insurance company or some other date mutually agreed upon—a "prior-acts" endorsement).

The broad categories of medical malpractice policies can be made to produce great variations and hybrids. Thus it is essential to review—preferably in advance—the nature and extent of coverage.[21]

On occasion it may appear that the doctor has no coverage for the particular claim made. Even so, the doctor should contact any insurance carriers he has anyway. Carriers sometimes provide coverage or at least a defense even if some technicality might allow them to avoid providing coverage. Carriers do so to avoid a reputation of proclaiming to cover everything when a doctor purchases a policy, but nothing when he or she makes a claim. Also, if a second suit by the doctor asserting valid coverage is brought, the company wants to (1) reduce possible damages by defending the original malpractice claim and (2) avoid a lawsuit based on the tort of "bad faith."

Initial notice to carrier

Immediately after being served with a summons (or notice of any claim made), the doctor or his attorney should notify the insurance carrier and provide a copy of the summons and any attachments. This is a particularly painful process for the doctor, who is often already suffering from acute professional paralysis induced by the trauma of being served with a summons. All policies include this requirement, however, so failure to give notice could enable the carrier to deny coverage.

A typical clause contained in malpractice policies provides:

> The insured [doctor] shall notify the Company, at its General Offices, ____________________, or its agent, as soon as possible, of any threatened claim, with full information relative to the services rendered; and in the event such claim is filed in court shall immediately foward any and all summons or process served together with the original or a copy of any and all other papers relating to said claim.[22]

Policies issued by St. Paul Fire and Marine Insurance Co. specify that:

> If there's an accident or incident covered under this policy you must:
> 1. Tell us or our agent what happened as soon as possible. Include the time and place of the event and the names and addresses of any witnesses and injured people.
> 3. Send us copies of all legal documents if you're sued or someone files a claim against you. . . .[23]

The notice requirements contained in the policy should be reviewed and followed explicity, remembering that reports can be revealed in court later. Because directions regarding notice may vary somewhat (even among policies issued by the same insurance company), it is important that the doctor review his own policy. If, as in the examples provided above, notice may be given to either the carrier or its agent, the notice should be sent to the company, with a copy of the notice and the enclosures to the agent. If the agent mentioned in the policy differs from the insurance agent with whom the doctor dealt when buying the policy, the doctor should notify his or her personal agent as well. As opposed to omitting important information, it's better to give too much notice than not enough. Send the notice "return receipt requested." Document the notification.

Although the policy may require a recitation of facts, the physician must remember these communications can be disclosed in court later. After the attorney is named, a thorough report can be made to him verbally.

The initial notice should be brief and to the point. Following is a suggested letter that would be sent by the doctor's personal attorney; it can be adapted if the doctor sends it personally, remembering to narrow the report as much as possible. This should be done in addition to a phone report, if one was made.

Insurance Carrier
Re: Dr. [Name]

Policy No. [Number]

Sir or madam:

Please be advised that I am the personal attorney of Dr. [Name]. Dr. [Name] is insured by your Policy No. [Number], a copy of which is enclosed.

On [Date and time], Dr. [Name] was served with a summons [or contacted by letter] alleging medical malpractice. A copy of the summons and attached complaint [or letter] are enclosed. I am hereby notifying you of this claim and providing you a copy of these documents on Dr. [Name]'s behalf.

Some general information about the claim is as follows:
Name and address of claimant: ______________________
Claimant's attorney and address: ______________________
Nature of claim: ______________________
Time, place and circumstances: ______________________
Known witnesses and addresses: ______________________
Other information: ______________________

If any further or different notice is required, kindly let me know. In the absence of such advisement, we will assume that this notice is sufficient to the policy's requirements.

I assume that, in accordance with the policy, you will immediately undertake the defense of this claim. I would ask that you confirm in writing that you will be undertaking the defense of this case and also advise me of the names of the attorneys from which list Dr. [Name] may choose for you to retain. If, for any reason, you will not undertake the defense of this claim, notify me immediately.

Dr. [Name] is in the process of preparing for your attorney a detailed statement regarding his current best recollection of the matter. This will be provided to the attorney as soon as possible.

The undersigned intends this letter only as compliance with policy notice mandates and does not intend by this letter to waive the traditional common law attorney-client or insurer-insured privilege and specifically reserves the right to object to disclosure of this letter or any communication referred to herein under applicable federal constitutional principles.

Thank you for your cooperation.

[Signature]

Copy: Dr. [Name]

The personal attorney will send this notice by certified mail, return receipt requested. This will provide proof of its receipt. The doctor should make certain to obtain copies from his attorney, and these should be kept in the doctor's own files.

If the doctor or his attorney does not hear from the insurance carrier before the 20-day period for answering the complaint expires, the doctor should have his attorney telephone the carrier to confirm that it will be assuming the defense of the case. If a response is not made, the court will assume the patient's claims should be granted. In the rare case that the carrier does nothing, the doctor's personal attorney should initially respond to the complaint.

Detailed statement

When the physician has calmed down—at least as much as possible until the case is resolved—it's time to study more exactly what the patient claims.

The doctor should thoroughly review the complaint and the charges it contains and obtain copies of and assemble all records related to the case. The records, including nurses' and other ancillary notes, should be gone over with the proverbial fine-tooth comb. Thereafter, with the assistance of the personal attorney, the doctor should prepare a detailed statement for the insurance carrier, and the attorney the carrier will retain to defend the case. This is NOT the time and place to bare all! That is done verbally with the attorney only. This report must be prepared realizing that it might be read to the jury in court.

Time usually permits preparation of a detailed statement. If it does not, a carrier's agent or the attorney it retains will contact the doctor to gather the facts. No interview should be granted without the attorney's permission. It is clearly better to prepare a detailed statement before talking with the insurer. When interviewed, the doctor may forget or misstate the facts. A detailed statement the doctor has had time to prepare will no doubt be more complete and accurate. The statement should be reread before and available at the interivew. Even if the doctor is interviewed first, he or she should prepare a detailed statement anyway and submit it to the carrier through the lawyer to make its records more complete.

Just what should be in the statement a doctor prepares will depend on the nature of the case brought. However, the doctor should keep in mind the four elements of a medical malpractice case, which the patient will have to prove:

- The treating doctor must have incurred a duty to care for the patient—***a doctor-patient relationship.***
- The doctor must have failed to perform or have breached that duty by deviating from the standard of care, usually that of the community —***negligence.***
- The patient must have been injured—***damages.***
- The negligence of the doctor must be the reason or proximate cause of the injury or damages—***causation.***[24]

Unless all four elements are present, no right to recover against the doctor exists. Therefore anything the doctor offers addressing these elements may be helpful to the defense.

In a sense, the statement should argue the case for the doctor. The statement is a necessary part of trial preparation. But under Pennsylvania's broad discovery rules, it can be brought into evidence at trial or at least reviewed by the other side's lawyer. As a document prepared "in anticipation of litigation," it will be assumed that it states the case most favorable to the doctor. Make sure it does so! Confession is good for the soul, but dreadful for the lawsuit.

This document should be prepared with the help of the attorney. The doctor's understanding of certain terms and certainly his understanding of the relative importance of some items will be different from that of the trial-wise lawyer. For example, if the patient telephoned the doctor years after the last office visit and if there is a statute of limitation defense possible, it will be important to emphasize in the report that the call did not involve the earlier treatment in any way, if it indeed did not.

Keeping these elements in mind, the following organization for a statement might be helpful to the doctor being sued.

- ***Introduction.*** Explain that this statement is being prepared to assist the attorney in defending the complaint filed against you. Provide any relevant background to the filing of the suit against you and its defense by the carrier. This would include your policy number, a copy of the summons and complaint served on you, the date the summons and complaint were served on you, and a copy of the letter notifying the carrier of the complaint, as well as the related return receipt from the post office.

- ***Doctor-patient relationship.*** Explain whether a doctor-patient relationship had been established. Consider these questions:

  Who was the patient?

  Is there any information the carrier should know about the patient or his family (psychological, financial, etc.)? If you have a credit bureau report on the patient or his family, provide a copy. Don't forget, when you are on trial, so is the patient.

Do you know of any other suits in which the patient or family have been involved?

When did you first start treating the patient for anything?

For what have you treated the patient in the past?

When did you first start treating the patient for the matter raised in the complaint?

When is the last time you saw the patient?

Are you currently treating the patient for anything?

- ***Negligence.*** Explain your reaction to the charge that you were negligent. Try to anticipate what the patient's attorney will say to build a case against you. Consider these questions:

What exactly is the negligence or form of medical malpractice claimed?

For what did you treat the patient?

Explain that the acceptable standard of practice for the treatment of a patient with the ailment involved was either met or exceeded.

How did you decide what the acceptable practice is? If it is based on any written documents (drug manufacturer instructions, hospital bylaws, books, etc.), provide copies. Be careful that you are documenting a standard of care, not optimal care, or care that may have avoided the result.

Explain or show how you followed the accepted practice.

If you did not follow the acceptable practice in all respects, explain the reasons.

How have you documented the treatment provided or not provided?

Reference the standard texts and journal articles that support your conduct.

- ***Experts.*** Because proof of negligence almost always requires expert testimony, identify the expert on which the patient may be relying. Consider these questions:

Did another doctor treat the patient at the same time you did? If so, who? This will be discoverable by the patient anyway.

Did another doctor treat the patient after you? If so, who?

Did another doctor or a nurse make any comments regarding your treatment of the patient that are already known to the patient? Don't volunteer additional evidence undiscovered by the plaintiff in this writing.

Are you aware of any other likely expert?

Do any of these doctors or individuals have any personal dispute with or grudge against you? This can be recorded if and only if you don't mind revelation in open trial. Otherwise, save it for the meetings.

- ***Damages.*** Explain your views on the injury or damages of the patient. Consider these questions:

  Explain the seriousness of the patient's prior existing problems, or lack thereof if the allegation is a failure to respond.

  Are you aware of any additional treatment that the patient will claim he had to undergo because of what is alleged you did or didn't do?

  If the patient was injured as claimed, what is the medical prognosis for that problem? To what degree and for what time should the patient be disabled?

- ***Causation.*** Explain that what you did or didn't do was not the actual cause of the injury or damages of which the patient complains. Consider these questions:

  Would the patient's condition be the same regardless of whether or not the alleged negligence occurred?

  If another physician is providing testimony against you, was the patient's injury caused by that other doctor? Be careful not to destroy multiple defendant unity without extensive consideration and planning.

  Did the patient take your advice on treatment, or did he or she refuse treatment?

  Do any alternative explanations for the outcome exist besides your treatment?

  How does the patient's alleged condition differ from what was expected anyway?

- ***Records.*** Provide copies of all your own records and those to which you have access (like hospital records) regarding the case, regardless of whether you consider them important, if they tend to exculpate you. Remember, documentation is almost always essential to a proper defense.

  Are there any important facts that will help you that are not documented?

  If so, what are they, and how can they be proved?

- ***Complaint.*** Review the complaint again and, paragraph by paragraph, provide any comments you have regarding each and every statement made. As you do, don't take the language used in the complaint too seriously. Much of the legal jargon is "boiler plate" language and words the law requires. The facts and both sides of the story will come out. To assure this, do not forget to mention any error in what is alleged in the complaint, however slight. Remember, if the patient makes very extreme allegations, they may be harder to prove and the patient's case may look ridiculously overstated to the jury.

- ***Attorney.*** Tell what you know about the attorney who represents the patient that is not slanderous. Consider these questions:

  Do you know the attorney?

  What other medical malpractice cases are you aware of in which the attorney was involved?

  Have you had any dispute with the attorney or any known friend of the attorney?

- ***Witnesses.*** Are there any witnesses or people with information about the claim who can help defend you who are not otherwise disclosed?

  Only in some situations should the doctor try to obtain information and learn attitudes from nurses and others involved. The attorney's advice on this should be sought.

- ***Summary.*** Conclude by offering to meet with the carrier's agent or the attorney selected to defend you at any time to discuss the case.

After completing the draft of the detailed statement, the doctor should have his personal attorney review it. If time permits, the doctor should reread it several times and add additional points as he remembers them. As time passes, one may recall more and more. However, it may as easily be forever forgotten if the doctor doesn't make notes. When the statement is completed, the doctor should have his personal attorney forward it to the carrier and request that the company or its attorney keep the doctor's personal attorney informed.

If a doctor remembers something after the detailed statement is submitted to the carrier or discovers some mistakes, a supplemental statement should be sent, with the same cautions and awareness of discoverability.

After being sued for medical malpractice, the doctor's highest priority should be preparing a detailed statement regarding a claim. The doctor should get it done and then get back to practicing medicine! Doctors shouldn't wait for telephone or personal interviews with the carrier's agent to disrupt the day and upset them. A detailed statement, if carefully and thoroughly prepared, will usually provide the carrier with most of the information needed. A brief interview can take care of the rest. A detailed statement will also provide a handy summary of the case when months or even years later the doctor must testify to remote events.

At the interviews, the carrier's representative will be doing something that the attorney will also have done or will do—assess the physician as a potential witness. It is important to present a professional, credible image. The insurance claim representative will leave the interview and make a written report, including the physician's prospects as a witness in his own behalf. The report can say, "Dr. Smith was knowledgeable about the case and the medical literature applicable. He was firm without overstatement and was entirely believable. He will make an excellent witness on his own behalf." OR the report can say, "This turkey will destroy us on the witness stand. Let's settle for whatever we can and get out of this one."

Carrier's response

Doctors, especially those experiencing their first claim, feel as if they are powerlessly adrift in a hostile legal sea. Perhaps for the first time in his life, the doctor is immersed in an alien discipline in which he is not the most knowledgeable expert. The doctor tends to look for emotional support from the insurer and its attorney.

In most instances the insurer will calm matters somewhat by contacting the doctor to say that it has undertaken the defense and selected an attorney to represent him. The attorney and a claims agent will then investigate the claims made in order to prepare a defense. As upsetting as the whole matter may be, the doctor should be candid and cooperate with both. Although motivated primarily to prevent any claim payment, they are trying to help.

Although the insurance carrier will normally undertake the defense of a case without question, disputes may arise. The doctor, already upset, may then be devastated if, for example, the carrier disputes coverage, thereby leaving the doctor to wage a two-front war against a former patient and the carrier. The carrier may notify the doctor that the potential exists for losses exceeding the policy limits. The company might be considering offering policy limits in settlement of a new bad case, telling the doctor that if he doesn't approve the deal, he'll be on his own.

A doctor's professional liability policy actually provides two distinct coverages: indemnity and defense. The indemnity provision requires the insurer to pay covered claims or any damages awarded to the former patient. The defense provision requires the carrier to provide, at its cost, legal counsel to defend or settle covered claims. Some policies are sold today offering one or the other; don't get caught with one of these and expect the company to provide both indemnity and defense costs.

The most common coverage disputes and problems arise in the area of indemnity. If a doctor fails to promptly notify the insurer of a claim, the insurer may deny coverage on the grounds that its ability to defend was hindered by late reporting. Another excuse for indemnity coverage denial arises when the patient seeks damages for allegedly intentional or dishonest conduct. Since many professional liability policies exclude coverage for illegal or otherwise fraudulent misconduct, the carrier may deny coverage if the doctor is accused of fraudulently concealing malpractice, intentionally causing injury, or violating controlled substances laws. Where multiple claims are made, a carrier may be required to defend all claims even though indemnity coverage extends only to some. As a matter of public policy, insurance cannot cover punitive damages.

Insurance companies do not always win in these disputes with their clients.[25] In fact, the contract of insurance will be interpreted adversely to the company that authored the policy in any close case. Thus companies will disturb their policy holders by notifying of reservation of rights not to cover whenever there is an excuse to do so. If the company doesn't dot all the i's and cross all the t's, it can lose.

If the insurer flatly denies both indemnity and defense coverage at the onset of a malpractice claim, the doctor's best action is to have his personal attorney or another legal specialist initially assume the defense of the case and attempt to resolve matters with the insurer. Most coverage disputes are not clear-cut, however. Consequently, most insurers will not flatly deny coverage but rather preserve the coverage question for resolution after termination of the underlying malpractice claim. Insurers do this by sending a "reservation of rights" letter.

When an insurer reserves rights under an insurance policy, the carrier provides a defense attorney to the doctor but reserves the right to determine whether to pay a possible judgment. If the malpractice claim is then successfully defended, ordinarily the issue is dropped. If a malpractice judgment is entered, however, the insurer may sue the insured and ask the court to determine whether coverage applies and whether the insurer must pay the judgment. Conversely, if the insurer wrongfully denies indemnity or defense coverage, the health care provider may subsequently sue the carrier for costs, expenses, and attorney fees incurred in defending the original malpractice claim, plus interest.[26] Whenever a coverage dispute involves a reservation of rights letter or a flat denial, doctors may find that years of premium payments leave them in the same position as if they had "gone bare." The cheapest policy may not always be the best policy.

Self-insurance: But I decided to go bare!

Very, very few doctors practice without medical malpractice insurance. Doing so is known as "going bare." Doctors who decide to go bare are on their own in defending a medical malpractice claim. In that case, a doctor must immediately contact his or her personal attorney. The attorney may choose to represent the doctor personally or refer the client to an experienced malpractice defense attorney. Of course, the doctor will be obliged to pay all fees and expenses out of his own pocket; there is no contingent defense fee. A large retainer also will usually be demanded up front.

While more and more doctors now consider dropping their medical malpractice coverage because of the exorbitant premiums, doctors should have coverage if they possibly can. Going bare is tempting, but defense costs and a modest judgment (based on what is "modest" in medical malpractice cases) could wipe out a doctor financially.

To make going bare useful, some doctors try to shield assets from potential claimants. In extreme cases, a doctor transfers all assets to the spouse or family and fully funds pension plans. While this may well work in some jurisdictions, a court in some instances can ignore these transfers and still allow creditors to go after the assets anyway, especially if the transfers were done after the doctor knew of the potential claim. The doctor also runs the risk that the spouse or the family may run off with the assets. In Pennsylvania, little or nothing can be hidden from the judgment creditor.[27] A doctor who plans to go bare should be certain to consult his personal attorney so the attorney can advise how to do it and describe the risks and uncertainties involved. If the attorney advocates going bare and the doctor is so inclined, the doctor should get a second opinion. One physician has said, "I want insurance because if I do make a mistake, I want my patient to be able to have a source available to get compensated."

Insurance companies, acting vicariously through hospitals, are attempting to make it impossible for doctors to even consider going bare. Hospital liability carriers are insisting, upon the threat of refusing to insure, that hospitals require each staff member to carry a certain level of insurance to maintain staff privileges. Hospital trustees and attorneys are also insisting on this. If both the hospital and physician are sued, the hospital wants a "partner" to share the defense costs and any payments that must be made.

The JCAH allows current evidence of adequate professional liability insurance as a professional criterion of medical staff members[28] but prohibits a hospital from unilaterally amending the medical staff bylaws to impose this (or any) requirement.[29]

Courts in some states have allowed such a requirement.[30] Although the issue has not been clearly resolved in Pennsylvania, a similar position will likely be taken.[31]

LEGAL ALERT

Hospital liability carriers are attempting to have included in the medical staff bylaws the requirement that doctors have certain levels of medical malpractice coverage. The purpose is to shift liability costs from the hospital to the medical staff. In most situations this effort should be opposed. If such a requirement is to be imposed, it would be better—from the perspective of any refuseniks on the staff—to have this requirement made a part of the bylaws of the hospital's board of trustees. A doctor would then have a better

chance of challenging the requirement if an effort were made to revoke the doctor's privileges on the basis of being uninsured or underinsured. If a staff agrees to a staff-imposed requirement, a court is more likely to tell staff members to follow their own rules. On the other hand, if physicians control the rule, the amount at which the requirement is set can be kept at an acceptable amount. One thing that must be avoided is indemnification of the hospital. If the physician or physician group is asked to sign such a commitment to pay the hospital's losses when the physician is at fault, run (don't walk) to the nearest exit. These agreements almost guarantee that the hospital will be a hostile party in any lawsuit.

Going bare is one thing, being scantily clad is quite another!

Doctors don't have to have medical malpractice insurance limits in the tens of millions of dollars. Indeed, some insurance companies discourage large limits or simply won't write them, as attorneys always want the limit when they try to settle a case and will usually accept the limit regardless of how severe the injury.

Furthermore, no law says that a doctor has to have his assets on a silver platter to serve the patient's attorney. Nothing is wrong with investing in assets that creditors cannot touch or suggesting that relatives leave inheritances in trusts that are not subject to creditors' claims. Some examples:

- Property held in trust for another is excepted from creditors' claims. Thus an educational trust for the children couldn't be taken if funded before anticipation of the specific claim or suit.[32]
- Let's say that a doctor's father plans to leave him an inheritance. On the father's death, the inheritance would normally pass through probate. The inheritance would then become part of the son's assets and subject to the claim of his creditors. Instead of giving it to the son outright, the father could leave it in a trust. The trustee could then be authorized to distribute all or any part of the trust assets to the son as the trustee sees fit. The trust would also provide, however, that it would not be subject to claims against the doctor. If a court ever held that claims could be made, then the doctor would lose the trust and the assets would pass to his family. If carefully drawn and the possibility of bankruptcy considered, the trust can give a doctor substantially all the benefits of ownership without any risk that creditors could ever take the assets.
- Certain insurance policies and proceeds are exempted. The policy should indicate that the proceeds and income therefrom are not assignable.[33] Some modern mixed-purpose life insurance policies could make this exception valuable.

Every doctor should consult a personal attorney about these kinds of suggestions to shelter assets regardless of whether the doctor has insurance. The possibilities are very limited in Pennsylvania. But what can be done, should. It's not going bare; it's just using good sense. But to be effective, these few ideas that are available must be carefully considered, implemented well before a problem occurs, and regularly reviewed with a personal attorney.

Endnotes

1. The steps suggested in this chapter should, to the extent appropriate, be followed if a doctor is contacted by letter regarding a possible medical malpractice claim.
2. An excellent book to read about the psychological impact of being sued for medical malpractice is *Defendant—A Psychiatrist on Trial for Medical Malpractice—An Episode in America's Hidden Health Care Crisis* written by Sara C. Charles, M.D., and Eugene Kennedy and published by The Free Press, New York. *See also* Wilbert, J., Charles, S., Warnecke, R. and Lichtenberg, R.: Coping with the Stress of Malpractice Litigation, **171** Ill. Med. J. 23, 1987.
3. Martindale-Hubbel Law Directory is published by Martindale-Hubbell, Inc., of Summit, N.J.
4. Belli, M.: Melvin Belli—My Life on Trial at 157, New York, 1976, William Morrow & Co.
5. 43 C.J.S. Infants §222 (1978).
6. The parents' interests may not be identical to that of the child.
7. Bertinelli v. Galonai, 200 A. 58, 118 A.L.R. 398 (Pa. 1938).
8. 20 Pa. C.S.A. §751(s) (Purdon 1975).
9. 42 Pa. C.S.A. §8301 (Purdon 1982). The power to sue on behalf of the estate is a part of the general power of the trustee. 20 Pa. C.S.A. §3332 (Purdon 1975).
10. Consortium has also come to refer to companionship and other benefits of family life, so that suits are filed for the loss of consortium of a child. Boarts v. McCord, 511 A.2d 204 (Pa. Super. 1986).
11. *See* Chapter 3 regarding failure to protect cases.
12. 42 Pa. R.C.P. Rule 1351 (Purdon 1975).
13. The 20-day limit is in Rule 1026.
14. Castel v. Mitchell, 423 A.2d 1375 (Pa. Commonwealth 1981). This, and the case cited in fn. 15, were appeals from the ruling of the chairman of a health care arbitrator's panel. The law creating these panels was declared unconstitutional in 1980. Mattos v. Thompson, 421 A.2d 190 (Pa. 1980). Additionally, the procedures involved were nullified because of the basic provision's unconstitutionality in 1984. Heller v. Frankston, 475 A.2d 1291 (Pa. 1984). But the basic notion of a default judgment for non-response both precedes and continues after the Arbitration Act.
15. Vrahas v. Challimar, 437 A.2d 809 (Pa. Commonwealth 1981).
16. 42 Pa. R.C.P. Rule 1021 (Purdon 1979).
17. Const. Art. 1, §6 (Purdon 1961).
18. 42 Pa. C.P.R. DR 5-107, A & B (Purdon 1975).
19. 42 Pa. C.P.R. DR 5-105 (Purdon 1987).
20. 42 Pa. R.C.P. Rule 4003.3. (Purdon 1987). In the past, documents and reports prepared in anticipation of litigation were protected. Cerney v. Brillson, 68 D. & C.2d 764 (Pa. Comm. Pl. 1974). In 1978, the rules were radically altered to protect only the lawyer's mental impression, conclusions, opinions, memoranda, notes, summaries, legal research, and legal theories, nothing more. Rule 4003.3, Explanatory Note-1978. The federal rules protected the same material when recorded by an insurance investigator, but Pennsylvania does not. *Id.* and Prio v. Bell, 25 D. & C.3d 668 (Pa. Comm. Pl. 1981), in which a physician's request for a protective order of a statement given his insurance company was denied. This rule is an abberation and should be changed.
21. Reviewing your insurance is discussed further in Chapter 8.
22. Taken from the policy forms of The Medical Protective Company, Fort Wayne, Ind., numbers TL-6-86 and CMI-10-86.
23. Taken from Form 40202 Ed. 10-78 of St. Paul Fire and Marine Insurance Co.

24. The elements of medical malpractice are discussed in detail in Chpter 2.
25. D'Allessandro v. Durham Life Ins. Co., 467 A.2d 1303 (Pa. 1983).
26. Unfair Insurance Practices Act. 40 Pa. C.S.A. §472 et seq. (Purdon 1987).
27. Examples of property exempt from execution on judgments are in 42 Pa. C.S.A. §8124 (Purdon 1982). Also see 13 Standard Pennsylvania Practice 2d, Chapter 74 (1983).
28. AMH/86 Accreditation Manual for Hospitals at 10.1.2.3.1.2.3.3, Chicago, 1985, Joint Commission on Accreditation of Hospitals.
29. The Accreditation Manual for Hospitals has been revised to provide in MS.2.1 that: "The bylaws and the rules and regulations of the medical staff are adopted by the medical staff and approved by the governing body prior to becoming effective. Neither body may unilaterally amend the medical staff bylaws."
30. *See, e.g.,* Pollock v. Methodist Hospital, 392 F.Supp. 3939 (E.D. La. 1975); Holmes v. Hoemako Hospital, 117 Ariz. 403, 573 P.2d 477 (1975).
31. See **7** A.L.R. 4th 1231 (1981).
32. Clark v. Clark, 191 A.2d 417 (Pa. 1963).
33. 42 Pa. C.S.A. §8124 (c) (4) (Purdon).

MEDICAL MALPRACTICE PRETRIAL PROCEDURES

Skirmishes

6

Synopsis

Almost everyone who is sued for the first time fails to understand that an attorney can't walk into court, explain why the claim is bogus, and have the case rejected on the spot. The system doesn't work that way. Few cases are obvious. Only if the plaintiff fails to state any basis on which relief could possibly be granted will the case be thrown out at this early stage. Months, perhaps years of pretrial skirmishes will usually take place before the case is resolved.

Meeting with the attorney

After a doctor notifies the insurance carrier of the lawsuit, the carrier will select an attorney who is usually from or familiar with the doctor's community. In some instances the carrier will allow the doctor to be represented by a personal attorney, or an attorney the doctor selects, but this is uncommon.

Although paid by the insurance carrier, the attorney selected is actually the doctor's attorney as well. This doesn't mean, of course, that the doctor cannot or should not keep a personal attorney involved in the case.[1] Unless the physician knows and has utmost confidence in the attorney selected, he should insist that his personal attorney be kept informed and allowed to participate, at the physician's expense, in the preparation of the case. Good defense counsel will welcome the help if the personal attorney does not become an irritant by looking over the other attorney's shoulder and second-guessing every step.

It is important for the doctor to establish good rapport with the attorney who will defend the case. To accomplish this, the doctor should begin by sizing up the attorney from every angle, just as one would a new patient. The doctor will be interested in the attorney's educational background, how long he has been in practice, what experience the attorney has had in malpractice cases, and what his record has been. One should particularly note whether the attorney has actively gone to trial or usually settles cases out of court. The doctor will also be interested in the attorney's reputation among his peers and the judges. If they don't get along with or have little respect for the attorney, this could adversely affect the case. Don't believe for a minute that judges are able to be totally impartial and that cases are not affected by mutual respect, past dealings, friendships, or animosities. The personal attorney can be of tremendous help in evaluating the attorney the carrier has selected, but only the doctor can decide whether the attorney knows anything about medicine or is capable of or willing to learn.

The attorney appointed by the insurance company will soon contact the doctor to discuss the case. If no contact is initiated within a few days after the doctor has been notified of the appointment, call the attorney's office and request an appointment to begin working on the case.

At the first conference the attorney will review with the doctor the facts of the case and the statements made in the complaint. The discussion will be greatly facilitated if the doctor has prepared a detailed statement about the claim, remembering that such a statement might be discovered later and examined by the other side.

At this juncture, an important purpose of the meeting with the attorney will be to help the attorney determine how to respond to the complaint. This is a particularly important time for the physician to make certain that the attorney understands just how vigorously the physician wants to fight the case. If malpractice is so apparent that even the doctor agrees that there was negligence, the attorney should be told the doctor wants to get out of the case as quickly and quietly as possible. If the claim is specious or a close call, the doctor should impress upon the attorney that he or she is expected to fight and win the case.

Attorneys often have a preference regarding in whose office they and the doctor will meet. At some juncture, it may be advisable to meet with the attorney at the practitioner's office. This arrangement will help provide the attorney the opportunity to evaluate the doctor, the doctor's practice, and even the doctor's staff. If the attorney is convinced that the doctor acted professionally, the attorney is likely to be more effective in defending the doctor. Initially, however, the physician should go to the lawyer's office as part of his assessment of his assigned representative.

Framing the defense

It may be obvious to the physician that a patient's complaint has no merit. This may not be as obvious to others, especially a judge or jury who may ultimately decide the case. It is essential that the best defense possible be presented on the physician's behalf; this may include educating the jury on the medical principles involved.

All court cases are defended both on legal grounds and on the facts. The legal grounds are often procedural and technical. They are to the attorney what medical details are to the physician—important responsibilities. For example, if the location of the trial court is unacceptable and the attorney fails to object at the outset, the objection is waived and there is no chance of getting it moved. At the initial stages of a case, legal grounds are the only way to have a claim rejected. At trial, the facts are critical. After trial, legal grounds can be the basis for appealing a decision or requesting a judgment notwithstanding the jury's verdict. Lawyers get sued for legal malpractice most often over the technical details, like missing a filing deadline.

The legal grounds on which a patient's suit can be rejected are numerous. The attorney, being skilled in the law, should recognize and pursue those "legal technicalities." Possible legal grounds include these:

- ***Statute of limitations expired.*** The case must have been filed before the statute of limitations expires. If the statute has run, the court will routinely dismiss the case.[2]
- ***Good samaritan statutes applicable.*** To encourage doctors to provide gratuitous medical care in cases of emergency, Pennsylvania has adopted a so-called good samaritan statute.[3] This statute can be a basis for throwing out the case, if the plaintiff has not alleged gross negligence or an intentional tort.
- ***Right of conscience.*** As a response to political pressure groups discouraging abortions, the Pennsylvania General Assembly passed the Abortion Control Act in 1982.[4] A part of this series of statutes is one stating public policy and legislative intent.[5] In one subclause, the General Assembly states: "It is the . . . public policy of the Commonwealth of Pennsylvania . . . to prohibit . . . imposition of liability . . . by reason of . . . refusing to act contrary to . . . conscience . . . in refusing to obtain, receive, subsidize, accept or provide abortions."[6] Rarely an attorney can attempt a motion for summary judgment on the basis of this statute.
- ***Failure to state a claim.*** The defense attorney will be alert to the possibility that, even assuming everything the patient has said is true, there may be no basis in the pleading such that a court would allow a jury to vote on the case. These cases are rare, but they do occur.[7] They are more likely at marginal areas of legal theory or when they name one of multiple defendants improperly and then strain to produce allegations.

The doctor sued for medical malpractice is of critical importance to the attorney in developing the facts necessary to defend the case. Essential facts helpful to the defense should already be presented in the detailed statement prepared for the carrier and the attorney. These facts may suggest certain defenses. Certain defenses require that allegations about the patient's behavior be made. The two most common "affirmative defenses" are contributory negligence and assumption of the risk:

- ***Contributory negligence.*** A patient may be responsible at least in part for the injury. A patient who fails to provide accurate and complete information needed for his treatment, ignores the doctor's advice, fails to keep appointments, fails to follow the directions given, or refuses treatment can greatly contribute to or indeed actually cause the injury. To be of significance, a patient's action or inaction must help cause the injuries. The patient's negligence usually will not defeat a claim, but it can reduce the amount of damages.[8] Pennsylvania is a comparative negligence state.[9] This means that damages are apportioned between parties on the basis of fault. (Under contributory negligence rules, a patient even partially at fault was barred from suing. Only those more at fault than the defendant are now so barred.) If the injured party contributed to the injuries to the extent of, say, 20 percent, damages are reduced by that amount. Therefore, a key point is whether any blame could be placed on the patient.[10]

- ***Assumption of risk.*** Some authorities suggest that a patient who is told through an informed consent of all the horrible things that could happen should not be able to sue if one of those things in fact happens. The theory is that the patient assumed the risk of injury by undergoing the treatment. This defense is available where the plaintiff knew and understood the risk he was taking and his choice was free and voluntary.[11] The parallels with informed consent are obvious. Traditionally, the defense was sufficient to prevent further suit.[12] It has been suggested that the defense is inapplicable because the plaintiff only assumed the inherent statistical risk, not the risk that the defendant would be negligent.[13]

However, usually the best defense is the most direct—simply that the physician did not act negligently. The medical record is there for all to see, although disputes will be raised about what was done in fact. Thus medical malpractice cases often revolve around the issue of standard of care.

- ***Standard of care.*** For a physician to be found negligent, he or she must have violated the standard of care, that is, acceptable practice in the same or a similar community.[14] The physician is in a much better position than the attorney to know what that is and why. The point is: What is the standard of care, and did the doctor conform to it?
- ***Causation.*** Although sometimes the key to the defense, this element is often a co-factor. The doctor can help enormously with information regarding the patient's prior condition, unmodified prognosis, and current expectations and disabilities.

The assistance that a doctor provides the attorney in assembling the facts of the case is extremely important in framing the defense. The doctor should take the time to be a real help. While "selling" your side to the lawyer is important, it is also important to retain enough objectivity to be able to point out any weak spots and to anticipate the patient's arguments.

Responding to the complaint

Motions directed to the complaint

Within 20 days after the doctor is served with a summons, the attorney will advise the court that he or she is representing the doctor. To do this the attorney files an "entry of appearance" or some other response to the complaint.

In most tort cases, an attorney will initially respond by filing a written motion with the court challenging the patient's right to bring or procedure in bringing a suit. A variety of other motions may also be filed, including, for example, a motion claiming that summons was not properly served, a request to have the trial moved to another county, or a request to have the patient give more particulars to enable the doctor to answer the complaint.

A motion is simply a request addressed to the court asking it to do something. The motion filed will depend in large part on the case involved. The most common purpose is to ask the court to dismiss the case for one reason or another. For example, the court might be asked to dismiss the case because of lack of conformity to law or rule of court.[15] Very often the attorney will argue that the facts alleged in the complaint are not sufficient to state a claim or cause of action against the doctor. In Pennsylvania, this is called by its ancient name—a demurrer.[16]

If the court grants a motion, it will then enter an order or decision to that effect. Sometimes a doctor is fortunate enough to have some defense that can cause the case to be thrown out immediately. Such instances are rare, however. More often a case might be dismissed, but then the patient is given an opportunity to correct the mistakes. The complaint can be amended.[17] When that is done, the motion process starts all over again until the complaint is sufficient to allege medical malpractice. This means that the complaint must state circumstances that, **if proved,** will legally and factually allow a finding that the doctor was guilty of malpractice.

To a person unaccustomed to how courts operate, these initial stages might seem more like the ritual of Oriental wrestlers than an expeditious way to settle disputes. But the doctor shouldn't become frustrated. These steps are important, often critical to the proper defense of a case. They are much simplified over the legal standards of the past. "Motions practice" was used then in an attempt to decide the case by endless and technically tricky filings, without even getting to trial. In some cases even today, the preliminaries can result in prompt termination of the case. Even if they do not end the matter, these motions can pin down the patient on the specific complaint. In the long run this information will make it easier for the doctor and the attorney to develop and defend the case.

Answering the complaint

The patient's complaint makes allegations of what the doctor supposedly did or didn't do. Eventually, the attorney will file what is known as an answer to these allegations. An answer simply responds to what is claimed.

Under Pennsylvania law the answer must explicitly admit or deny each fact stated in the complaint, paragraph by paragraph.[18] The answer will thus be a series of statements that refer to each paragraph of the complaint and either admit or deny each. Denial is also accomplished by denying sufficient knowledge to form a belief regarding the statement.

When an answer is filed, the case is said to be at issue. This means that the complaint and the answer, when examined together, tell what the parties dispute.

Other pleadings

The answer is often the only pleading filed by a medical malpractice defendant other than perhaps some preliminary motions. Under some circumstances other pleadings may be needed. The nature of other pleadings may vary considerably. Some are included as part of the answer itself. Examples include:

- ***Affirmative defenses.*** An affirmative defense is some matter that could result in the patient's claim being denied even if the claim's assertions are true. For example, if the case had been settled and the patient signed a release, the existence of the release would be an affirmative defense.[20] Affirmative defenses are pleaded as "new matter" extrinsic to the plaintiff's case against the physician.[21]
- ***Counterclaims.*** If the doctor has some reason to countersue the patient, that may be done as part of the same case. The doctor's claim is called a counterclaim.[22] Although it is rarely done, if the patient owed a bill, the doctor could counterclaim for the amount owed. A doctor sued for medical malpractice often wants to "counterclaim" against the patient or the patient's attorney for bringing suit. However, it will be dismissed as a counterclaim since it doesn't arise from the facts in the plaintiff's suit, but from the suit itself.[23]
- ***Joinder of parties.*** If other defendants are involved in the case, the doctor may have some claim against them. He may plead that these other defendants are in fact at fault.[24] For example, a doctor may have followed some drug manufacturer's instructions explicitly, and still the patient was injured. If both the doctor and the manufacturer are sued, the doctor may sue the manufacturer for any damages imposed against him. Plaintiffs are ecstatic when this happens. It means they can watch the various defendants point fingers at each other and make the case for the plaintiffs. In other states and in federal court, these are called "cross claims."
- ***Third-party complaint.*** A third-party complaint is a suit filed against another person who is not a party to the case. It is referred to as a joinder of additional defendants.[25] These suits serve a purpose similar to joinder of parties (above) where the person sued is not already named in the case. The defendant who joins or brings in an additional party is essentially saying, "Here is the person responsible for the harm you accuse me of causing."
- ***Jury demand.*** The patient will probably have requested a jury trial. If not, and if the doctor wants a jury trial, the doctor's attorney can demand one when answering the complaint. If the patient has already asked for a jury, the doctor need not do so.

If other pleadings are filed, the patient or other person against whom they are directed will have an opportunity to answer or reply.

The ill-fated review panels

Unlike many other states, Pennsylvania does not require that a review panel consider medical malpractice cases before or after they are filed. There are no required panels to filter out frivolous claims or arbitrate those claims generally. The Pennsylvania Supreme Court declared the heart of the 1975 medical malpractice arbitration panel legislation uconstitutional.[26] More recently, all of the arbitration procedures were declared invalid.[27] The heart was taken when the state's supreme court exercised plenary jurisdiction to reach down, pick up, and decide a case pending in superior court. The justices quoted statistical analysis of claims filed with the arbitration panels' administrator and found that the procedure created constitutionally unacceptable delays in plaintiffs' right to a trial.[28] Therefore the exclusive original jurisdiction of the arbitration panels in medical malpractice was rescinded—plaintiffs could once again go straight to court. Under the procedure, now unused, a panel composed of an attorney, a health professional, and a lay person would consider the merits of a claim and determine a fair and just compensation for any injury caused by malpractice.[29] The panel could appoint its own expert witness.[30] The determination was subject to rejection by any of the parties. They were then entitled to a trial in the Court of Common Pleas, where the panel's findings of facts could be introduced as evidence.[31] Similar panel procedures have been upheld in other jurisdictions where the delays were not so great. The Pennsylvania experience influenced physicians in other states to cooperate, participate, and help to move arbitration panel proceedings along.

Discovery

Generally

When the pleadings stage is completed or well underway, the parties begin "discovery." Attorneys use this process to find out or discover information relevant to the claims made. The early investigation of a case on both sides is somewhat informal. After suit has begun, formal methods enforceable by the court apply. The methods of discovery include written interrogatories, oral or written questions, discovery or inspection of documents, and physical and mental examination of people.[32] Failure to comply with discovery requirements can subject a party to court-imposed sanctions ranging from imposing punishment for contempt to preventing a party from maintaining a claim or defense.[33] Expenses and attorney fees may be granted in certain instances.

Discovery is intended to narrow the issues for trial and to prevent surprise. The parties have ample opportunity to learn about the other side's case, but should not be permitted to "go fishing" for anything they want. Theoretically, discovery should encourage settlement or dropping of cases.

Just what may be discovered in a case is very broadly construed; about anything goes. A patient may obtain from the doctor and the doctor may obtain from the patient any matter relevant to any claim or defense. No discovery or deposition will be permitted which (1) is sought in bad faith (as when the attorney is really trying to turn up new cases), (2) would cause unreasonable annoyance or burden, (3) is related to privileged matter, or (4) would require an unreasonable investigation by any party or witness.[35] The court may enter an appropriate order—a protective order—regulating discovery to prevent unreasonable annoyance, expense, embarrassment, burden, or oppression.[36]

Confidentiality extends to all proceedings and records resulting from evaluation by professional health care providers for the quality and efficiency of services performed.[37] This QA/peer review information is not discoverable and may not be used in evidence. However, if the documents are available from some other source, the protection is lost and they can be used.[38] This provision doesn't protect other records, such as the doctor's application for staff privileges.[39] The purpose of this limit or use of peer review material is to improve the quality of care, reduce morbidity and mortality, and control costs.[40]

It is worthy of note that those attending these QA/peer review meetings cannot be called as witnesses regarding the review proceedings.[41] They can be witnesses otherwise, but cannot be asked about the peer review committee hearings.

Interrogatories

Interrogatories are written questions regarding the case submitted by one party, such as the patient, to another party, such as the doctor. Within 30 days after these questions are served, the person to whom they are directed must answer them in writing, under oath.[42]

If the patient asks the doctor to respond to interrogatories, the doctor should take time to seriously consider the importance of the answers. When the attorney receives them, he or she will usually send them to the doctor with the suggestion that initial answers be prepared. The attorney then will sit down with the doctor to review the answers. After that the attorney will translate the answers into "legalese," saying only a minimum and in the way that will best support the doctor's position. The prepared answers will then be submitted to the doctor for a final review and signature.

A doctor should not underestimate the importance of properly answered interrogatories. Patients' attorneys develop elaborate questions to trap the doctor into helping them make their cases.[43] Only the specific question must be answered, not what the attorney "should" have asked, and only as minimally as posible. The doctor should carefully review the questions, prepare preliminary answers, think about them for a couple of days, and review them again, making certain that the answers are exact and volunteer nothing. A doctor shouldn't rely on memory for anything that can be verified from records. The doctor should also make certain the answers do not conflict with the records. Under some circumstances it may be appropriate to simply attach a copy of the records. Doctors who answer carelessly will find that months later the patient's attorney will use those answers against them.

The doctor's attorney will usually decide whether the client should submit interrogatories to the patient or other parties. Interrogatories are best used to obtain data and objective information, such as the amount of bills incurred, other doctors consulted, collateral sources of compensation, and the like. It is important that the doctor have the patient disclose the names of any anticipated expert witnesses. Their identity and their opinion (and basis for that opinion) in summary form can be discovered.[44] However, the doctor doesn't want to give the patient a better opportunity to frame the offense—specific questions might suggest a line of inquiry or point of vulnerability that will otherwise remain unrecognized by plaintiffs.

Depositions

Depositions are a commonly used method of discovery in medical malpractice cases. Unlike interrogatories, which are questions submitted and answered in writing, depositions involve questions posed and answered orally, under oath, and recorded verbatim.[45] A deposition may be taken of a party to the case as well as any other person having information relevant to the case, such as expert witnesses or nursing staff present during the alleged malpractice. In somewhat more pleasant circumstances, a doctor may have had a deposition taken in connection with a patient's personal injury or a worker's compensation claim against someone else. Even then, he should have been on guard—such cases have been known to become malpractice cases after the attorney obtained more information. The defendant's depositon is both a hazard and an opportunity. The doctor must be as careful as a six-point buck on opening day.

A doctor should be very cautious when called to testify by deposition in a malpractice case if not named as a defendant, but only as a treating doctor. In such a case the doctor should consider being represented by an attorney and reporting the case to the insurance carrier. The patient's attorney may attempt to drag the doctor into the case after he has given testimony without being fully prepared (because the doctor saw no danger of being named a defendant).

Depositions are taken before a wide group of "officers" or other persons empowered to administer oaths and take testimony.[46] A record of everything said is transcribed and, if necessary, is used in court.[47] Formal notice must be given a reasonable time before a deposition is to be taken.[48] In practice, the attorneys informally agree on a time and place where a deposition will be taken. Subpoenas are necessary only if the deposition is of a nonparty to the suit.[49] Depositions are most often held in an attorney's office, which is more anxiety-provoking than the physician's own office, but is less likely to be near potentially damaging documentary evidence. The attorney's office is better practice for trial and its pressures.

Before the case is heard by the judge or jury, a deposition will usually be taken of all parties to the case, as well as others who will likely testify at trial, including expert witnesses. The physician's attorney should attend all depositions, even in multiparty cases. Although some attorneys are inclined to try to make these informal and candid bull sessions, the doctor shouldn't be fooled. Depositions are extremely important, and the doctor should take them very, very seriously. What is said at depositions may be the basis for having the case resolved without a formal trial.[50] Depositions can also be used to impeach or contradict testimony at trial, as an admission of some information, and infrequently, as actual testimony of witnesses who do not appear.[51]

When a deposition is taken of the patient, an expert witness, or some other person, the doctor should attend unless the attorney gives him a good reason not to. By being present, he will get a good feel of the case and what is likely to be said at trial. Also, with the doctor sitting across the table, it may be harder for the person deposed to be as harshly critical as when the defendant is absent. The doctor, being the best expert and factual witness, can greatly assist the attorney in correcting or clarifying facts and applying medical knowledge to what is being said. While present, the doctor should remain calm and talk only when his attorney requests it. A doctor who wants to talk with his attorney should simply whisper or request a private conference in another room.

When notified that he or she must give a deposition, the doctor should take a number of steps. Before giving the deposition, the doctor should:

- Have a meeting with the attorney, who will brief the doctor on what to expect. If the attorney doesn't insist on this, a new attorney is needed. The doctor should prepare for the deposition in much the same way as preparing for trial. While preparing, the doctor shouldn't withhold anything from the attorney, who must clearly understand everything about the case to properly defend it. While a written statement is discoverable, the attorney's notes on what the doctor says are not.
- Review everything about the case in advance, including the detailed statement already prepared, all the patient's records, the complaint and the answer, answers to interrogatories, depositions of others, etc. The doctor should think of the questions he or she would ask another doctor to determine if the care rendered was proper. This is a time for the doctor to impress upon the opposing attorney that the practitioner is not some fumbler but a qualified, competent, and concerned doctor. The doctor should show the patient's attorney he or she will be his or her own best witness.
- Review the standard works pertaining to the medical situation involved and provide copies to the defending attorney. The doctor can and should educate his counsel as to the medical science in the case.

- Discuss with the attorney how to handle discrepancies in the material reviewed, should they come up.
- Unless the deposition is at the defending attorney's office, meet the attorney at his or her office and travel to the place of the deposition together. If it is at the doctor's lawyer's office, the doctor should arrive early, see where the deposition will be held, and confer with counsel.
- Be courteous but serious upon arrival at the deposition. This is not the time to discuss golf scores and tell jokes. It's also not a time to be arrogant or cocky. The patient's lawyer will recalculate his own estimates of the chances of winning or losing depending on the physician's attitude and the impression made, as well as what is said.
- Ask the attorney where to sit. He should review the procedures involved and remind his client that he is entitled to request breaks if he feels tired or becomes rattled. The plaintiff's attorney will not be able to harrass or exhaust witnesses in court without signifiant risk; it is unnecessary for the physician to demonstrate that he can "take it" endlessly without rest.

Giving the deposition:

- When the deposition begins, the notary public will ask the doctor to raise his right hand and swear to tell the truth. And when testifying, the doctor should do just that. Tell the truth! The inadequately prepared physician may suddenly feel a wave of anxiety as he realizes the seriousness of the deposition. He should have been readying himself for a serious, important session well in advance. He should feel confident that the truth is his friend and will help to exonerate him.
- The opposing attorney will then proceed to ask questions. The doctor should make sure he or she understands the question completely before answering. If need be, the doctor should consult records before answering. The practitioner shouldn't guess and should avoid the natural tendency to conceal misunderstanding. The questions should be answered directly and specifically, but the doctor shouldn't volunteer information. After all, the patient's attorney wants the doctor to do just that, and the attorney will give the doctor plenty of rope to hang himself. Answer the question asked, not what should have been asked. The doctor should remain calm and not lose his temper. If the practitioner didn't hear or understand a question, he or she should ask that it be repeated or clarified. The behavior of a doctor-defendant is a source of amazement and dismay at too many depositions. The cause may be the doctor's natural desire to be helpful or a naive belief that simple explanations will straighten the whole problem out.
- During questioning, the opposing attorney may ask the doctor whether a particular book is authoritative.[52] The attorney wants to use the text to establish what care should have been given. By "authoritative" the attorney will mean "perfectly accurate and unquestionable"; the doctor may mean "pretty good." Therefore, unless the doctor clearly be-

lieves the book is authoritative, he or she shouldn't agree that it is. Virtually no text is accepted in all respects and over time. It's preferable to note that no text can deal with all the circumstances that arise in practice and cannot be considered correct in all respects. If it is a famous book and the physician feels constrained to recognize its worth or would appear foolish in failing to do so, the term "authoritative" should still be avoided. Physicians can admit that they read and use certain texts and journals without having to accept every phrase taken out of context. This avoids the foolish appearance of denying the worth of everything.

- The opposing attorney may attempt to lead the doctor into particular answers—the leading question—or try to get the doctor to agree that certain broad generalizations are correct. The physicians should think before answering these and avoid being tricked into generalization or the answer the opposing attorney wants. In general, avoid saying "never" or "always." If the physician is successful in avoiding this, the attorney may turn to truths so universally recognized that no one could deny them: "Doctor, this patient was not perfectly healthy, was she?"
- While questions are being asked, the doctor's attorney may object to some questions. If this happens, the doctor should take his attorney's direction as to whether to respond. The doctor shouldn't argue (for example, "No, I want to answer that question!"). If the doctor's attorney objects to a question, the opposing attorney may then ask that the court reporter "certify" the question and allow the court to determine whether the doctor must answer it.[53] The doctor shouldn't answer too quickly, but rather give the attorney time to consider and voice any legal objections. In most cases after an objection, the defense lawyer will advise the physician to answer the question. The objection is now on the record and may be argued to try and keep the question out at trial.
- The doctor's attorney may also ask the doctor questions. However, this is usually done only to correct or clarify something the doctor has said. There is no reason to give the opponent more information than requested.
- The doctor should use this opportunity to practice explaining the important medical facts in layman's terms. When the case is ultimately heard, laymen will hear it. Technical jargon won't impress them. They will like, understand, and believe a doctor more who explains things so they can appreciate his position.
- When the deposition is concluded, the doctor will be asked whether he or she wishes to waive "notice and signing" of the deposition.[54] The doctor's attorney will usually make that decision. When a deposition is taken, the doctor has a right to review it. Any changes in the form or substance that one desires to make will be entered upon

the deposition with a statement of the reasons given for making them.[55] The right to sign a deposition is frequently waived. A doctor who wants to review the deposition should let the attorney know in advance.

- The doctor's attorney will obtain a copy of the deposition. The doctor should see that the attorney provides a copy of the deposition (as well as all others) for the doctor's own files.
- If the doctor thereafter reviews the deposition and finds a misstatement, the defending attorney should be notified. He or she will know the best way to correct or clarify it.

Depositions are normally taken only for discovery purposes. However, depositions may also be taken for use as evidence at trial. The procedures for taking evidence depositions are not different in Pennsylvania, but their use as such is highly restricted.[56] This is because of the strong general rule that the jury should see witnesses to pass on their credibility. Evidence depositions are seldom allowed unless an important witness is unavailable for valid reasons. However, in 1979, Rule 4020 (a) (5) was added, allowing a medical witness, other than a party, to testify by deposition even if available. Cost and inconvenience were cited, but objections have been raised to the use of testimony other than by personal appearance in medical malpractice cases.[57] The use of videotaped depositions of medical witnesses is permitted, even if the opponents were not given a copy of the medical report first.[58]

Inspection of documents

In connection with interrogatories or depositions, a request is usually made to inspect or receive copies of documents, objects, or tangible things relevant to the case.[59] In medical malpractice cases, of course, the patient's attorney should already have obtained all hospital and medical records. Thus the exchange of these requests may be of greater help to the doctor's attorney who may request such things as reports received relative to the patient's injuries, financial information, photographs, prior condition, and the like. As with all discovery, "fishing expeditions" are not allowed—the information sought must be reasonably calculated to produce, or lead to, evidence that might be used at trial.[60] One court said fishing is necessary but, "(w)hat we do condemn is the attempt to fish with a net rather than with a hook or a harpoon."[61] For example, because of confidentiality requirements, medical records of patients not a party to the case are not given to the party attempting to discover them.[62]

Physical and mental examinations

If a person's physical or mental condition is in dispute, as it often would be in a medical malpractice case, discovery rules allow the doctor to obtain, at his or her expense, a physical or mental examination of the person. A copy of the examination report must be provided to the person examined.[63] Clearly, if the nature and extent of a patient's injuries are in question, a physical or mental examination is appropriate. The sanctions generally available to penalize noncompliant litigants in the discovery process are more limited regarding a party to a suit who refuses a physical examination.[64]

Admissions

To expedite the trial of a case, a litigant may request another party to either admit a fact or the genuineness of documents.[65] An admission avoids the need for further evidence on the point. Requests for admissions are particularly helpful in establishing data (for example, income). If the party requesting the admission doesn't get a positive response, then he may be able to get compensation for the costs of proving that fact.[66]

Enlisting defense experts

With few exceptions, a doctor's guilt or innocence of medical malpractice will depend primarily on what experts in the field say. Experts establish the standard of care and comment on causation; a patient usually needs expert testimony to make his case.[67] To properly defend a case, the doctor must enlist expert testimony to support his position. Although doctors can be their own experts,[68] they shouldn't think for a minute they can simply tell their side of the story and expect to be vindicated.

Colleagues sometimes shun a doctor who is sued. However, they should realize that they are probably next and help one another. If a doctor is sued, other doctors should offer to help by reviewing the case and serving as an expert or even by helping to obtain another expert. Even if the cáse is one of clear negligence, another doctor may be helpful in getting the case settled in the most favorable and expeditious manner. The support can be important psychologically, and the educational benefits to the helping physician, who learns a great deal about the process, can be significant.

Even if the doctor's attorney has a stable of professional expert witnesses who make a career of testifying at medical malpractice trials, the task of getting appropriate experts will be an important and critical one. Although it may seem as if this task should be easy, defendants have a different problem from plaintiffs. Doctors have a natural reticence to testify against a colleague. On the other hand, doctors do not want publicly to be supportive of less than perfect care. But the defense needs a reasonable, credible expert—not an angry peer who will say anything to try and help "get" the plaintiff or "get off" his friend, the defendant.

The task of securing a defense expert is sometimes made difficult because other doctors who might be willing to be expert witnesses cannot devote hour after hour to something for which they are not well paid. Most insurers are willing to pay for expert witness services, but will not be as liberal as plaintiffs. It may happen that an expert goes into a deposition or even a trial cold, without any preparation, and not knowing what to expect. Even an expert who was initially briefed will be at a distinct disadvantage if he or she is the only witness who does not hear the preceding testimony at trial. An expert who is aware of the tone and direction of the adverse testimony can word and emphasize his own testimony to refute more directly the expert testimony offered by the patient.

The doctor can assure the best expert testimony possible by working with the attorney in selecting the experts. The attorney may have some ideas based on earlier cases, but so may the doctor. Also, the doctor should make certain that any expert is satisfied with his compensation. If a squabble develops between an expert and the carrier on this, the doctor should be willing to personally guarantee in writing that he will pay the fee if necessary. For example, the doctor should have an expert clock every hour devoted to the case, including time sitting around waiting to be called or in thoughtful contemplation of the case at home, and pay him at least on the same per-hour basis as the attorney. Expert fees run from $75 to over $200 per hour or up to $1500 per day plus expenses. Insist to the insurance company throughout, however, that they must pay this cost eventually.

The most important qualification of any expert witness selected is that he will help convince the judge and jury in the doctor's favor. Many factors are involved in making this decision, so the doctor should:

- Make certain the expert is of the same category of doctor or health care provider as the defendant-doctor and is qualified to testify as to the acceptable practice of care.[69] If a specialist in a different field is needed to testify, then that expert should be in addition to the same specialty witness.
- Make certain the expert has been given all records relative to the case. The doctor also should ascertain whether the expert considers the records complete, or whether some of them would not support the opinion the expert will render on the doctor's behalf. Selective submission of records will come out at trial and weaken the witness' credibilty.
- Make certain the expert agrees with the doctor on the appropriate methods of diagnosis and therapy and concludes that the doctor was in compliance with the standard of care in the treatment of the patient. Will the expert say that, despite meeting the standard, the care was suboptimal? That he would have done it differently? Can another expert be found? What is the most favorable credible testimony that can be obtained?
- If at all possible, find an expert in active practice, preferably having years of experience and practicing in the same area. Often doctors are impressed with doctors with academic backgrounds, but often academicians tend to be critical of the average doctor in practice and forget that the standard of care is what the doctor of ordinary skill and care would do, not what is taught at the most prestigious teaching hospitals. A doctor should avoid the academic type who is overly impressed with his own paper credentials, likes to pontificate, and is

out of touch with the realities of everyday medical practice.[70] On the other hand, a realistic well-spoken academician can be very helpful, especially with the right kind of jury.

- If possible, avoid an expert who is too directly associated with the doctor personally or professionally. If the two are friends, the patient's attorney will attempt to discredit the expert's testimony on that basis.
- Before retaining an expert, make clear that in addition to the trial, he or she must be willing to devote considerable time to the case, including predeposition and pretrial preparation. If the expert cannot spare this much time, it might be wise to search for another. However, if the expert's testimony is vital, the doctor should take what he can get but consider adding another expert as a reserve or addition. Again, the doctor should make certain the expert is adequately compensated for time devoted to the case.
- Check the expert's credentials and background, including testimony he may have given in other cases. Make certain the expert is what he or she claims to be. Exaggerated or falsified credentials can completely negate the testimony of the expert.
- As much as possible, make certain the expert is "clean." That means he has no skeletons in any closets, such as an arrest for drunken driving; treatment for substance abuse; loss or suspension of license for any reason, including narcotics violations; loss of hospital privileges; or any criminal or civil violation other than minor traffic tickets. The doctor can be certain that the opposing attorney has thoroughly checked the background of the witness. If the witness is not "clean," the patient's attorney may well be able to impeach the testimony. Past history of testimony is critical; transcripts should be reviewed if available.
- Review any books or articles the expert has written or in which he's been quoted. The doctor should make certain that statements made support rather than conflict with the doctor's position.
- Make certain all experts are paid. During deposition and at trial, the attorneys often ask the experts how much they are being paid. The experienced expert will answer simply and directly, explaining in addition that the fee is for his time, not his testimony. If the expert wants to be paid up front, before testifying, don't resist. Testimony to that effect will make the independence of the expert clearer to the jury. The jury may be surprised that the physician's expert is being paid so much, but plaintiff's expert will be getting that much or more. Free testimony, even if available, runs the risk of appearing to be given out of friendship or other biased reason.
- Make certain the expert is prepared for the questions usually asked regarding board certification. If the expert is not certified, the doctor should ensure that the witness has a ready and acceptable answer if the patient's attorney tries to use this to discredit him.

- Take a realistic look at the expert. The doctor should have an eyeball-to-eyeball meeting with him. The doctor should make certain that the expert has the persuasive attributes the doctor wants to project to the judge or jury. Let's face it, to a great extent successful medical malpractice defense is a theatrical production. The way the team looks, acts, and expresses itself sways the jury.
- Keep in mind that although it helps to have experts who are experienced as witnesses, the doctor doesn't want an expert who has testified so frequently that he appears to be a professional witness for doctors sued for malpractice, a "hired gun." Also, the prior sworn testimony can be brought up to discredit the witness, if it conflicts.
- Get the expert involved as the case progresses and make certain that he is thoroughly familiar with the case before testifying either at depositions or at trials. The expert should have copies of all relevant documents and be made aware of how the patient's attorney might attempt to challenge his testimony. He should also be told of testimony preceding his, even though he may not be allowed (on motion of the plaintiff) to sit in on the trial.

While the doctor has nothing to do with the selection of the patient's expert witnesses, the doctor should review these same points with respect to them. Regardless of the apparent thickness of the armor on opposition witnessses, the doctor should personally check them out. It's surprising to see what is sometimes overlooked. A trip to the hospital or community where they work (and play), or an inquiry by the doctor's attorney to a leading law firm in that city frequently turns up some very interesting and useful information. The doctor's insurance carrier will also have files to assist in this review. Hiring a private investigator has been tried, and it led to a lawsuit by the expert for invasion of privacy.

The doctor's personal involvement in selecting and evaluating experts is critical. Don't let the lawyer "take care of it" alone. Make sure your sword is sharp, your magazine full, before you go into battle.

Summary judgment

The importance of the pretrial skirmishes becomes evident when the doctor realizes that they may be the basis for a judge summarily ruling on a case without a formal trial. The judge does so by entering a "summary judgment." A summary judgment is entered when it is clear that one or the other side should win. Summary judgment will be granted, for example, if it is evident that expert testimony is required to prove the patient's case and none is obtained after numerous opportunities.[71]

To request a summary judgment an attorney will file a motion with the court. Unless the right to a summary judgment is clear from the complaint and answer, which it seldom is, affidavits or sworn statements will be filed to fill in the facts.[72] Significantly, answers to interrogatories, discovery depositions, and admissions of the parties also may be used for this purpose.[73]

A court will not enter summary judgment if there is any factual dispute existing that requires a full hearing in the case. It will do so only if, based on the affidavits filed and discovery taken, no material issue of fact remains. Most summary judgment motions are denied because there is an issue regarding a fact affecting the disposition of the case.[74]

In medical malpractice cases, it is quite common for the doctor's attorney to file a motion for summary judgment. The courts do grant them in proper cases, but very infrequently. For example, if the problem with the plaintiff's case can be cured by amending the papers filed, the court will allow this, rather than grant summary judgment.[75] But to a doctor sued for medical malpractice who actually obtains a summary judgment, it is a welcome vindication.

Endnotes

1. See Chapter 5 on the insurance company's lawyer's potential conflicts of interest and on the value of a personal attorney.
2. *See* Chapter 4 for a discussion of the statute of limitations in medical malpractice cases.
3. 42 Pa. C.S.A. Section 8331 (Purdon 1982).
4. 18 Pa. C.S.A. Section 3201 et seq. (Purdon 1983). Also see, Note, Toward Constitutional Abortion Control Legislation: The Pennsylvania Approach, **87** Dick. L. Rev. 373 (1983).
5. 18 Pa. C.S.A. Section 3202 (Purdon 1983).
6. *Id.* at (d). This is the Right of Conscience wording, adopted, of course, not to help physicians suffering in a moral quandry, but to do everything allowable constitutionally to discourage abortions.
7. Craddock v. Gross, 504 A.2d 1300 (Pa. Super. 1986).
8. 42 Pa. C.S.A. Section 7102 (Purdon 1982).
9. *Id.*
10. This could be a touchy issue, tactically. The lawyer may not want to risk angering the jury by blaming the hurt/sick/crippled/dead plaintiff. But the defense should still be raised in the pretrial papers, even if it is only a possibility. Defenses and objections not raised are irrevocably waived. 42 Pa. R.C.P. Rule 1032 (Purdon 1975).
11. Keeton, Prosser and Keeton, On Torts, 5th Ed., 480 (1984).
12. *Id.,* at 481.
13. Fala, The Law of Medical Malpractice in Pennsylvania, *36* U. Pitts. L. Rev. 203, 235 (1974). The defense is clearly available in Pennsyvlania and acts as a bar to plaintiff's suit where successful. Plaintiffs always plead negligence, however, so the issue of whether or not the harm was negligently caused will still go to trial. If the harm was the result of an inherent risk in the procedure, the physician should be relieved anyway, even without the defense of assumption of the risk. But the public too often expects perfect results. Plaintiff's lawyers are very skillful at suggesting that because something went wrong, something was done wrong. The Pennsylvania General Assembly may have meant to cover assumption of risk in the comparative negligence statute—they added a clause to it to say that assumption of the risk will still apply to ski resort cases. 42 Pa. C.S.A. Section 7102 (c) (Purdon 1982).
14. *See* Chapter 2 for a discussion of the standard of care.
15. 5 Standard Pennsyvlania Practice 2d Section 25:45 (1982).
16. *Id.,* at §25:59.
17. *Id.,* at §25:73.
18. 42 Pa. R.C.P. Rule 1029 (Purdon 1975).
19. *Id.,* at (c).

20. 5 Standard Pennsylvania Practice 2d §26:46 (1982). This comes under the heading of "Accord and Satisfaction". Two common affirmative defenses, assumption of the risk and contributory negligence, are explained above.
21. 42 Pa. R.C.P. Rule 1030 (Purdon 1975).
22. 42 Pa. R.C.P. Rule 1031 (Purdon 1975). The term *counter-claim* is used in any cross-action, whether set off, recoupment, etc., as long as it arises out of the same subject matter as the plaintiff's suit.
23. Hershey Estates v. Magriney, 52 D. & C. 2d 570 (Pa. Comm. Pl. 1971). See also 14 Standard Penn. Practice §80:64(1983).
24. 42 Pa. R.C.P. §2229 (Purdon 1975).
25. 42 Pa. R.C.P. §2252 (Purdon 1975).
26. Mattos v. Thompson, 421 A.2d 190 (Pa. 1980).
27. Heller v. Frankston, 475 A.2d 1291 (Pa. 1984).
28. Mattos, supra. n. 26, at 196.
29. 40 Pa. C.S.A. §1301.308 (Purdon, 1987).
30. 40 Pa. C.S.A. §1301.507 (Purdon, 1987).
31. 40 Pa. C.S.A. §1301.509 and 510 (Purdon, 1987).
32. 42 Pa. R.C.P. Rule 4001 et seq. (Purdon 1975).
33. 42 Pa. R.C.P. Rule 4019 (Purdon 1975).
34. *Id.*, at (e) and (f).
35. 42 Pa. R.C.P. Rule 4011 (Purdon 1987).
36. 42 Pa. R.C.P. Rule 4012 (Purdon 1987).
37. 63 Pa. C.S.A. §425.4 (Purdon 1987).
38. *Id.*
39. Fowler v. Piris, 34 D. & C. 3d 530 (Pa. Comm. Pl. 1981).
40. Robinson v. Mageovern, 83 F.R.D. 79 (ED Pa. 1979), specifically addressing the Pennsylvania Peer Review Protection Act. The legislature expected doctors to be more willing to criticize their colleagues with this protection in place.
41. 63 Pa. C.S.A. §425.4 (Purdon 1987).
42. 42 Pa. R.C.P. Rule 4006 (Purdon 1987).
43. Books have been written to instruct attorneys on developing interrogatories for medical malpractice. Some of these are listed in Chapter 8.
44. 6 Standard Pennsyvlania Practice 2d §34:32 (1982).
45. 42 Pa. R.C.P. Rule 4007 (Purdon 1975).
46. 42 Pa. R..C. Rule 4015 (Purdon 1975). The officers may be authorized to administer oaths by state or federal law. Even notary publics are authorized. 57 Pa. C.S.A. §164 (Purdon).
47. 42 Pa. R.C.P. Rule 4017 (Purdon 1975).
48. 42 Pa. R.C.P. Rule 4007. 1(a) (Purdon 1975).
49. 10 Goodwick-Amram 2d §4007.1 (aq):1 (1979).
50. How the deposition will be used at a hearing on the pretrial motion is up to the local court. 10 Goodwick-Amram 2d §4020:3 (1979).
51. 42 Pa. R.C.P. Rule 4020 (a) (Purdon 1975).
52. The general rule is that a book cannot be introduced as evidence unless "authenticated" or recognized as authoritative by a witness. It may be used for cross-examination purposes only if recognized as authoritative. Foster v. McKeesport Hospital, 394 A. 2d 1031, 1034 (Pa. Super. 1978).
53. When improper questions are asked, the attorney may tell the witness not to answer. This happens infrequently, as the attorney doesn't want to risk the other side getting another "crack" at his witness. When it does happen, an argument between counsel usually ensues as to whether or not the lawyer controls the witness. This may conclude by the lawyer defending the deposition indicating that he only advises the witness. The physician should take the advice. If he wants the answer brought out it can be brought out later after lawyer and client confer. The risks of refusal are the costs and attorney fees involved in coming back if the refusal was wholly unjustified. 10 Goodrich-Amnan §4019 (b): 2 (1979).
54. 42 Pa. R.C.P. Rule 4017 (b) (Purdon 1975).
55. 42 Pa. R.C.P., rule 4017 (c) (Purdon 1975).

56. 10 Goodrich-Amram 2d §4020 (a) 16 (1979).
57. *Id.,* at §12.3.
58. 10 Goodrich-Amram 2d §4017.1:1 Supp. (1987).
59. 42 Pa. R.C.P. Rule 4009 (Purdon 1975).
60. Estate of Townsend, 241 A.2d 534 (PA 1968).
61. Brownstein v. Philadelphia Transp. Co., 46 D. &. C. 2d 463, 464 (Pa. Comm. Pl. 1969).
62. Stark Dental Associates, P.C. v. Medical Service Association of Pennsylvania, 11 D. & C. 3d 699 (Pa. Comm. Pl. 1978).
63. 42 Pa. R.C.P. §4010 (Purdon 1975).
64. 42 Pa. R.C.P. §4019 (c) (4) (Purdon 1979). The sanction of contempt is not to be applied to those refusing an exam. Orders regarding presumption and evidence are still allowed, however.
65. 42 Pa. R.C.P. §4014 (Purdon, 1975).
66. 42 Pa. R.C.P. §4019 (d) (Purdon 1975).
67. *See* Chapter 4 for a discussion of the requirement of expert testimony in the evaluation of a case by the patient's attorney.
68. Meyer, Pennsylvania Trial Advocacy Handbook, 189, Philadelphia, 1976 Bisel.
69. *See* Chapter 2 regarding these requirements.
70. Meyer, fn. 68, at 188-89.
71. Brophy v. Brizuela, 517 A.2d 1293 (Pa. Super. 1986).
72. 42 Pa. R.C.P. Rule 1035 (Purdon 1975).
73. 6 Standard Pennsyvlania Practice 2d §32:1 (1982).
74. *Id.,* at §32:9.
75. *Id.,* at §32:10.

MEDICAL MALPRACTICE TRIALS

The doctor's tribulation

7

Synopsis

Getting to Court
- Pretrial Conference and Trial Setting
- Final Settlement Efforts
- Other Pretrial Actions
- Personal Preparation

Beginning the Trial
- Opening Court
- Picking the Jury
- Opening Statements

Presenting the Evidence
- Generally
- Testimony Regarding the Standard of Care
- Being a Witness

Final Arguments

Jury Instructions

The Verdict

Post-Trial Activities

Post-Trial Motions
Reduction of Damages
Prejudgment Interest
Appeal
Payment of Damages

Suits for Malicious Prosecution

The day for the trial nears. Whatever the preparation, it will be one of the most emotionally trying times of the doctor's life. Those personal reactions to being sued, which may have been put out of mind temporarily, now return with ferocity.[1] This will not be an easy time.

Getting to court

Pretrial conference and trial setting

After the doctor has answered the patient's complaint, a judge may review the case from time to time with the attorneys to determine if the case is ready for trial. This is done at pretrial conferences.[2]

The judge can call for the conference or either attorney can request it.[3] Court rules don't provide a means of enforcement, but the judge can act against the case of the plaintiff who doesn't appear at the conference.[4] By order of the Commonwealth's Supreme Court, the trial judge has to call one pretrial settlement conference, unless he finds it unnecessary.[5]

At a pretrial conference the attorneys consider with the court what can be done to expedite the trial.[6] The conference will consider (1) possible simplification of the issues, (2) possible need for amendments to the papers filed with the court, (3) admissions that might avoid unnecessary proof, (4) limiting the number of expert witnesses, (5) possibly referring part of the case to a "master" (a type of judge) to find some issues, (6) anything that may aid in disposition of the case.[7] For example, in some cases a doctor may admit fault and desire only to contest the amount of the damages, or perhaps the parties have settled all aspects of the case save one or two.

Sometimes, the judge tries to "strongarm" a settlement. He privately tells the plaintiffs how weak their case is and how little chance they have of winning. He then calls in the defendants and reviews their weaknesses and emphasizes plaintiff's strengths. He tries to get each side to move its best settlement offer toward the other's demands.

After the pretrial conference the court will place the case on a trial docket. If the case will be heard by a judge, the setting will be specific. If the case will be heard by a jury, the setting merely states when a jury will be hearing cases. The jury will take up cases in the order they appear on the docket, unless they are settled or for some other reason removed from the docket. Thus the doctor's attorney will have a good idea when a jury case will be taken up but can't be certain. Sometimes, continuances are requested for tactical reasons, which further aggravates the physician defendant, but the delay also must be supported by valid reason.[8]

Final settlement efforts

The Pennsylvania Supreme Court rule ordering pretrial conferences specifically uses the term *settlement*.[9] In fact, the term *settlement conference* is used about as often as the more general term *pretrial conference.*

After pretrial discovery is completed, the parties and their attorneys will have an idea of their respective chances of winning. One side or the other will usually initiate some settlement discussions. Settlement discussions usually take place well before the pretrial conference. At the pretrial conference, the judge will at least inquire whether settlement has been attempted. If the answer is yes or if that settlement is impossible, many judges do little more. When a jury case is involved, some judges do much more, going over the facts and even giving an idea how the case should be settled. An effective judge can do much to get cases settled that should be settled.

It is sometimes assumed that the first person to blink—to initiate settlement discussions—believes his case is weak. Certainly if the patient's attorney considers the chances of winning slim, that attorney will bring up settlement unless he is holding on, praying that defendants will bring it up. Similarly, if the doctor's position is indefensible or just weak, the insurance carrier may suggest settlement. In such cases, the attorneys want to strike the best possible deal without incurring further costs. Many times settlement is initiated because the attorneys are simply realistic about the legal system, particularly juries. When juries go behind those closed doors, they are the law. They can decide to throw the patient out of court, put the screws to the doctor or, as they often do, effect their own settlement of the case. Jury trials are often referred to as a roll of the dice.

Medical malpractice insurance carriers like to settle cases before they go to trial. They contend that settling is less costly and avoids the risk of an excessive judgment. Most insurance policies allow the carrier to settle cases without the doctor's consent if the carrier considers this appropriate.[10] Others provide that the carrier may not compromise any claim without the doctor's consent.[11] If the doctor's consent is required, however, the policy may limit the carrier's liability to the amount for which the claim could have been settled.[12]

In some instances settlement is appropriate. However, an expedient settlement does nothing to preserve the doctor's reputation except ending the adverse publicity with one last damaging announcement. Patients' attorneys, of course, want to balleyhoo the settlement in hopes of generating other cases. Carriers often suggest that a settlement is neither a reflection on a doctor's competence nor an admission of guilt, but only a business decision. This is not entirely correct, at least insofar as the doctor is concerned. The first reaction of many doctors when sued is to resolve to fight 'em all the way to the Supreme Court! This is not universal, however. Doctors with low policy limits or those threatened with punitive damage claims may panic and demand that the insurance company settle up to the policy limits immediately. Settlement is an emotional issue. Yes, it is a little bit like admitting something was done wrong. And yes, it's grossly unfair that settlement should be considered where there was little or no error in fact. But catecholamine surges and systolic pressure elevations do no good at this point and may do harm. The physician must absolutely be level-headed and hard-headed about this decision. All the variables must be taken into account, not simply the relative chances of winning at trial. Especially important to realize are the individual interests of all the players in the game.

Consider, for example, "nuisance settlements." Insurance companies can lay out $50,000 for defense of a big case, so early settlement looks good to them. They also know that an early settlement is a cheaper settlement—not just in terms of cost but also because the "value" of a case rises with time, discovery, and pretrial progress. The company will tend, therefore, to recommend settlement, even in some cases in which the chances of winning are good. But the doctor's interests are different. He doesn't have to pay the defense costs and the reputational damage of a small settlement may be significant.

The lesson is clear! The doctor should resist the insurance carrier's urging of a small settlement for its "nuisance" value, particularly if the claim is frivolous and has no merit. A doctor should avoid being intimidated into surrendering these cases. The reputational damage and possible adverse effect on staff privileges or applications are personal reasons. In addition, the general effect of many of these settlements is to encourage nuisance suits. The cost to the attorney of preparing initial papers and filing suit is well worth the potential one-third share of 10 or 20 thousand dollars.

Although the insurance carrier may have the right to settle a case without the doctor's consent, the far-sighted company wants that approval. Before a doctor agrees, the attorney the carrier has selected—the doctor's attorney—should give an "informed consent" of all facts and circumstances necessary for a free and intelligent decision regarding settlement. The attorney-client relationship between the doctor and the attorney imposes upon the attorney the same professional obligation that would exist had the doctor personally retained the attorney. If approached by the attorney about settlement, the doctor should take the time to evaluate the case carefully after reviewing all discovery available. Some attorneys want to settle every case out of court and are actually afraid to try a case. They may be "crepe hangers" who paint the worst possible picture both to justify settlement and to justify their own failure to achieve a better result. The doctor who has this kind of attorney must take the attorney's suggestions with a grain of salt. Conversely, some attorneys don't want to settle anything. They are either unwilling to take the time to negotiate an appropriate settlement, preferring to leave it up to the judge or jury, or they believe their incomes and reputations depend on trying cases and not settling them. They may also just like a good fight or want the extra income the trial will produce.

Given all this, can the physician get any useful information from his attorney's assessment? For the most part, the answer is a qualified "yes." The situation is not exactly comparable to that of a patient to whom surgery is recommended. The patient knows that the surgeon only earns a fee if he does the operation. The patient in part relies on the surgeon's ethics, trusting that the surgeon will not recommend unnecessary surgery just to generate a fee. The doubting patient may turn to his family doctor for advice or seek a second surgical opinion. The modern health care consumer also "grills" the surgeon and tries to assess the options him or herself.

All of these techniques are also available to the consumer of legal services. The physician should "grill" the lawyer for both objective data (what little there is of it in law) as well as opinion. What's been the history of similar cases in that court? What track record do both the attorneys have? What subsequent discoveries could help or hurt the case? The second opinion from a personal lawyer can be valuable when settlement is being considered. The attorney himself can be asked if others in his firm working on the case or if the insurance company's representatives assess it differently. What are their recommendations?

For the insurance carrier, the case is a business matter. For the attorney, the case is just another suit. But for the doctor, the case is a significant personal and professional battle that will have ramifications for the rest of the doctor's life. A doctor who reasonably doesn't believe the case should be settled should make certain that the attorney and the carrier know that. The doctor who logically balances all the data and concludes that settlement is the best course should cooperate with the company's efforts. A doctor must give opportunities to settle a great deal of calm, careful thought.

Other pretrial actions

A variety of other pretrial actions may be taken on the eve of trial. They generally serve the purpose of preventing the parties from being surprised at trial by some unanticipated evidence or argument. These are often resolved at the pretrial conference. Some of these actions are:

- ***Supplemental interrogatories.*** Once interrogatories are asked, the party to whom they are directed has an obligation to update them before trial, where the previous response becomes incorrect or invalid.[13] Thus, for example, if the plaintiffs add an expert witness, they must supplement their previous interrogatory response.[14]
- ***Compelling attendance of witnesses.*** If the doctor needs someone or something (e.g., records) at trial to present a defense, the doctor can compel the necessary person or item to be present at the trial. If the person is not a party to the case, the attorney will subpoena him.[15] If the person is a party, the attorney will simply notify him to appear.

- ***Pretrial orders.*** The judge has broad discretion to control conduct of the trial. He may limit the number of attorneys or witnesses, the length of addresses to the jury, etc.[16]

In addition to these activities, time will be devoted to making certain that all of the doctor's evidence, including the testimony of expert witnesses, is prepared and ready for presentation. The doctor's attorney will orchestrate these activities, but the doctor must be actively involved.

Personal preparation

The doctor must resist his natural inclination to let the attorney guide him and prepare him. An aggressive personal program of preparation will pay off.

If at all possible, the doctor should try to witness an actual medical malpractice trial weeks before his case is heard, either in his own community or a comparable one in Pennsylvania. An ideal situation would be an opportunity for the doctor to observe his own attorney or the patient's attorney in action. The doctor might need to travel to another city, but it would be worth the time and expense to have firsthand knowledge of what happens. At a bare minimum, the doctor should insist on being taken to the courthouse and shown where the trial will probably be held. The doctor should become familiar with the physical aspects of the room and have the attorney point out where all the participants in the case will sit as well as explain the protocol of the trial. Any avoidable discomfort adds unnecessarily to the risk that the jury will regard the physician as mendacious or guilt-ridden.

When observing a trial, a doctor quickly will note that every attorney has a personal style of trial technique. Full-time litigators almost all have tremendous egos. Many trial attorneys take pride in improvisation. If the doctor's attorney has this style, the practitioner would be wise to point out that health care professionals by inclination and training are basically rote actors and feel more comfortable with a script outline. The doctor wants to know exactly what questions the attorney will be asking and those the attorney anticipates the patient's attorney will ask. The doctor also wants to know the essentials of the preferred answers. A memorized response that sounds rehearsed is not believable, but is better than a stuttering, stammering, damaging admission.

To help find out what questions may be raised, a doctor can ask his attorney to find out whether any relevant discussions exist in *Bender's Deposition Strategy, Law and Forms,* or *American Jurisprudence Proof of Facts.* These books, discussed in further detail in Chapter 8, contain sample testimony to assist in preparing for and proving the facts important in a case. Because the patient's attorney will likely have reviewed these or similar books, it can be like knowing the questions to be asked in advance.

It perhaps goes without saying that a doctor should be completely familiar with all the facts and records in the case. He should be certain to review all depositions and other information obtained or given in discovery to avoid contradicting previous statements of his own or his witnesses. If the judge and jury aren't convinced that the doctor knows what is going on now, they won't be persuaded that the practitioner knew what was going on back then. No doctor can honestly remember the events as well as some patients claim to recall them, but the records must be gone over repeatedly and understood thoroughly.

The doctor should realize that in the trial, no detail should be overlooked. This includes such things as dress, decorum, and body language. The way questions are answered is particularly important. The doctor should be aware of voice and mannerisms. He or she should avoid talking down to the judge and jury and should try to sound sincere and believable. Let the physician's natural concern for the patient show through. The doctor's attorney will have some practical tips on these points based on his experience. Some attorneys are fearful that too much preparation will make their client sound unnatural and rehearsed. The cure for this is more preparation and more rehearsal!

The doctor might consider having the attorney go over the testimony in a videotaped dress rehearsal. The doctor can then study it and gauge his own reaction to the testimony. The doctor should ask, "Would you let this person treat you?" The doctor's testimony must persuade the judge and jury that the doctor is competent and was competent in this particular case. A doctor who has a problem speaking should consider taking some instructions from a professional. The testimony shouldn't sound rehearsed, but rather competent and professional.[17]

Does this sound like too much? Is it ridiculous? Not if the physician wants to win. Litigants who can afford it for big money or precedent-setting cases are holding full-scale mock trials to practice for the real one. Demographic experts research the likely jury characteristics. Psychologists analyze juror posture and body language. Although medical malpractice insurers don't expend resources to this degree in preparation, there are cases in which they wish they had. The physician can rely on his attorney, luck, and justice—or he can do everything in his power to prepare.

A doctor preparing for or in the midst of a trial should never forget that the successful conduct of a trial basically involves an exercise in public relations. Because the doctor and his attorney will likely be strangers to the judge and jury, the techniques of public relations will greatly influence the outcome of the trial. Even if the judge or jury has an unfavorable opinion of doctors, or if the doctor or defending attorney is not held in particularly high esteem, with proper "PR" the judge and jury can be won over. To put it simply and bluntly, a trial is really a play in which each set of actors tries to put on the performance most pleasing and convincing to the jury. At this stage, the evidence is sometimes not as important as the manner in which it is presented.

In most courtrooms, the jury is favorably impressed if the doctor is neatly and conservatively dressed. It is no accident that the most hardened criminals, who are pictured in the newspapers as discheveled, raunchy, long-haired characters, appear in court neat, clean, barbered, and attired in Brooks Bros. suits. Attorneys are conscious of the fact that clothes and personal appearance make a difference. Little things may affect the jury, such as a beard or a mustache in a community that dislikes unshaven men. Some research, albeit soft, addresses credibility and reactions to appearance. For example, men with beards or brown suits are less trusted.

An exception to this rule might be a trial in a depressed, poor area. If the patient is an appropriately dressed local resident and the doctor brings in a flashy attorney with a sharkskin suit, a 5-karat diamond ring, and an alligator briefcase, the jury might be completely alienated despite the attorney's ability.

The doctor should definitely discuss the appropriate public relations techniques with his attorney, particularly in light of what type of judge and jury the doctor expects to hear the case.

Beginning the trial

Opening court

At long last the day of the trial arrives. The doctor should ask the attorney how long the trial might last and free his schedule accordingly. A trial could take a day, but more likely it will take several. The doctor shouldn't have anything else that must be done because the jury could construe squirming in the chair (eager to get back to patients or whatever) as the body language of guilt.

The doctor and the attorney usually will meet at the attorney's office and go to the courthouse together. The doctor should take his files.

At the courthouse, the doctor should follow the attorney's directions. If the case is delayed, a conference room will often be available in which to wait and privately discuss the case with the attorney. The doctor should be courteous to the patient, the patient's attorney, his attorney, or any family and witnesses that may be present but shouldn't wait or talk with them.

Immediately before the case begins, the attorneys will usually meet with the judge to discuss any final procedural matters. Frequently last-minute settlement discussions occur "on the courthouse steps." Ultimately, the judge will determine that the case is ready to begin and will direct that the parties assemble in the courtroom.

When the case begins, several people will be in the courtroom, including the parties themselves, their attorneys and witnesses, prospective jurors (if a jury trial), and court personnel. The court personnel include a court clerk to maintain the court's records and evidence presented, a court bailiff to maintain order, and a court reporter to keep a transcript of the hearing or monitor the tape-recording. The clerk will announce the judge's arrival and, out of respect for the court, will direct that those assembled stand while the judge enters. The judge will then ask everyone to be seated. The doctor should hold his head up high with self-confidence, but not appear arrogant. Posture should be erect and interested. The doctor shouldn't appear aloof. The jury may read a hostile reaction formation or coping mechanism of minimalizing as casualness. Such a reaction may suggest a lack of interest. This runs the risk that the jury will feel that they shouldn't care about what happens to the doctor.

The judge will first take up some housekeeping tasks. These include such things as stating what the case is and who the parties are. The judge will then ask if the parties are present, represented by counsel, and prepared to proceed. The doctor's attorneys will make statements "for the record." The record means what is being taken down by the court reporter or taped. Things that appear quite obvious to those present would not be so obvious to another court that might be asked to review the record later. "Preservation of the record" is an important function of lawyers and looks ahead to possible appeals.

Picking the jury

Cases are heard either by a judge or by a judge with a jury. Either party has the right to have a jury trial and would have made this demand early in the case if desired. Patients generally request juries because juries are more likely to ignore legal technicalities and allow their emotions to justify finding for patients and awarding large judgments. Depending on the disposition of the jury, however, this can backfire, and the jurors can see through a patient simply seeking something for nothing. A jury might also be prejudiced against an obnoxious person, something the judge tries to ignore in the interest of fairness. If a case is to be tried before a jury, the first task in the trial will be to select the members of the jury.

Physicians are not automatically exempt from serving on juries.[18] However, even if the local court excuses physicians, a doctor who is asked to serve on a jury should forego the exemption and be willing to serve. It is an excellent experience and a chance to learn from the inside just how a jury works. Also, a basic problem with the jury system in this country is that too many good people avoid serving.

In each of Pennsylvania's judicial districts except the First, a jury selection commission of three members is appointed.[19] Prospective jurors are randomly selected from the list of registered voters. The list may be supplemented by appropriate additional sources, such as the telephone directory or tax rolls.[20] The master list is updated annually and must be available for public inspection. Those randomly selected may thereafter be asked to complete information forms so that a determination can be made whether they are qualified.[21] The names of those qualified are placed on a wheel. Upon receipt of a court order, the commission publicly selects at random the number of names required.[22] These prospective jurors are then required to come to court and may be called as jurors. For that reason the prospective jurors are sometimes referred to as "veniremen" because *"venire"* in Latin means "to come."[23] The group thus called makes up the array from which the actual jury selection will be made.

From the prospective jurors summoned, the court and attorneys will "impanel" the jury. This process involves seating, examining, challenging, passing, and accepting jurors for the case. The attorney can challenge the entire array, but this right is rarely utilized in medical malpractice cases.[24]

The prospective jurors then undergo what is known as *voir dire*. The term literally means "to speak the truth" and denotes the preliminary examination of prospective jurors to assess their competency, interest, or any matter affecting their qualification as jurors.[25]

Judges vary on how they handle the *voir dire* examination. In general, however, the judge will ask some questions and then ask questions that the attorneys have asked be posed.[26] Some judges will also allow the attorneys to ask questions directly.

The selection of the jury is one of the most important tasks in the trial of any jury case. It is so important that in recent years the legal process has given rise to individuals who do nothing but assist in the selection of jurors. One method involves defining the ideal juror for a particular case and then trying to assure the selection of 12 "ideal jurors" through the use of such clues as psychological considerations and body language.[27]

Because doctors by intuition and training are good judges of human behavior, a doctor can be of considerable help to his attorney in the selection of jurors. For example, a doctor may recognize a prospective juror as a satisfied patient or relative of one. Conversely, a doctor might also recognize a disgruntled patient, a deadbeat, or someone who has caused trouble for other doctors. Because the doctor is being sued for medical malpractice, he should be especially cautious if a prospective juror has an obvious physical defect. As time permits, prospective jurors should be checked out as much as possible in advance.

A prospective juror can be challenged. The three types of challenges are:

- ***Challenge for cause.*** This usually involves a juror who has a relationship with a party, attorney, or witness in the case, acknowledged bias, or preconceived notion about the case.[28] There is no limit to the number of people who can be challenged for cause. It is within the discretion of the judge whether to grant the challenge or not. These challenges are only rarely available, but attorneys still try to use them on people they don't want to be jurors for other reasons.
- ***Peremptory challenge.*** Each side is entitled to four peremptory challenges. These are highly valued and are not used if a prospective juror can be challenged for cause. A peremptory challenge is an objection to a juror without showing any cause or reason. Thus, to a limited extent the doctor has an absolute right to exclude some prospective jurors. An attorney will normally look over the entire group of pro-

spective jurors to avoid wasting peremptory challenges. There may be others the patient would especially like on the jury whom the doctor absolutely would want to keep off.

After the jury is selected, it is sworn to try the issues in the case. The oath may be administered by the judge or the clerk of the court. Thereafter the judge will often advise the jurors of the importance of their function and thank them for serving, even though they are compelled to do so.

Opening statements

As soon as the jury is empaneled, the patient's attorney will make an opening statement. The doctor's attorney will follow. Most authorities regard the opening statement as the most critical part of the lawyer's job at trial.[29]

Opening statements constitute the typical scene shown in television courtrooms (other than perhaps "The People's Court"). The judge is presiding, the doctor and his attorney are at one table, and the accuser and his attorney are at another table. The jury is in the jury box.

The opening statement provides an opportunity for each attorney to explain his side of the case to the jury. The patient's attorney will attempt to convince the jury at the onset that the doctor owed a *duty* to the patient and that the doctor *breached this duty* by not treating the client *in a manner accepted and standard to the community,* that the doctor *injured* the patient, and that the doctor was the *proximate cause* of the injuries. Therefore, it will be argued, the patient is entitled to a lot of money. The plaintiff's opening statement is, in a sense, a promise to prove the assertions made. The attorney will try and so impress the jury that their minds close to the doctor's side of the case.

The doctor's attorney will attempt to convince the jury that the doctor was not negligent. In doing so, the attorney may argue that the doctor had no professional duty to the patient, that due care was exercised, that the patient was not injured, that any injury was not caused by the doctor, or that the patient simply is trying to "get rich quick." Although the doctor's attorney may argue all these points, he probably will focus on the best defense and emphasize it. This is what insurance company trial attorneys call "going for the poison." Usually the doctor's attorney will argue that the patient can't prove at least one element and that the jury thus has a duty to render a judgment for the doctor regardless of sympathy. The defense lawyer tries to plant doubt about the plaintiff's assertion and reopen the jury's mind. Although the doctor may want his attorney to attack the patient, rarely is this wise. The patient will be presented as sympathetically as possible. A jury may overlook lack of negligence or cause if angered by the attack on the patient.

Presenting the evidence

Generally

After the opening statements, the patient's attorney will begin to present the patient's evidence. At this juncture, the evidence presented by the patient's attorney is called the patient's case-in-chief. In the American judicial system, evidence is presented by question and answer. Only infrequently does the judge ask questions.

The testimony of the patient or the patient's witnesses should not come as any surprise. The doctor knows that the patient or anyone else having direct knowledge of the facts of the case will testify along with the patient's expert witnesses. The doctor has heard what they will say in discovery so the doctor shouldn't try to act surprised; it rarely appears genuine. The patient's attorney presents evidence by "examining" the witnesses and requesting that documentary evidence be presented. The doctor shouldn't forget that he may be called as an adverse or hostile witness.

Throughout the patient's case the doctor's attorney may make technical objections to the testimony and also has the right to cross-examine the witnesses. The doctor's attorney will want to discredit the case presented and set up the patient's witnesses for the evidence to be presented on the doctor's behalf. Some disputes are resolved immediately. For example, an objection may be "sustained," which means that the judge agrees with it, or it may be "overruled," which means that the judge rejects it. Arguments between counsel may occur at the bench or "sidebar" out of the jury's hearing. For other disputes, the jurors will be taken from the courtroom until the disputes are resolved. Objections are not made because the witness is lying or mistaken. Cross-examination, referred to as "that great crucible of truth," and defense evidence address these problems.

The little skirmishes that take place in the courtroom may seem important, but many are not. Sometimes they are merely tactics intended to break a spell cast on enthralled jurors. The doctor may want his attorney to object to practically everything said. In reality, it's the overall picture or impression that will win or lose the case. Jurors and even many judges have difficulty following technical testimony. Judgments often are made on a more personal level, such as a belief that the doctor did or did not do everything possible under the circumstances of the case.

At the end of the patient's case, the doctor's attorney normally will ask for a directed verdict. This is something like a summary judgment, but it is not granted until after the patient has had the opportunity to "give it his best shot." Now that the judge has heard the patient's actual case (not just what the patient said it would be), the judge can enter a judgment in favor of the doctor. This will be done only if the plaintiff has not offered proof of all the required elements of the case. For example, the patient's attorney may not have presented needed expert testimony or proof that the doctor caused the injury complained of. If a jury is involved, the judge may have some questions about the case but will prefer to let the jury render a decision and, if appropriate, only then override the jury's verdict. The judge is less likely to be overturned on appeal if he is able to simply affirm a jury finding.

After the patient's case has been presented, it's the doctor's turn to present evidence. The method will be similar to the presentation of the patient's evidence.

As the doctor's evidence is presented, he should keep in mind that if a jury is hearing the case, it should be the prime audience to whom the performance is directed. And, since the jury is composed of laymen, the more interesting and understandable a doctor can make the testimony, the better. For example, while the spoken word is important in selling a point of view, persuasion is often materially assisted with visual aids, such as photographs, drawings, and items such as anatomical models or medical or surgical equipment. The jurors always feel more involved if the doctor's attorney can put something in their hands for close inspection.

Recreating events in the courtroom is also informative and impresses the jury. The doctor's attorney should be encouraged to use these modes and to provide them for the doctor. The practitioner should explain to the attorney how dull a medical presentation is if the speaker does not have slides and an electric pointer. People learn and understand better when all five senses are stimulated at the same time. "Show-and-tell" testimony works well.[30] A doctor can be certain that the patient's attorney will use "Day in the Life" videotapes or other demonstrative evidence when it will bolster the patient's case—a tie should go to the defense.

After the doctor's evidence is presented, the patient's attorney will have another opportunity to present evidence. This evidence is designed to rebut the doctor's evidence. New evidence is not permitted, but the court has wide discretion to allow reopening.[31] In cases heard by judges, the parties can go back and forth several times. Judges are not as liberal in jury trials. Regardless of how many times the parties go back and forth, the patient's attorney is entitled to go last because the patient has the burden to prove his case.

Testimony regarding the standard of care

As evidence is presented, a focal point will be the standard of care in the case. Doctors must clearly understand what that term means.

Earlier we stated that *standard of care* is a legal term referring to that level of care required of a person to avoid tort liability when injury results to another person. In other words, it is that level of care above which a person can say, "Even though I might have injured you by my conduct, I am not at legal fault."[32]

The problem with the term *standard of care* in a medical malpractice action is that a witness is often called on to testify to "the standard of care," since testimony in these terms is essential to establish what care was required. And despite the term being a legal term of art that should ideally not be posed in those words to a witness, one hears over and over in the courtroom questions such as "doctor, what did the standard of care require doctor X to do under the circumstances?" Or, "doctor, didn't the standard of care require doctor X to obtain a lung scan at 8 o'clock that night?"

When doctors who are not experienced expert witnesses are posed such a question, they usually are not really familiar with the phrase "standard of care" and begin to answer the question by whatever benchmark they find most comfortable. They might analyze the question by asking themselves what they would do under the circumstances. Or they may answer by determining what would be the ideal approach, or an approach that would have avoided the outcome complained of. However, neither of these truly represents the standard of care. The standard of care is what the average reasonable doctor would do under the circumstances. It is not the ideal. It is not what the greatest, most renowned doctor would do. Nor is it simply the average or lowest common denominator. It is what the ordinary reasonable doctor would do.

Keeping in mind the general rule that the standard of care is what the ordinary doctor would do under the circumstances customarily, the doctor should observe a few guidelines when testifying about the standard of care, either in his own case or in another practitioner's case.

First, doctors must remember that in many situations, no defined method of practice exists. Doctors testifying as witnesses should not hesitate to state in such circumstances that no defined practice, method, or standard exists and that care becomes a matter of exercising judgment. That judgment, even if erroneous, does not necessarily constitute malpractice. Therefore, in answer to a question posed about the standard of care in such circumstances, the doctor would answer, in substance, that the standard of care didn't "require" the particular action the plaintiff is saying should have been done. Care was a matter of judgment.

Second, doctors should not fall into the trap of being asked what they would do in a given situation and then be led into suggesting that their practice represents the standard of care. This may misleadingly suggest that only one type of practice represents the standard of care when a variety of practice may well be acceptable. Remember Pennsylvania's strong adherence to the two schools of thought doctrine. A doctor's own practice may, of course, be within the standard of care or within the range of customary practice, but it may not necessarily be the only acceptable practice.

Third, doctors should constantly keep in mind the common *actual* practices of practicing physicians, not the ideal. The former represents the standard required. The standard is not the optimum. This is one reason why plaintiffs have better luck with academicians as experts—it is not just their credentials the plaintiff wants but also their demanding insistence on the highest possible standards for their residents, their students, and even themselves. This is admirable, but wrongly applied in a tort lawsuit. It is not what the law requires.

Finally, the standard of care is not determined by simply analyzing the case in retrospect and determining what would have avoided the outcome. A poor outcome does not equal malpractice. The standard of care takes into account what doctors would do in the circumstances as they existed at the time, before the outcome was known.

Being a witness

Whatever the preparation for being a witness, the doctor will be nervous. At this stage, about to take the stand, a few final considerations should be kept in mind.

At some point in the trial, the doctor's attorney will call on the doctor to testify. When that attorney asks the doctor questions, this is known as direct examination. This is the doctor's opportunity to give his side of the story. Thus the doctor should:

- Remember when testifying that the spotlight is on him and he should make it count. Often, regardless of the allegations made, judges and juries want to believe the doctor. The doctor wants to leave them with the impression not only that the patient was treated in an acceptable manner, within the standard of care, but also that the doctor did the best that could be expected of any doctor under the circumstances. The jury must be allowed to see the physician as a caring, concerned, serious professional.
- Realize that his attorney is on his side. Don't treat these questions as hostile. The doctor should answer the questions posed in a solid and credible manner.
- Remember that his own attorney may not ask what are known as leading questions. Leading questions suggest the answer. Through preparation, however, the doctor should know virtually all the questions to be asked by his attorney and the answers to be given.
- Be very attentive to the questions asked. If the doctor doesn't hear a question or was confused by it, he should ask that it be repeated. The attorney will get the message and may withdraw the question or ask it in a different way.
- Witnesses often have dry throats from nerves or climate control. It is okay to ask for water. This is better than sounding nervous.
- Refrain from going beyond the question asked when answering. Even though the doctor knows what points are to be made in the defense, the attorney should be allowed to bring out the facts in his own way and in his own time. He should be allowed to stage manage this performance.
- Avoid talking down to the judge or jury. Personality means a great deal in a trial.
- Keep in mind the general theme of the defense. A jury should end up with the same general impression of the case as the doctor proposes. Keep it simple and straightforward. The doctor shouldn't get

bogged down on minor points that may mean very little to the jury.

- Keep calm. While the doctor's attorney is asking questions, the patient's attorney may make various objections. The doctor shouldn't let these be upsetting or, more importantly, appear to be upset. The doctor should let his attorney handle them.

When the doctor's attorney finishes questioning him, the patient's attorney will have the opportunity to ask questions. This is known as cross-examination. The patient's attorney can also call the doctor to testify as an adverse party.[33] This would be done while the patient's case is being presented and should be handled the same as cross-examination. The doctor should:

- Listen carefully to the questions asked.
- Most importantly, remember that the patient's attorney, unlike the doctor's attorney, can ask leading questions. As the name implies, these questions can lead the doctor to the answers the patient's attorney wants. The patient's attorney wants the doctor to admit being in the wrong or that something should have been done other than what was done. The doctor should be very, very cautious and think before answering a question.
- Respectfully but firmly avoid supporting the patient's position even though that's what the attorney wants. The physician's habitual predisposition to be helpful must be thwarted. The doctor's answers should support the general defense being raised in the case.
- Avoid appearing hostile or unfriendly to the patient's attorney or the patient. Depending on how the patient's attorney acts and the doctor responds, jurors may be sympathetic to the doctor (because of very aggressive cross-examination) or believe the doctor is dodging questions (because of attitude or unwillingness to answer questions).
- Let the attorney handle any objections. The doctor's attorney may make objections while the doctor is being questioned. When the attorney makes an objection, he must handle the discussion until the judge decides the objection. The doctor shouldn't interrupt his attorney and should try hard not to answer before his attorney has a chance to object.
- The physician witness, while not making objections, should assert himself where necessary. The most common situation where this arises is when the plaintiff's attorney buffaloes the physician into giving yes or no answers. "Just answer the question, doctor." The attorney will then start asking unanswerable questions along the line of "Have you stopped beating your wife?" It is perfectly all right for the physician to say "I can't answer that question yes or no;" or "It would be misleading to answer without explanation."

Final arguments

After all evidence has been heard and all witnesses called, each side presents a final argument. This is basically an opportunity for the attorneys to summarize what each contends the evidence has shown and to persuade the judge or jury that his client should prevail.

The patient's attorney speaks first. As at the beginning of the case, the patient's attorney will attempt to convince the jury that the evidence showed that the doctor owed a *duty* to the patient and *breached this duty* by not treating the patient*in a manner that is accepted and is standard in the community,* that the doctor *injured* the patient and was the *proximate cause* of the injuries. Although the evidence will be the heart of the closing argument, other subjects will be addressed. The credibility of the witnesses will be stressed. The amount of money that should be awarded and the basis for that calculation will be a subject of prolonged discussion.[34] The attorney will then urge the jury to find the doctor guilty of malpractice and suggest that they force the doctor to pay a huge amount of money.

The doctor's attorney then will attempt to refute these accusations and persuade the jury that the doctor is not guilty of malpractice. The attorney's final argument or closing statement will usually focus on one or two shortcomings of the patient's evidence. If the patient made a favorable impression, the doctor's attorney may admit that patient is a nice person, perhaps even an injured nice person, but that recovery should be denied because an essential legal element is lacking. If the patient has been exposed as a liar or gross exaggerator, the doctor's attorney may address the entire argument to the jury's duty not to reward the deceit that has monopolized the court's time and taken the jurors from their own families and jobs. Finally, if the doctor made a good impression on the jury, his attorney will use this fact just as the patient's attorney tried to engender sympathy for a poor, injured, innocent client. The doctor's attorney will tell the jury that in a few hours they will return to their homes and families and forget all about the case, but that for the doctor, the case will affect the rest of his life; that after enormous effort, expense, and tireless devotion to the community, this is how the doctor is repaid. This admittedly theatrical approach is not within the abilities of all lawyers. If it can be carried off successfully, it is often just what the doctor ordered, so to speak, because many, many jurors hold the average doctor in high esteem. The attorney will end by pointing out that he will not have another chance to argue the case.

Because the patient has the burden of proof, his attorney will again have the last say, a last-ditch effort to undo the closing statement of the doctor's attorney. Some lawyers save their best for the final pitch. Only rarely will the attorney use the dramatic and risky tactic of disdainfully stating only that nothing further need be said and sitting down.

The whistle blows and the players leave the field. Have the impression it's like a big game? Good observation—and the game isn't over yet.

Jury instructions

If the case has been heard by a jury, the judge will instruct the jury as to the law or rules to be applied in the case. While a jury decides on the facts of the case, the judge determines the law or rules by which those facts are to be judged. The judge instructs the jury through formal jury instructions read after final arguments are made.

Before the trial reaches this stage, the judge will have directed the attorneys to prepare suggested instructions. These instructions are to state the law correctly and be phrased so that every juror can understand them. The judge will then determine which instructions to present to the jury.[35] Many judges write their own instructions, attempting to avoid bias.

Most jury instructions are "patterned," that is, they are variations on a form used previously. Some jurisdictions have officially published pattern instructions.[36] Depending on the state, these are models that courts must or may use if appropriate. If suitable instructions are not available, they must be custom drafted. The language may be taken from previous court opinions, if translated into language understandable to a lay juror. It is valuable for the doctor in reviewing a case to know just what the jury will hear before it makes its decisions. Therefore the doctor should ask his attorney for a copy of the instructions that will likely be used.

The instructions are critically important. First, the judge pronounces them. The jury has been sharply attuned to any indication of the judge's attitude and will continue to be. Second, the instructions are the last thing the jury will hear before beginning deliberations.

The instructions will begin with some general cautionary comments. Jurors are told, for example, that neither sympathy nor prejudice should influence them and that they are to consider only the testimony of the witnesses and the exhibits offered and received.[37] Various other instructions are given, including those pertaining to evaluating the evidence, determining negligence, and establishing damages.

Of particular interest to doctors are those instructions specifically pertaining to malpractice. A review of examples of these will give the doctor some idea of how the law is presented to the jury. These instructions would, as appropriate, be given along with other instructions applicable to the case.

Throughout this book, reference has been made to the duty of a doctor.[38] A jury instruction that might be given in a malpractice case describes that duty as follows:

> A physician who is not a specialist is required to possess and employ in the treatment of a patient the skill and knowledge usually possessed by physicians in the same or a similar locality. He must give due regard to any advances in the profession at the time of the treatment. He is also required to exercise the care and judgment of a reasonable physician in like circumstances.[39]

In an old case, the Pennsylvania Supreme Court reversed a lower court trial judge who instructed the jury that, in treating a broken leg, the physician had to "... make it straight and of equal length with the other when healed, and if he did not, he was accountable in damages, just as a stone-mason or bricklayer would be in building a wall of poor materials, and the wall fell down ..."[40]

Where the defense has presented testimony that the physician chose one of multiple acceptable methods of treatment, the jury may be instructed:

> A physician does not have to employ any particular mode of treatment. When the medical profession recognizes more than one method as proper, it is not negligence to choose any of these recognized methods.[41]

Plaintiffs will ask for instructions on damages that segregate the different elements of damages:

> You are instructed that if your verdict is in favor of the plaintiff, then it is your duty to award the plaintiff such sum as will fairly and reasonably compensate him for all the damage suffered by him which proximately resulted from the negligence of the defendant. You are further instructed that absolute certainty of prospective continuation of any injury need not necessarily be established. It is sufficient if the probability of that damage continuing is reasonably certain, in which event allowance should be made therefor.
>
> In fixing the amount of the award to the plaintiff, you will consider the elements of damage I will now mention:
>
> (a) The reasonable value, not exceeding the cost to the plaintiff, of the examinations, tests, attention, and care by physicians and surgeons, reasonably required and actually given in the treatment of the plaintiff, and the reasonable value of any further treatment that you find from the evidence is reasonably certain to be required.
>
> (b) The reasonable value, not exceeding the cost to the plaintiff, of hospital accommodations and care, medication, and orthopedic appliances, reasonably required and actually given or used in the treatment of the plaintiff;
>
> (c) If you find that there was some physical injury, then such sum as will reasonably compensate him for the pain, discomfort, and mental anguish that under the evidence was shown to have been suffered by him as a proximate result of the injuries in question and for such pain, discomfort, and mental anguish that you may find under the evidence he is reasonably certain to suffer in the future from the same cause;
>
> (d) The reasonable value of time lost by the plaintiff since his injuries when he has been unable to pursue his usual occupation. In determining this amount, you should consider the evidence of

the plaintiff's earning capacity, his earnings, and the manner in which he ordinarily occupied his time before the injury and find what he was reasonably certain to have earned in the time lost, had he not been disabled;

(e) Such sum as will reasonably compensate him for any loss or diminution of earning power occasioned by the injuries in question, from which you find under the evidence that he has suffered and is reasonably certain to suffer in the future. In this connection, you are instructed that earning power is related to capacity to do work and earn money, and it may be impaired even though plaintiff's earnings have not yet been reduced. In fixing this amount you may consider such factors as the plaintiff's health, physical ability, and earning power before the accident; the nature and extent of his injuries, whether or not they are reasonably certain to be permanent, or if not permanent, the extent of their duration. You may also consider the plaintiff's age, life expectancy, occupation, talents, skill, experience, training and industry, all to the end of determining the effect of his injuries upon his earning capacity to date and in the future;

(f) Such sum as will reasonably compensate him for the extent to which the injuries received by him have impaired and deprived him of, and which you will find from the evidence will in the future impair and deprive him of, the ability to engage in and enjoy the nonoccupational activities and pleasures in which he formerly engaged.[42]

For a juror to listen to all that and not feel that he is being instructed to award something is not possible. So the defendant may, if he is unsuccessful in getting the judge to withhold or rewrite that instruction, ask the court to ameliorate the effects with:

> The fact that I have instructed you on the issue of damages must not be considered by you as any indication of plaintiff's right to recover damages, or as any indication of the court's view on the issue of liability or as to which party is entitled to your verdict. I have instructed you on the issue of damages to guide you in the event that you find from the evidence that plaintiff is entitled to recover damages, since it is my duty to instruct you fully on all the law in the case. However, if you should determine from the evidence that plaintiff is not entitled to recover damages, then you should entirely disregard all instructions I have given you on how to determine damages.[43]

Judges have a great deal of discretion in what they will and will not say to a jury. One judge, instructing on pain and suffering damages, said to the jury, "see what you think the pain and suffering . . . are worth."[44] The judge was upheld on appeal!

Judges also may review the evidence and summarize it for the jury. It is in doing so that the judge must be most careful to avoid communicating his own opinion to the jury. Consider the difference between:

> Dr. Smith, the plaintiff's witness from New York, said that the defendant was wrong and caused the alleged injuries. Professor Jones, the chief of the Department at University Hospital testified that the defendant acted within the standard of care.

and:

> Dr. Smith testified that the defendant's treatment of the plaintiff fell below the standard of care and was the cause of plaintiff's injuries. Dr. Jones said the defendant was not negligent.

The parties may object later, but the instruction won't be overturned or a new trial granted unless there was an "abuse" of the judge's discretion.

The court will also give summary instructions:

> If you find from all the evidence that the plaintiff has met the burden of proof on each of the issues concerning which the burden of proof rested upon him (and that the defendant has failed to meet the burden of proof on any of the affirmative defenses) then you should return a verdict in favor of the plaintiff.
>
> If, on the other hand, you find that the plaintiff has failed to meet the burden of proof on any of the issues concerning which the burden of proof rested upon him (or that the defendant has met the burden of proof on any of the affirmative defenses) then you should return a verdict in favor of the defendant.[45]

It should be apparent that the case can be won or lost on the instructions. The physician must insist that his attorney try hard for every possible advantage in the wording and choice of instructions. This is not a time to let down and coast. "It ain't over 'til it's over."[46]

It should be apparent that once enough words are thrown at the most conscientious of jurors, they all begin to blur. Thus anything the jurors can take into deliberations with them will stand out. Last impressions, the figures on a blackboard used in closing arguments, the way the judge emphasized a certain word at one point, all may have an inappropriately significant impact on the jury's decision, if their minds are not already made up. This is why jurors are usually not allowed to take notes and then carry them into the jury room.

Example

Mrs. Reichman went to see Dr. Wallach about a pelvic mass. He recommended surgery, but she hesitated. A month later, the mass had grown, and Dr. Wallach again recommended a total hysterectomy. She agreed to the operation. She bled post-operatively and had to be re-explored. After the two surgeries, Mrs. Reichman developed abdominal pain, nausea, vomiting, anorexia, weight loss, and abnormal liver enzymes. She was hospitalized four times in the next 7 months, without a diagnosis. About a year later, ulcerative colitis was discovered. The jury awarded her $429,960.

Dr. Wallach appealed on the basis of a blackboard. The jury had asked for the blackboard on which the plaintiff's lawyer had calculated damages. It was rolled into the jury room. Dr. Wallach claimed this was prejudicial error. The superior court agreed that the better practice is not to consider such notes as evidence; but it upheld the verdict. In part the court made this decision because it didn't have the blackboard to review and "it is the complaining party that has the duty to preserve the record . . ."[47]

After the jury is instructed on the law and rules to be applied, the judge directs that the bailiff take the jurors to the jury room, where they will deliberate in private until they reach a decision. It is a good idea for the doctor and the doctor's attorney to try to make eye contact with all jurors as they exit for deliberations. This is the doctor's only opportunity before learning the verdict to assess the impact of the evidence and closing arguments on the jury.[48] If the jurors intentionally avoid any eye contact, this may signal a patient's verdict. The importance of assessing eye contact is underscored because if settlement is discussed during jury deliberations, all data is potentially useful.

The verdict

Because a jury's deliberations are held in secret, there is little to dictate just how jurors proceed in reaching a decsision in a case. However, the most common practice is for jurors to select one from their number to serve as a foreman to preside over the jury's deliberations. Under the foreman's directions, the jurors may take an initial vote to see if there is initial agreement.

In reaching a decision, the jurors will weigh the evidence. The jury must conclude that the patient did or did not prove his side of the case by what is known as a "preponderance of the evidence." This means that the jurors must be persuaded that the evidence presented by the plaintiff balanced the scales at least slightly in favor of his side. It's much like requiring a side to win "51 to 49." It is not necessary, as it is in criminal cases, to prove a case "beyond a reasonable doubt."

The decision reached is called a verdict. Once it is reached, the judge is informed and the parties called. The parties assemble again, and the verdict is then announced, usually by the foreman of the jury.[49]

In Pennsylvania, the jury's verdict need not be unanimous. It is clear in both the Constitution and statute that 5/6 of a jury may agree and render a verdict.[50] Furthermore, the parties may agree on a specific number, even a bare majority.[51]

If any doubt exists that it is the decision of all jurors, each may be polled and asked whether he joins in the verdict.[52] A jury that is unable to reach a five-sixth's decision is called a "hung jury." In the case of a hung jury, a new trial is ordered. A hung jury is rare in civil cases because if nothing else, the jurors haggle among themselves until they reach a "settlement figure" for the litigants.

Damage awards in medical malpractice cases with multi-defendants who are not joint tortfeasors must be apportioned. Basically, separate verdicts are rendered.[53]

After the verdict is returned, the court will enter a judgment. The judgment is the formal conclusion of the trial.

Post-trial activities

Post-trial motions

After the trial, a party can file a post-trial motion within 10 days after the jury's verdict.[54] The purpose of this motion is to ask the judge to throw out the jury's decision because of some technicality or because it is clearly erroneous. A similar motion can be filed in cases in which the judge hears the case without a jury.[55] The judge will consider the motion and enter an appropriate order, which could even include ordering a new trial.

Reduction of damages

Within 10 days after a judgment for malpractice is rendered, a motion may be filed with the court to reduce or increase the verdict.[56] The jury's verdict has to be clearly beyond what's justified by the evidence before a reduction will be granted. The amount must be so excessive as to "shock the conscience."[57] The trial judge can also use his power to order a new trial to force one side or the other to accept an altered verdict, in effect a post-trial settlement.

Although physicians may suffer a "shocked conscience" and other maladies at the amounts awarded in malpractice cases, reduction in damages is uncommonly granted. Fortunately, an increase in damages is even more rare.

Prejudgment interest (or delay damages)

In an effort to move cases along and reduce court congestion, Pennsylvania requires that interest be added onto awards.[58] Of the civil cases filed, only 38% go to trial and only 25% to verdict.[59] Of those settled before trial, many are concluded after trial is scheduled or even on the courthouse steps. Part of the reason is the lack of incentives for early settlement and even the practical fact of incentives for delay by defendants. A big payout of the same amount in a few years allows the insurance company to use the money in the interim and generate interest for themselves. This is a major feature of the insurance business.[60]

The court adds 10% per annum, not compounded, to the verdict for compensatory damages.[61] It is computed from the time the plaintiff filed the initial complaint or 1 year after the negligence occurred, whichever is later.[62] The calculation is to the date of the verdict. There is no indication that the amount may be increased or recalculated after a year or two of appeals. This is a strong inducer of early settlement offers. This rule was passed in 1978 when interest rates were higher. Then, 10% meant the defendant broke even or came out a little ahead by keeping the money until after trial. In 1987, 10% meant the defendant lost by delay. In other states, amounts provided for damages for delay range from 6% to 9%.[63]

An offer of settlement can cut off the prejudgment interest. The rule provides that if the defendant makes a written offer and the plaintiff fails eventually to win at least 125% of that offer, no delay damages are awarded from the date of that offer.[64] The physician's attorney will point this out when urging submission of a settlement offer as early in the case as possible.

The rule should have made some provision for fees and costs, but it does not. As tort reform is considered in Pennsylvania, the following point seems minor, but it can have great impact in medical malpractice cases. If a physician has made an offer of settlement and the patient then loses or wins only 75% or less of that offer, then the physician ought to be entitled to recover attorney fees and costs or have them deducted from the award, up to 25% of the offer of settlement. In multidefendant litigation such a rule would have significant impact. If the other health providers are found negligent and the physician defendant found non-negligent or responsible for only a small percentage of the judgment, he should be able to take advantage of such a rule.

The stakes in an unjustified malpractice suit are so one-sided that they need to be balanced a bit. In some cases, the physician bets his whole pot, but the patient only "antes." Reform is needed because of the ease with which patients can bring and pursue frivolous claims, just on the miniscule chance that they can scare out a settlement or even win a jury's sympathy. This reform can be accomplished without blocking patients' rights to sue for just cause.

Appeal

In lieu of or in addition to a post-trial motion, the judgment can be appealed. However, the trial court's post-verdict review can be requested for more and different reasons than appellate reviews.[65] There is a right to appeal the case to the Superior court.[66] After a decision is rendered by the appellate court, the Pennsylvania Supreme Court may or may not be willing to consider the case. The right to an appeal is an important policy in the Commonwealth, more strongly and dearly held than in some other states.[67]

If the doctor wins the case, the patient may threaten or even file an appeal. This could well be a ploy to get some settlement to recoup expenses and/or stave off a suit for malicious prosecution. After what the doctor has gone through, he shouldn't give the patient a cent, even if part of the claim was just. Instead, the doctor should almost always take a chance on the patient's appeal because once a judge or especially a jury rules against the patient, the decision is statistically unlikely to be reversed on appeal.

If the patient wins the case, the doctor will consider with his attorney whether to appeal. A not inconsequential number of judgments against doctors are reversed on appeal. If a sound technical basis for the appeal exists, it should be filed. In some cases, the doctor might consider an appeal as a method to negotiate downward the damages awarded.

Payment of damages

Once the judgment is finalized, the successful plaintiff can begin to collect. In most cases, the insurance company will make out a check. But where the policy limits are exceeded, the company is insolvent, or the physician "went bare," the plaintiff's lawyer has to try to get the award from the physician himself. Declaring bankruptcy won't help! The court's judgment is a debt that survives bankruptcy proceedings. The lawyer can collect in the same way a doctor might collect on a judgment that a patient owed him money. Assets can be attached and sold. Wages or other money owed the defendant can be garnished or made to be paid over to the plaintiff. If the insurance company is only being recalcitrant, the plaintiff's lawyer can garnish the debt of indemnity the company owes its insured doctor.

Suits for malicious prosecution

Because of the emotional and professional scars that result from virtually any medical malpractice case, a doctor who is sued will usually consider bringing suit against the patient or the patient's attorney.[68] To protect people from unjustifiable litigation, the law allows actions for malicious prosecution. They should be at least thought about in every medical malpractice case. Unfortunately, in Pennsylvania they have very little chance of success. The physician usually wants to "get at" the patient's lawyer, who might have some assets, but countersuit is even less likely to succeed against the attorney, rather than the patient.[69]

As a threshold for even considering a claim for malicious prosecution, the physician must first win the case brought by the patient.[70] Thus even considering a possible claim for malicious prosecution is premature until after the suit against the doctor is concluded.

In Pennsylvania, two related wrongs can be the basis of such a suit. Abuse of process is the misuse of legal process for unlawful purposes.[71] This would be the proper action to file if the plaintiff's lawyer, during the malpractice case, had filed a complaint regarding competency of the defendant doctor with the state board, in an effort to force settlement. Malicious prosecution addresses the wrongful initiation of a suit.[72] Doctors most often consider these countersuits.

The required elements of a suit for malicious prosecution are successful conclusion of the first suit, lack of a reasonable basis for filing the first claim, and malice. These might be arguably present in some malpractice actions. What kills a physician's hope of countersuit in Pennsylvania is the requirement that, to prevail, the physician must show that he was either arrested or deprived of property.[73] The reader who has been paying attention will say, "But having to leave my practice and pay lawyers deprived me of property." Unfortunately, that's not enough—a seizure of property must occur. The loss must exceed the costs associated with any legal proceeding.[74]

Before a doctor devotes the time and energy needed to pursue a malicious prosecution case, much less the money, he should be certain the case is worth pursuing. Few are. A doctor who files a malicious prosecution case faces an uphill battle. The possibility should be considered, and reform from the legislature or courts hoped for, but to date in Pennsylvania, no physician has won such a case.

When the doctor talks with his attorney about a malicious prosecution case or claim for attorney's fees, the attorney will probably suggest the doctor forget it. "Be happy you didn't get stuck by some fluke and get back to medicine," the attorney will say. As much as the doctor may not like it, that's usually good advice. It also avoids yet another possible suit against the physician—one for malicious prosecution brought by the patient who lost the first case, but who wins the second case, the malicious prosecution suit brought by the physician.

Endnotes

1. *See* Chapter 5 regarding personal reactions upon being sued.
2. 42 Pa. R.C.P. Rule 212 (Purdon 1975).
3. 7 Standard Pennsylvania Practice 2d §41:2 (1982).
4. *Id.*, at §41:3.
5. 1 Goodrich-Amram 2d §212:1 supp., citing Order of the Supreme Court 9 Pa. Bull. 3936 (12/1/79). This applies only to civil suits, which include medical malpractice cases.
6. 7 Standard Pennsylvania Practice 2d §41:2 (1982).
7. 42 Pa. R.C.P. Rule 212 (Purdon 1975).
8. 42 Pa. R.C.P. Rule 216 (Purdon 1975).
9. *Supra.* n.5.
10. *See, e.g.*, St. Paul Fire and Marine Insurance Co. Physicians' Professional Liability Protection—Claims Made Policy Form 40294 Ed. 11-80.
11. *See, e.g.*, The Medical Protective Co., Claims Made Policy Form CMI-10-86.
12. *See, e.g.*, The Medical Protective Co., Policy Form TL-6-86.

13. 42 Pa. R.C.P. Rule 4007.4. (Purdon 1975). Goodrich-Amram 2d §4007.4:1 Sup. (1986).
14. Philadelphia Electric Co. v. Nuclear Energy Liability—Property Ins. Assoc., 10 D. & C. 3d 340 (Pa. Comm. Pl. 1970).
15. 42 Pa. R.C.P. Rule 234, referencing Rule 1357. (Purdon 1975).
16. 8 Standard Pennsylvania Practice 2d §48:4 (1982).
17. A helpful book in preparing for trial is *Belli For Your Malpractice Defense* written by Melvin M. Belli and published by Medical Economics Co. Inc., Oradell, N.J. It contains numerous anecdotes from Belli's half-century career in medical malpractice litigation, primarily suing doctors. His personal observations and advice on proper and productive courtroom etiquette is worth the cost of this book.
18. 7 Standard Pennsylvania Practice 2d §47:3 (1982).
19. *Id.*, at §47:8.
20. *Id.*, at §47:9.
21. 42 Pa. C.S.A. §4521(d) (Purdon 1987). In counties where qualification forms are not mailed out, information is collected by summons.
22. 42 Pa. C.S.A. §4524 (Purdon 1981).
23. Black's Law Dictionary (ed. 5) at 1395.
24. Meyer, Pennsylvania Trial Advocacy Handbook, 95, Philadelphia, 1976, Bisel.
25. Black's Law Dictionary (ed. 5) at 1412.
26. Meyer, *supra*, n. 24 at 96.
27. One book discussing these techniques is written by doctor-lawyer William J. Bryan, Jr., titled *The Chosen Ones, or The Art of Jury Selection* published by Westwood Publishing Co., Glendale, Calif. Many generalizations are in Meyer, *supra* n.24, at 104-6.
28. Meyer, *supra*, n.24, at 107.
29. *Id.*, at 109-10.
30. *See* Belli, M.: Belli For Your Malpractice Defense at 179, Oradell, N.J., 1986, Medical Economics Company Inc.
31. Meyer, *supra*, n.24, at 186.
32. *See*, Chapter 2 regarding the standard of care.
33. 42 Pa.C.S.A. §5935 (Purdon 1981).
34. Meyer, *supra* n.24, at 244-52.
35. *Id.*, at 257-62
36. **6** Am. Jur. Trials 927-8 (1967).
37. **23** Am. Jur. Pl. and Pr. Forms (Rev) Trial Form 124 (1973).
38. *See* Chapter 2 regarding the standard of care of doctors.
39. Adapted from Donaldson v. Maffucci, 156 A.2d 835, 838 (PA 1959).
40. Fala, The Law of Medical Malpractice in Pennsylvania, **36** U. Pitts. L. Rev. 203, 209 (1974). Quoting from McCandess v. McWho, 22 Pa. 261 (1853). In defense of the trial judge, it should be pointed out that the clear mandate of today to analyze malpractice claims by negligence, not contract, principles was not then pervasive.
41. *Id.*, quoting Donaldson, supra n.39.
42. **5** Am. Jur. Trials 1022-4 (1967), adapted from a plaintiff's jury instruction by Jacob A. Stein.
43. **23** Am. Jur. Pl. and Pr. Forms (Rev.) Trial Form 131 (1973).
44. **5** Am. Jur. Trials 1022, fn. 2, citing Herb v. Hallowell, 154 A. 582 (Pa. 1931).
45. **6** Am. Jur. Trials 948 (1967)
46. Yogi Berra.
47. Adapted from Reichman v. Wallach, 452 A.2d 501 (Pa. Super. 1982). The jury had awarded against both Dr. Wallach and the hospital, but the judge threw out the case against the hospital, leaving Dr. Wallach liable for the whole amount.
48. "You can observe a lot just by watching." Yogi Berra.
49. 10 Standard Pennsylvania Practice 2d §60:5 (1982).
50. Pennsylvania Constitution, Art. 1 §6 and 42 Pa.C.S.A. §5104 (Purdon).
51. 10 Standard Pennsylvania Practice 2d §60:17 (1982).
52. *Id.*, at §60:41.
53. *Id.*, at 60:41.
54. 42 Pa. R.C.P. 227.1(c) (Purdon 1985).

55. *Id.*, at (2).
56. 10 Standard Pennsyvlania Practice 2d §60:75 (1982).
57. *Id.*
58. 42 Pa.R.C.P. Rule 238 (Purdon 1984).
59. 1 Goodrich-Amram §238 Commentary (1987).
60. This analysis justifying pre-judgment interest ignores the perception of many insurers that they can settle a case cheaper if settled earlier. Lectures, Tillinghast Associates, 1985-6.
61. 42 Pa.R.C.P. Rule 283 (a) (1) (Purdon 1984).
62. *Id.*, at (2).
63. 1 Goodrich-Amram, *supra* n. 59.
64. 42 Pa.R.C.P. Rule 238 (3) (Purdon 1984).
65. Meyer, *supra* n. 24 at 270.
66. Pennsylvania Rules of Appellant Procedure, Rule 1101 (Rules Service Co., 1977).
67. Pa. Constitution Art. V. §9 (Purdon 1969).
68. Annotation, Medical Malpractice Countersuits, 84 ALR 3d 555 (1978). An excellent review is found in Logan, An Eye for an Eye, a Tooth For a Tooth, Etc. **32** Med. Tr. T. Q. 153 (1985).
69. See generally, Annotation, Liability of Attorney Acting For Client for Malicious Prosecution, **46** A.L.R. 4th 249 (1986). Also see 1 Standard Pennsyvlania Practice §4:69 (1981).
70. Smoker v. Ohl, 6 A.2d 810 (Pa. 1939). Counterclaim is not appropriate. 14 Standard Pennsylvania Practice §80:64 (1983).
71. Shaffer v. Stewart, 473 A.2d 1017 (Pa. Super 1984).
72. *Id.*
73. McGee v. Feege, 510 A.2d 822 (Pa. Super 1986).
74. *Id.*, at 825.1

8

RESPONDING TO THE MEDICAL MALPRACTICE CRISIS

Back to medicine?

Synopsis

Reviewing the Disease and Etiology

Prophylaxis

- Having a Personal Attorney
- Improving the Doctor-Patient Relationship
- Practicing Good (and Defensive) Medicine
  - Generally
  - Identifying Areas Warranting Defensive Medicine
  - Picking Patients Carefully
  - Thinking Before Commenting on Prior Treatment
  - Thinking Before Commenting on Current Treatment
  - Developing Office Defensive Medicine Techniques
  - Defensive Medicine Checklists
- Learn About the Law
- Reviewing Your Insurance Coverage
- Seeking Constructive Legislation

Back to Medicine? Absolutely—But Better Prepared!

The negative impact of the medical malpractic crisis on patient care is unquestionable, except by the plaintiff's bar. Lawyers who make their living suing doctors will claim that malpractice litigation improves patient care. But any doctor who has been through the hard-knocks schooling of a medical malpractice case will never practice medicine quite the same as before. If a patient recovers by verdict or settlement, the physician who gave proper treatment feels victimized. Even doctors who are willing to admit error through inadvertence, lack of training, or even clear negligence, often believe that the legal system unjustly enriched the patient or that the jury process was unnecessarily humiliating. And perhaps most unfair, even doctors who win a case carry scars from an embarrassing, costly, and time-consuming legal battle. They feel victimized by the system of justice itself.

Faced with the medical malpractice crisis, some physicians regard every patient as a potential litigant, and altruistic inclinations are stifled. The physician-patient relationship becomes adversarial. Other doctors are simply refusing to practice under threat of medical malpractice suits that now confront them. It may not be that doctors are going into farming or the restaurant business, but they are avoiding many of the high-risk areas of practice. One example is the growing number of qualified obstetricians who are refusing to deliver babies because of the increasing number of suits. Will first-rate care be available if eventually the care of the parturient falls back to the time when midwives performed this function? Who do the plaintiffs' attorneys think will deliver their child or grandchild? This concern is critical, particularly in rural communities.

Reviewing the disease and etiology

How do physicians respond to the medical malpractice crisis? How do doctors get back to concentrating on medicine? For most physicians, the suggestion of Dick, the butcher, from Shakespeare's "King Henry VI" would surely suffice: "The first thing we do, let's kill all the lawyers."[1] Hopefully, less drastic measures will do. Some solutions are found within the current system; others will require changes.

At the beginning of this book we said that the disease that we as health care providers must confront is the medical malpractice crisis. The etiology is the universal desire for money or the common wish for revenge. Short-sighted greed is a perversion of the driving force behind the American economy. Like some other diseases, the chances of infection with the affliction depend on exposure to the innoculum—as the number of potential dollars involved rises, more of those exposed fall prey to the temptation to take advantage of the opportunity. Co-factors in spreading this epidemic are found in the legal system and its changes. The contingency fee is like a free sample from a dope-peddler: "Try it—no risk or cost." The relatively new freedom lawyers have to advertise and the technical changes in the law, such as breakdown in the strict locality rule, have lowered society's resistance to the disease.

Although it is ironic to the point of pathos, the greatest stimulant of the spread of the malpractice disease is the fault of medicine and its practitioners themselves. We do not mean to say, as do the plaintiffs' lawyers, that the cause is poor medical practices. Rather, the cause lies in historically recent benefits in medical care. Out of the stunning successes and major advancements of medical care in the last four decades have come unreasonably high expectations. People no longer regard themselves as doomed to die—we seem to live in oblivious disregard of the universal mortality of humans. A fatal cancer might have been diagnosed earlier. The brittle diabetic could have been more aggressively advised of the need to lose weight. The patient should have been tested for that rare disease at the outset.

In addition to astronomical expectations of the health care system, willingness of most people to question and second-guess has generally risen. No professional (except perhaps a plumber) is accorded respect as in years gone by. The general rise in consumerism in society has meant that people demand perfect behavior from professionals in all walks of life. Combined with high expectations for excellent results, high expectations for flawless professional behavior have caused patients and families to question their health care providers with increasing frequency.

Granted, many of these societal changes are improvements and have great beneficial results. But they are changes, and the full effect has yet to be seen. How far can it go? Hopefully, most physicians will not yet have confronted the extreme of expectations evidenced by a patient's family member, who reacted to a diagnosis of heart attack in the 77-year-old man by suggesting that his doctor had failed him. The doctor had seen the patient, who had no history of risk factors, on a routine office visit a year previously![2]

There are no vaccines for this disease. Both good and bad practitioners have been assailed. But the known risk factors can be addressed. Our suggestions to doctors are:

- Have a relationship with a personal attorney before a suit is filed
- Improve the physician-patient relationship
- Practice good (and defensive) medicine
- Learn about the law
- Review your insurance coverage
- Seek constructive legislation

Prophylaxis

Having a personal attorney

We have emphasized in this book the need for a personal attorney. From the day a doctor graduates from medical school, he should have a personal attorney.

The personal attorney should have essentially the same relationship with the doctor that patients have with their family doctors. The attorney should, first of all, be someone the doctor trusts. He should be not only an attorney but also a confidant. While the attorney may not be able to carry out all of the doctor's legal work, he will be able to refer the physician to appropriate specialists, just as a family doctor would.

A physician who has a personal attorney will feel free to call the attorney on a wide variety of questions, many not directly related to medical care. Early legal involvement in many kinds of potential problems can be helpful. The doctor will learn about the law, and the attorney will be encouraged to keep abreast of the law of medicine. The attorney can also supply lists of physicians and hospitals being sued locally and the names and backgrounds of the attorneys doing the suing. As the physician-attorney relationship matures, the attorney can keep the doctor informed on the inner workings of the legal community.

To make this arrangement work, the physician should insist on paying for the attorney's services. Lawyers don't think well on credit or when they are not being paid. The best way may be to pay the attorney a regular retainer, which could take care of routine advice and services, or against which services can be billed. Court appearances, collections, and detailed legal services would be billed separately. Alternatively, the doctor could simply pay the attorney on a straight hourly basis for the services performed.

Some doctors and attorneys essentially trade services. Income tax problems aside, this isn't a good idea. This never comes out even and seldom even close to it. If the attorney or his family has the client as a doctor, it's better if the doctor charges for services, perhaps at a reduced rate. And it's better if the doctor pays the attorney as well for legal services.

If the doctor and the attorney work out an equitable financial arrangement, both will be comfortable and satisfied. You want the lawyer taking serious care with your legal needs, just as you take seriously the health needs of patients with whom you have other dealings.

Improving the physician-patient relationship

Although the legal profession bears considerable responsibility in the current medical malpractice crisis, the medical profession must shoulder some responsibility as well. Doctors' worst failing in this regard is that they have made medical care far too impersonal. Some doctors do not communicate very well at all with their patients. They are sometimes discourteous and lack tact. The high and proud priests of arcane knowledge sometimes can't be bothered to relate to patients as if those patients were human beings. In sum, doctors have allowed the deterioration of the traditional doctor-patient relationship, often developed over many years.

A malpractice claim, although perhaps warranted, seldom will be filed if the doctor is considered a trusted friend; the patient accepts the fact that the doctor did his best. The trend toward specialties and technology has enhanced expectations of miraculous recoveries; when they don't occur, patients demand recompense from the doctor they saw only briefly if at all. Within the establishment of the specialty of family practice, an aggressive effort is being made—as it should be—to regain confidence, respect, and tolerance of doctors' shortcomings. The common cynical disbelief of a physician's ethical motivations can be assuaged by sincere and open communication.

Practicing good (and defensive) medicine

Generally. The goal of every doctor is to practice good medicine and health care. But today, good medicine is simply not enough to survive the medical malpractice crisis. We must also practice "defensive medicine" or, as we prefer to call it, "survival medicine."

Defensive medicine has been defined as:

> The alteration of modes of medical malpractice, induced by the threat of liability, for the principal purposes of forestalling the possibility of lawsuits by patients as well as providing a good legal defense in the event such lawsuits are instituted.[3]

For some people, *defensive medicine* is a term that connotes cowardly, demeaning, or ethically and economically unjustifiable practices. As the definition quoted previously indicates, defensive medicine only requires a reasoned response to the constant threat of malpractice actions that doctors face.

As with everything else, there are good and bad kinds of defensive medicine. All conscientious practitioners will shun anything that unnecessarily adds to a patient's risks, suffering, or even costs and that is designed only to protect the physician. Insurance counsel and much of the defense bar will disagree with this strict formulation. Physicians who feel the threat of malpractice litigation most acutely will be tempted to transgress the edges of this rule. But the alternative is the abandonment of the traditional standard by which medical decisions are made: What is in the best interests of the patient? It is reasonable to suggest that the regard and faith still visited upon the medical profession by most of the public are the result of years of strict adherence to this most basic of principles. Surrender this and the major justification for the tremendous responsibility and license of the physician is surrendered. If it becomes generally accepted that physicians may make practice decisions based on their *own* interests where those interests conflict with a patient's, then the medical malpractice crisis will have done far more damage than it has heretofore.

But certain things can be done, rationally and in good conscience. Generally, these measures involve effort, time, and/or expense for the physician. Acceptable defensive practices provide no absolute bar to malpractice lawsuits, but they clearly help. They are designed to prevent suit and, failing this, to prevent successful suit by patients.

Not only must the doctor's practice conform to medically accepted methods, but for a successful defense, the doctor also must be able to prove, often many years after treatment, that the care was rendered properly every step of the way. The burden at trial is on the patient to prove his case by the "more probably than not" standard. But even allegations alone can shift the burden over to the physician to prove that everything was within the standard of care. A successful defense includes not only showing that proper data were gathered through a history and a physical examination, to make possible a reasonable assessment of the patient's condition, but also that appropriate laboratory tests, x-rays, and other diagnostic methods were used. The defense must demonstrate that all the data were given consideration and that a reasonable diagnosis or plan was formulated. The doctor's successful defense must show that the patient was properly informed of the risks, benefits, and alternatives of available therapeutic methods to enable the patient to make an intelligent decision whether to undergo the proposed treatment. It must be provable that the therapeutic methods selected were acceptable at the time and properly used. Even sufficient manual dexterity and skill may have to be shown. A successful defense in court also includes showing that the patient had been adequately instructed and counseled about participation in his own care. All these ingredients of a successful legal defense are part of the recipe for defensive medicine.

Constant attention to detail and documentation is a must. Unfortunately, the type of medicine indirectly required by the courts may be perfect first-class medicine, even when this is unrealistic because of patient costs or the realities of day-to-day medical practice. Nevertheless, until the threat of ruinous medical malpractice actions subsides, doctors must deal with these threats through defensive medicine techniques.

Patient's attorneys are taking the position that defensive medicine, whatever the cost, is a good thing. Suits do have a good aspect insofar as they, or the threat of them, encourage physicians to (1) keep more meticulous records; (2) study the professional literature more regularly; and (3) attend more continuing education programs. But where the response is more tests or refusal to treat risk-laden patients aggressively, defensive medicine is not necessarily good. Where fear of suits inhibits the exercise of medical judgment in the patient's best interests, patients lose.

Identifying areas warranting defensive medicine. The forms of medical malpractice with which individual doctors or health care providers should be concerned can vary somewhat based on the nature of the practice. The scientific background of the physician will cause him to recognize these data as "soft" but they are, for now, the only basis for rational decision. Insurance companies, medical societies, specialty boards or colleges, and others often maintain statistics highlighting the allegations made in malpractice claims. The Medical Protective Co. of Fort Wayne, Ind., and St. Paul Fire and Marine Insurance Company of St. Paul, Minn., for example, each distribute newsletters—"The Protector" and "Malpractice Digest"—that regularly include this information, both generally and with respect to particular specialties or types of claims. The recent federal General Accounting Office (GAO) report has been criticized in its methodology but is still useful.[4] Other sources are cited later in this chapter.

Examples of conclusions reached on available statistics include:

- ***Anesthesiology claims*** commonly involve adverse reactions to the anesthesia or damage to the teeth. Other typical claims include cardiac arrest resulting from anesthesia, postoperative complications, and improper monitoring or treatment.[5]
- ***Dental claims*** most often arise from fee disputes after allegedly unsatisfactory dentures, crowns, or restorations. Claims also involve periodontia (diagnostic failures, improper or incomplete treatment); contingent damage (lacerations, damage to adjacent teeth, broken needles, equipment failures, fractured or dislocated jaws); aspirations and ingestions (materials, teeth or bone fragments, parts of instruments); assaults (extraction or treatment of wrong teeth, slapping recalcitrant juvenile patients); infections; endodontia; roots in antrum; orthodontia; nerve injury; and reactions (antibiotics, anesthetics), among others (spillage of medications or other substances damaging clothing or exposed skin, incomplete work).[6]
- ***Emergency medicine claims*** most commonly involve a failure to diagnose a myocardial infarction. Diagnostic failures related to abdominal pain also represent a large number of claims. Potentially critical conditions such as abdominal aortic aneurysm, appendicitis, ectopic pregnancy, ruptured or perforated viscus, gastrointestinal bleeding, hemorrhagic pancreatitis, perforated diverticulum, and intestinal obstruction warrant consideration. Fractures, meningitis, and wounds account for many claims as well.[7]
- ***Gynecologic claims*** overwhelmingly stem from a failure to diagnose either breast cancer or cancer of the cervix.[8]
- ***Internal medicine claims*** commonly involve misdiagnosis of breast, lung, or colon cancer. Misdiagnosis of myocardial infarctions, pulmonary emboli, acute abdomen, and ectopic pregnancy are also significant. Other claims are based on drug injuries and cardiac catheterizations.[9]
- ***Neurology claims*** usually involve misdiagnosis of some sort, often brain-related misdiagnoses. Drug overdose claims are increasingly significant. Many of the overdose cases have involved the use of Dilantin.[10]
- ***Neurosurgery claims*** usually involve spinal surgery and laminectomy/

myelogram procedures. About one-fourth involve nerve injuries, often causing paralysis. Failure to diagnose cases, commonly a fractured spine or hematoma, are also significant.[11]

- ***Obstetric claims*** most often involve accidental injury to a fetus during birth. To a lesser extent claims involve the death of a fetus or mother during delivery, diagnostic failures, and failure to do a cesarean section.[12]
- ***Ophthalmologic claims*** usually involve loss of vision. Two-thirds of these claims arise in the wake of surgery, typically cataract surgery, correction of a strabismus, or removal of a foreign body. Of claims not involving surgery, most result from an alleged failure to locate foreign bodies in the eye, failure to diagnose a detached retina, or abrasions during routine examination.[13]
- ***Orthodontic claims*** usually involve unsatisfactory work. These claims are often motivated by a patient's concern over the bill. To a significantly lesser extent, cases involve diagnostic failures and extractions of wrong teeth.[14]
- ***Orthopedic surgery claims,*** naturally, most often arise from improper treatment of fractures. To a lesser extent, surgical error, diagnostic failure, nerve injury, infection, unsuccessful laminectomy and myelogram, retrieval of foreign bodies, and equipment defects are alleged.[15]
- ***Otorhinolaryngology claims*** usually involve surgical work on the nose and throat. The more serious claims, however, involve the nose.[16]
- ***Pediatric claims*** usually involve diagnostic failures. Many of these involve meningitis or hip dysplasia. To a lesser extent, cases involve hypoglycemia, phenylketonuria (PKU), and hydrocephalus.[17]
- ***Psychiatric claims*** usually involve suicidal patients and whether an attempted or actual suicide could have been prevented. A growing number of claims allege improper sexual involvement.[18]
- ***Radiologic claims*** usually involve failure to diagnose cancer, fractures, or other conditions. Injuries during radiation therapy and adverse reactions to contrast media are also common claims.[19]

Information regarding claims can be extremely helpful to doctors in developing personal defensive medicine techniques. Consider these examples:

- According to one study, more than one-fourth of anesthesia claims involve dental damage. Of these more than half the dental damage occurred in the recovery room, when patients awakened and bit down on oral airways. If oral airways are removed as soon as patients start to awaken and nasal airways put in if necessary, these incidents would likely be reduced.[20]
- One of the most common claims made against emergency physicians is failure to diagnose myocardial infarctions. For this reason, before a patient with chest pain is sent home, emergency physicians are well

advised to clearly document a finding that a patient did not suffer a myocardial infarction.[21]

- Dental claims, particularly those involving orthodontic patients, are commonly precipitated by fee disputes.[22] Accordingly, dentists and orthodontists should discuss fees with patients in advance to avoid allegations of unsatisfactory work thereafter. For major treatments, a written disclosure or schedule may be appropriate.
- Obstetric claims most often involve an impaired baby. Although most hospitals do not routinely examine the placenta or umbilical cord, it has been suggested that a pathologic examination soon after birth can help pinpoint why the baby was born impaired. Impairment attributed to a doctor's negligence may actually be due to genetic, environmental, or other medical causes rather than birth trauma.[23]

These examples merely demonstrate the practical use that a doctor, applying defensive medicine, may make of this statistical information. The information is indeed a potential, non-traditional source of information about quality foci, as well.

Just as doctors must keep abreast of developments in medical practice, they must also be alert to trends in malpractice claims. Patients' attorneys, eager to expand doctors' responsibility, will develop new theories of liability or variations on those that are well recognized. Prescription or medication-related claims, for example, have increased dramatically in recent years.[24] Defensive medicine techniques must be monitored and improved to respond to the types of claims that are currently being made against doctors.

Picking patients carefully. If any defensive medicine suggestion is difficult to actuate but potentially priceless in value, this is it: A doctor should pick patients carefully! Many physicians, because they are under contract or because of referral patterns, cannot do this. Although this policy is philosophically distasteful to many doctors (and perhaps rightly so), freedom from medical malpractice claims (not necessarily medical malpractice itself) requires excellent rapport with both patients and their relatives. Where the physician, such as a primary care practitioner, has the time and personnel to intake "screen" his patients, he should.

The distinction between good and bad defensive medicine is admittedly less clear here. What if everyone recognized and refused these patients, producing a social-Darwinism selection process? But the recommendation here is to avoid going into a relationship with these dangerous people. Once they do become patients, they must be treated very carefully.

People vary in their propensity to sue. Some patients are just plain litigous. They are often demanding patients who never pay their medical bills. Others wouldn't sue a doctor regardless of what the practitioner did. Most patients fall between these extremes. It is important to recognize who is who during the first professional visit.

Certain signals should alert the doctor to litigous patients. For example, the doctor should look out for the patient or family who is critical of past doctors, hospitals, or the health care system in general. The doctor should politely tell this type of person that he doubts he can do any better and, without getting involved in a referral or any doctor-patient relationship, suggest that the patient return to his last doctor, or to a teaching center, or to a large, nationally known referral center.

Also, the doctor should beware of the patient who always complains about prices. Some individuals would never be satisfied, even if the doctor treated them for free. They should be avoided. However, the doctor must distinguish them from the elderly person who is concerned about prices but may actually be a responsible person who intends to pay. The doctor shouldn't be embarrassed to explain the financial aspects of care, or to have a capable member of the staff do so.

A doctor's aptitude for assessing people and conveying sensitivity, ability, and credibility is more instinctive than learned. Sometimes, the only warning a physician gets is a "funny feeling." It is important that a doctor be able to recognize from simple visual and facial expressions, together with subtle remarks, when a person simply does not like the doctor and never will. The doctor must have the good sense not to take this person as a patient.

To pick patients wisely, a doctor should:

- Ask at least once, but not dwell on: Is this patient a potential litigant?
- Establish the best possible rapport with the patient, family, and even concerned, obviously influential friends, remembering and respecting principles of confidentiality.
- Study the patient, family and associates. The doctor should also determine whether these people are hostile to doctors and the health care system or have a negative, antagonistic attitude toward life in general. If a doctor is treating such a person, the professional relationship should be tactfully terminated as soon as possible.
- Become a member of the local credit bureau in the area and investigate every prospective patient, preferably before entering into a doctor-patient relationship. If a patient has poor credit, shows a history of litigation or is criminally inclined, the doctor should not accept him as a patient. These people often seek something for nothing, are demanding, are never satisfied, and will sue at the drop of a hat. An attorney won't give them the time of day unless he can smell a contingency fee or secures a large retainer.
- Notices in some local newspapers identify medical malpractice plaintiffs. The doctor should open a file on those people. If the office has a computer, the names of every medical malpractice plaintiff should be entered into a program that allows alphabetical sorting for instant identification of litigous patients. If a doctor accepts the professional plaintiff as a patient, the patient will try to sue. If the doctor has time, he should obtain the list of all medical malpractice cases that may be

available in the courthouse. In some large cities, such as Chicago, services exist that will supply names of patients and attorneys who have sued doctors. Other information that a doctor reads or hears about patients or possible patients should be put in files or in computers.

- Use extra caution when dealing with transient patients or those involved in accidents or fights. These patients are particularly prone to sue.
- Recognize that a physician who refers a disproportionate percentage of dangerous patients is no friend. Is the business generated from this referral source sufficient to justify the risk?

Thinking before commenting on prior treatment. Perhaps the greatest misunderstanding about defensive medicine that doctors should recognize is that defensive medicine does not require them to place blame elsewhere. Doing so does not alleviate their own risk.[25] As a good "bad" example, consider the following. The doctor should never write or dictate:

> This patient had a cholecystectomy on Sept. 2, 19XX. Before leaving the hospital, the patient felt like his incision broke loose, but the surgeon said everything was OK. The patient now comes in with an obvious large postoperative incisional hernia.

The doctor could simply have noted: "Abdominal bulge, right upper quadrant," listing cholecystectomy as past history. A doctor should never criticize another practitioner to a patient. Share your concerns with the peer review committee. A doctor who has something to say to a colleague should call the colleague on the telephone or mention it when next they meet. A doctor should always get the previous doctor's version of what happened before making judgments. A practitioner should even consider bringing the surgeon back into the case, if possible, and letting him explain the problem to the patient.

Attorneys have criticized doctors for a "veil of silence" because no doctor wants to testify against another. Responding to specific questions may well warrant explicit answers, but there is certainly no need to encourage a suit. Things do happen. Doctors shouldn't take the unrealistic attitude that it's their duty to see that another doctor is "punished" by having to face a civil suit. What doctors should do, as professionals, is seek an improved profession without bringing in the plaintiffs' lawyers as police. The proper disposition of some problems may be peer review or licensure proceedings. Once the lawyer is consulted, he will consider naming the criticizing physician as a defendant, too. He's afraid the second physician will turn out to have been at fault. He also wants to try and pressure the second physician into acting as a witness for the plaintiff in return for an unreliable promise of being released from the case. Moreover, a second doctor's comments to a patient may motivate the patient to do such a thorough job of reviewing the treatment that yet a third doctor will be asked to find something wrong in the second doctor's care. He may invite other doctors to retaliate by criticizing the second doctor's work.

Comments about prior treatment usually relate to some other doctor, but not always. According to a true story,[26] a doctor was examining a woman's throat one day and noticed that the right pillar, both anterior and posterior, were completely scarred and distorted.

The doctor asked, "Who the devil did that to you?"

"Why you did, doctor, some 6 years ago," was the woman's reply.

The point is obvious. A doctor must think before commenting on prior treatment. He may be putting his own head in a noose. Even if he doesn't damage himself, he's aggravating the crisis in physician-patient relations and malpractice litigation.

Thinking before commenting on current treatment. As important as not commenting on prior treatment is the admonition to think before commenting on current treatment, including a doctor's own. In one case, a doctor exclaimed, "It broke!" apparently referring to the patients' tooth, which had broken during extraction. But the patient thought the remark referred to a needle and subsequently filed suit. Although the case was successfully defended, legal fees amounted to $3,000 a word.[27] Even worse is the doctor who says to the patient after some mishap, "Oh, that's why I have insurance." What a doctor says about treatment, in embarrassment or whatever, can and probably will be used against him. Rash comments are a good way to signal patients that a doctor should be sued.

Developing office defensive medicine techniques. To effectively practice defensive medicine, a doctor must involve the office staff in the effort. A doctor's care will be for naught if the staff is careless when assisting in treatment, is rude or discourteous to patients, makes snide remarks about the doctor or other doctors, fails to maintain adequate records, makes medication errors, mislabels bottles, etc., etc. It's up to the doctor to pick good people as employees and to make certain that they do good work. The doctor must take the time to instruct them in defensive medicine techniques.[28]

Defensive medicine checklists. In Chapter 3 we discussed the forms of medical malpractice. Defensive medicine techniques may be used to avoid medical malpractice claims in each of those categories. Here are checklists of specific defensive-medicine suggestions regarding forms of medical malpractice commonly alleged. Very general or otherwise uncategorizable items lead off. Read through these, giving each the time it deserves in the context of your own practice set-up. Use this risk management checklist to alert yourself to areas where action is needed or available. Put the one-year anniversary of today on your long-range planning calendar and commit now to reread this checklist on that date.

General

☑ Do you think about the fact that every patient is a potential litigant before taking on a patient? Pick your patients carefully!

☑ Have you thought through the forms of medical malpractice that could be alleged against you and the defense that you would present?

☑ In all professional endeavors, certain results are unacceptable to patients. If techniques, procedures, or tests are available that are not dangerous to the patient and that effectively eliminate the possibility of adverse outcome, do you use them? The doctor who fails to use them does so at his peril. If the cost to society of the technique, procedure, or test is great, do you also analyze the risk-benefit ratio purely from the viewpoint of the individual patient? That is what a jury will do. A rare risk that remains very rare statistically will loom large in court if a patient sues over that rare risk's actual occurrence, and talks about it at trial for 5 days.

☑ The best way to prove something is to show a contemporaneously created, dated, signed (and even witnessed) record. Do you carefully document what happened whenever you anticipate the possibility of having to defend a malpractice claim?

☑ After examining and treating a patient, do you routinely look at the medical record to see that it is complete? Relevant positive and negative complaints and findings should be noted. How will that record stand up in court 2 years from now?

☑ If you do something (procedure, test, therapy, dosage, consultation) in treating a patient that ordinarily would not be done or would not be done that way, do you document carefully the reasons for your decision?

☑ If you omit something (procedure, test, therapy, dosage, consultation) in treating a patient that ordinarily would be done, do you carefully document the reasons for your decision?

☑ Do you consider the worst possible cause of the patient's problem or worst possible complication of your therapy? Make certain that all elements of care are documented, including information about the worst possibility conveyed to the patient. Then, if a suit is filed, you will have a better chance that the medical care as documented will be acceptable. For example, when a person is referred or proposed to have surgery, do you realize that the person might die or have other major complications resulting in permanent injury? Make certain that indications for the procedure are documented in terms of history and physical findings, and that any laboratory or diagnostic work required and consultations needed are obtained.

☑ Are you aware of how medical experts review charts for possible suit? Can your charts withstand such scrutiny?

☑ Is your documentation written with at least the possibility of a jury review in mind? How would a lay person react to the care given? Remember, don't put anything in a patient's record that you would not be willing to have read in a courtroom, because there is a distinct possibility that this will happen. For example, say the patient was disputacious and that there were problems in communicating. You must document why you urged the patient to seek another physician. It's clear that the patient was an S.O.B., but if you write it in that way, what will the jury think?

☑ Do you try to enhance the doctor-patient relationship through proper communication with the patient and the patient's family, as appropriate?

☑ Do you believe that your patients understand your instructions? If verbal instructions are given, they should be noted in the patient's chart. Printed instruction sheets may be helpful. Do subsequent events indicate that you're not getting through to your patients? Can your nurses help?

☑ Do you consider what a patient might say about the care rendered or how the patient may interpret the care received? Do you look at it from the patient's viewpoint?

☑ Are you prepared to discuss your fees with a patient? If a procedure is expensive and elective, does the patient have a clear understanding of the fees in advance?

☑ If you do examinations of people for employers or insurance, do you understand that this is not a physician-patient relationship? Does the patient understand this? Do you do anything in these situations that might allow a court to decide later that you had actually entered a relationship or were treating the patient?

☑ If the results are less than satisfactory (irrespective of reason), do you refrain from sending letters or statements demanding payment? Do you have a follow-up system in place to assure that accounts which concern you for any reason are withheld from collections? Does your agreement with your collections agency allow you to pull accounts out of the collection process whenever you wish?

☑ Do you refrain from billing patients for services required to remedy an injury that you caused? Some doctors worry about signaling a guilty mind by not billing, but where error is obvious, nothing is to be gained by restraint.

☑ Are you up to date on the care customarily rendered in particular circumstances? Are you satisfied with (better yet, proud of) your record?

☑ If a problem arises from a patient's care, are you careful what you or your staff says to the patient or the patient's family? Are all your current staff trained and "in sync" with your attitudes on this? Do they support you fiercely? What is said may be just what motivates a patient to sue. Hospitals in particular make this mistake. As part of "quality control" or even risk management, they send out junior administrators or others to make some remark to the patient about the patient being "injured" or there being some "mishap." One purpose of these contacts is good—to nip suits in the bud. But as practiced in a few hospitals, these discussions fertilize suits. Do the hospitals where you treat patients monitor and supervise Quality Assurance/Risk Management personnel adequately?

Consent

☑ Do you refrain from examining a patient of the opposite sex without someone of the same sex as the patient present? Do you avoid examinations of the genitalia of a patient or the breasts of a woman without someone of the same sex as the patient, or at least a nurse, present? At the extreme of the spectrum, simply decline to take as patients flirtatious individuals of either sex.

☑ Are you especially alert to the possible need to have a witness present when dealing with a psychiatric patient or a patient with psychological problems?

☑ When examining a patient, if you detect any reluctance on the part of the patient or from the parent if the patient is a child, do you more carefully review and explain your diagnosis and recommend treatment, together with the possible complications and alternative treatment? Don't hesitate to ask why the patient seems recalcitrant. A patient's anxiety is often relieved with simple communication. If the patient's reluctance persists, seriously consider insisting on a consultant for a second opinion.

☑ Does the informed consent improve communication with the patient and family? If a doctor has explained the adverse outcomes that can be expected from a procedure, the patient or family are more likely to accept a bad result. Bad results have been the number one allegation in professional liability claims.[29] If a bad result is an anticipated risk, the patient is less likely to believe the doctor was negligent when a bad result occurs.

☑ Are you satisfied that your patient is an adult and otherwise legally able to consent? If any doubt exists about a patient's competency, consult a friend or relative of the patient to obtain background information on the patient, remembering the constraints of confidentiality.

☑ Are you aware (in advance of a crisis) of your patient's religious beliefs and whether proposed treatment or procedures run counter to them? Do you discuss resuscitation measures with the patient and family before they are needed?

☑ If there is any question about the competency of a patient, do you have any consent *also* executed by the patient's next of kin? Consider encouraging the appointment of a legal guardian.

☑ If a patient has appointed an agent, do you carefully review the power of attorney to determine the agent's authority, and do you keep a photocopy in the patient's file? Further, the patient's personal consent should be obtained in addition to the representative's whenever possible.

☑ If a patient refuses recommended treatment, do you obtain a written waiver signed by the patient and, if possible, next of kin? Does your waiver specify the treatment recommended, state that the doctor has recommended the treatment and informed the patient of the possible consequences of refusing treatment, acknowledge that the patient has nevertheless knowingly refused or declined the treatment, and state that the patient releases the doctor from any responsibility or liability for any consequences resulting from the patient's decision? It is important to have a witness present during your conversations with the patient and when the waiver is signed. "Informed refusal" cases are becoming more common.

☑ Do you always have a witness, such as your nurse, present when you are informing a patient, and do you have the nurse sign any consent form as a witness?

☑ If the patient is usually accompanied by or has a close relative, and if the patient allows it, do you explain to the relative that you have discussed the case thoroughly with the patient and have obtained the patient's consent? It is usually not a good idea to have the relative witness the giving of the consent as he could be another witness to dispute your version of what took place. Many malpractice claims are encouraged by relatives.

☑ In difficult or problematic situations, do you consider tape recording the informed consent? However, the recorder should be in plain view, the patient advised while the tape is running that a tape is being made, and the consent of the patient to the tape recording obtained and recorded. If you are inclined to treat a patient who has sued another doctor in the past, this might be an appropriate extra step.

☑ Do you use, at a minimum, both verbal and written consent forms? Some doctors have prepared or purchased audio- or videotape disclosures. Methods and the extent of informing patients must be individualized.

☑ Do you allow and indeed encourage the patient to ask questions?

☑ If you detect any reluctance on the part of a patient or a relative, do you seriously consider insisting that a second opinion be sought even for routine treatment or surgery?

☑ Do you know better than to rely entirely on a written consent form to establish an informed consent? This is particularly important when the informed consent is obtained in the hospital. Patients are quick to testify that a multitude of forms were placed in front of them, and they signed them all without reading them. Jurors have probably had that very experience. Doctors, accordingly, should document the informed consent by noting in the chart that an informed consent conversation took place with the patient; when it took place; where it took place; whether any witnesses were present; that the benefits, alternatives, and risks of the proposed procedure were explained; that all questions were answered; that the patient consented (or stated that he would think about the procedure, etc.); and that a written consent form was then signed.

☑ Do you keep a copy in your office file of the signed consent form and the hospital record page (or your own record) substantiating that consent was informed?

☑ If an informed consent is obtained in a doctor's office, does further discussion take place in the hospital? The hospital record should note the discussion in the hospital and that an informed consent was obtained in the doctor's office. If the only mention of an informed consent is in the doctor's own records, attorneys may claim it was altered and should not be believed. Many hospitals in Pennsylvania insist on this two-step process.

☑ If any doubt exists about a person's age, particularly if a major nonemergency procedure is involved, do you insist that some identification, such as a birth certificate, be provided?

☑ If a minor is involved, do you obtain the consent of the minor's parent or guardian for any treatment? Statutes abbreviate this need in certain situations. See Chapter 3.

☑ Where a minor has authority to consent and you intend to rely on that consent, are you satisfied that the statutory or regulatory requirements allowing the minor to consent are complied with? Read the statute or regulation itself; don't rely on what you believe it says.

☑ If the parents are divorced, do you obtain a consent from both parents or confirm the authority of one parent to give consent unless emergency treatment is involved? The authority of a parent will be stated in the divorce judgment or some related agreement. In the absence of specific authority, custody papers are enough. This is so even if the other parent is paying. In view of the ease with which documents can be altered through photocopying, certified copies may be desirable. Communications to the noncustodial parent may be a violation of confidentiality. Remember, the parents have likely been through litigation already and they may go through it again. Don't get caught in the middle.

☑ Do you refuse to depend on the advance consent that camps and schools obtain from parents? This type of consent is designed primarily to protect the camp or school, not the doctor. Except in an actual emergency, do you contact the child's parents?

Diagnosis: general considerations

☑ Do you refuse to make a diagnosis over the telephone? Have a patient who telephones go *directly* to the emergency room for diagnosis and treatment if there is any possibility of a significant problem.

☑ Do you avoid making a diagnosis at social gatherings or informally? Attorneys handle these situations with a standard: "Call my office for an appointment!"

☑ If you practice in a community where the hospital does not have an emergency physician and you're on call, do you invite trouble by diagnosing on the basis of a patient's or nurse's description? Examine the patient personally.

☑ Do you insist on doing a thorough job of working-up all your patients? Some doctors are tempted to try and save money for friends or friends of friends. Give away your time if you wish but don't do a "half-posteriored" job.

☑ Do you document your telephone conversations with the patient in the patient's chart? Does the documentation demonstrate that you didn't make a telephone diagnosis? ("Now hold the receiver over your right carotid artery, Mrs. Jones.")

☑ If a diagnosis is made, do you consider that you may be wrong (although you seldom will be)? Do you instruct the patient to be alert for unexpected signs and instruct on what to do if those signs develop? Do your patients understand what to do if they fail to progress as expected? For example, if a patient consults an emergency physician for abdominal pain and the physician concludes that the patient has a gastroenteritis, the physician still considers the possibility of appendicitis. The patient is told what the doctor believes the problem is, but that if it is something else, such as appendicitis, this is what will happen. Therefore, the patient is advised to watch for various conditions and be instructed on what to do if they occur. Very simply, every field has its commonly found diseases based on particular symptoms. However, the second and third diagnosis on the differential list deserve consideration.

☑ Do you document the reasoning process used in reaching a diagnosis and instructing the patient? A doctor is less likely to be considered negligent for misdiagnosis or even a delay in diagnosis if appropriate instructions were given to the patient that would initiate a review of the problem. The proof of the appropriateness of those instructions is found in the record.

☑ Do you retain any x-rays or reports or other laboratory records used in making or rejecting a diagnosis? Obtain copies if possible, or make copies if you are required to release originals, but keep your file fit to defend you.

Failure to refer

☑ Do you insist on and make liberal use of consultants?

☑ Are you careful to avoid taking a case if you are not needed or are not professionally or emotionally qualified? It's better to lose a patient than gain a lawsuit. Be cautious and refer or get another opinion where you are hesitant.

☑ Do you refrain from treating a patient for a condition that you have never handled before without assistance, especially if qualified consultants are available? If the situation is an emergency and you have to go ahead, document the emergent circumstances. If you are in a rural community, strongly recommend (and document) consultation in a referral center and offer to make the necessary arrangements. If the patient refuses, document this and have a witness sign your records. If the patient does not respond to your treatment, recommend consultation *again* and *again*. Document your further recommendations as well. How will it look in court if you are forced to admit you'd never done that procedure or cared for that problem before? It's done all the time, but obtaining assistance is the safer course.

☑ Those of you from the "old school" who try to save the patient money, forget it! Few appreciate the economy. There's a reason why the demand for health care is inelastic. Patients want the best. If the expense is needed and justified in the best interests of the patient, go ahead. "Cost containment" is not a sufficient excuse for failure to perform a medically indicated procedure or test. Do you provide all necessary care, regardless of cost?

☑ Particularly keep the use of specialists in mind when you have a patient who may be in danger of dying or suffering major complication. Are you certain of having one or even more other qualified doctors to back you up—even if you are well-qualified to take care of the patient alone?

Treatment: guaranteed results

☑ A basic rule: Are you careful never to tell a patient or anyone else that you "guarantee" or "warrant" a result? Always state just the opposite: "Nothing is guaranteed in medical care. Medicine is an inexact science, and although we carry out a procedure on several patients, the result may not always be the same." This is especially important when cosmetic surgery or other purely elective procedures are involved, since those patients are more likely than others to expect a guarantee. Only if you must, specify what you hope to accomplish.

☑ Are you careful when trying to reassure the patient and family? It is much better to tell the truth and, if necessary, condition them for the worst. If there is a medical reason to refrain from telling someone a bad prognosis, be extraordinarily careful to document this and the reasons for it. Many patients and families will let you know when they're ready for you to tell them, but in some situations you have to try to warn them, ready or not. Be sure to caution your staff about this pitfall as well. Out of a kind desire to allay patient anxiety, your personnel may commit you to at least an arguably binding guarantee. Do you state clearly in any written consent forms that a particular result is not guaranteed?

☑ Do you always state in your office record and also in any hospital record that you told the patient, spouse, and relative at hand that nothing has been guaranteed and complications are possible?

Procedures

☑ Do you know who your patient is? Charts, patients, and tests can get mixed up. Before treating a patient, make certain the patient and the records match. Do you have a routine that you consistently follow, even when rushed, to avoid this kind of simple error?

- ☑ Do you give the patient written instructions? You may be constantly available by phone and you may remember every patient perfectly, but what about the patient's problems that might not even trigger a call from the patient? Besides, the patients will realize you're an especially caring, careful physician.
- ☑ When providing instructions, either verbally or in writing, do you take into consideration the patient's native or preferred language and literacy? Can you satisfy a jury that your routine assures patient or responsible party understanding?
- ☑ Do you carefully document instructions given? The adequacy of medical treatment may often be determined on the adequacy of instructions.
- ☑ Do you avoid treatment or therapy by telephone whenever possible or risky?
- ☑ If for some reason you do provide treatment or therapy, or even chat about the patient's health by telephone, are you certain to note the substance of your conversation with the patient in the patient's chart?
- ☑ Do you insist on and make liberal use of consultants before procedures?
- ☑ Do you have a relatively liberal hospital admission policy? When in doubt about a patient's condition or when dealing with areas of common error, do you recognize that you, too, can make a mistake? Admit the patient to the hospital and deal with utilization review later.
- ☑ Do you make use of pathology to establish reasons for adverse results? It has been suggested, for example, that adverse results to fetuses and infants attributed to negligence on the part of an obstetrical team during delivery may actually result from genetic, environmental, or other medical causes rather than birth trauma. Placenta or cord pathology could aid malpractice defense in such cases.[30]
- ☑ Are you very certain that equipment used is in good working order, both the hospital's and that in your office?
- ☑ Do you do any procedures in your office that require a checklist? Well, do you have one and do you use it?

Prescriptions

☑ Are you satisfied that your patient understands how medications are to be taken? Many patients can't read, or what they read, they don't understand. If a patient is unable to take his own medicine, arrange for it to be administered by a family member or friend of the patient. Document your instructions to the family member or friend. If your staff does this for you, is it documented by someone?

☑ Have you considered providing your patient with printed instructions about medications?

☑ Are you in compliance with all applicable regulations and laws regarding dispensing medications?

☑ Before prescribing medications, do you invariably check the patient's drug sensitivities? The patient's record should prominently note these sensitivities. It's also advisable, in addition, to always ask the patient whether he has any known drug sensitivities.

☑ Do you know generally the manufacturer's instructions about any medications prescribed, including usual dosage, common and serious side effects, allergic reactions, cross-reactions and incompatibilities, and other idiosyncracies? Don't forget that these may be changed from time to time, so be certain to keep abreast of the latest uses and warnings. Also consult data about available drugs from sources other than drug manufacturers. This is "do-able" for the limited list of drugs you most frequently use. Do you take the time to look up the ones you're unfamiliar with before prescribing?

☑ If medications are prescribed other than in accordance with the manufacturer's instructions, do you always have a good reason for doing so and document it? It's not illegal or necessarily wrong to prescribe a marketed drug for an unapproved indication. The U.S. Food and Drug Administration's Bulletin of October 1972 notes that: "The labeling is not intended either to preclude the physician from using his best judgment in the interest of the patient, or to impose liability if he does not follow the package insert." However, a doctor must be prepared to prove why his judgment differed from the insert.

☑ When prescribing medications, do you consider the added problems of generic substitutions? If a substitution is made, the doctor may be obligated to follow the manufacturer's warnings for both the drug actually prescribed and the substitute. The warnings may vary.

☑ When treating a patient on medication prescribed by another doctor, are you careful to confirm why the medication is being taken and exactly what it is? In many cases, it's advisable to visually inspect the drugs themselves to make certain that the drugs are what has been prescribed.

☑ Do you use written prescriptions whenever possible? The list that follows comprises the ingredients of a properly written prescription in most cases:

- Use a large printed pad that includes your name, address, telephone number, medical degree, and license number. Some authorities suggest printing the narcotics number, but most physicians are justly concerned about its misuse.
- Write or print *legibly.*
- Give the name of the drug, dosage form, route of administration, strength, and quantity.
- Indicate specific directions for use and frequency of administration. *Do not* write "as directed" or use some other generalized instruction, depending on the patient to remember what you said.
- Ideally, you could list side effects that would direct the patient to stop taking the medication and call you.
- Some warnings are so standard that you can print them on the pad: "Pharmacist: Please label 'not to take if driving or with alcoholic beverages.'"
- Prescribe only as much as will be needed for a reasonable time with none left over. Never give enough to cause death to a potentially suicidal patient.
- Specify either no refills or a thought-out, limited number of refills.
- After writing the prescription, read it.
- Send one copy of the prescription to the pharmacist, keep one in the patient's chart, and ideally put the third in a sequentially numbered file of all prescriptions that you write.

Verbal prescribing in any form is risky. Most hospitals require that any orders or prescriptions given over the telephone be signed by the doctor within 24 hours. In some communities it is a frequent practice of doctors to call in prescriptions and refills for patients without examinations. To complicate the possibility of liability, the prescribing doctor never sees or signs a written prescription. If you must prescribe over the telphone, first write out the prescription and then read it over the telephone. Have the pharmacist read it back to you. Ideally, send or deliver it to the pharmacist, retaining the two copies as recommended above for written prescriptions. Do you always record prescriptions in the patient's chart in some form unless they are phoned? If the pharmacist contacts you for any prescription clarifications, go over the entire prescription again.

☑ Is your office staff, all of them, aware that they are not authorized to permit refills when a pharmacist calls? Are you monitoring your people adequately on this?

☑ If the patient does not follow your directions about taking medications, do you note that in the patient's chart? You should, but then you must be careful to act in accordance with awareness of this problem with this patient from then on.

Abandonment

☑ If you decline to accept a patient after an initial discussion, do you record this decision in a chart and that you advised the person to consult another doctor? If the person's condition is serious, it is advisable to also confirm this in a letter.

☑ Are you having to cancel too many appointments? If a patient must be rescheduled, see the patient as soon as possible. If the patient requires care earlier than you are able to reschedule, arrange for a competent substitute.

☑ If you will be temporarily unavailable to treat a patient, do you let the patient know and arrange for a competent substitute? This is necessary for your hospitalized or very sick out-patients.

☑ If a patient possibly will need continued treatment or the condition is serious, do you schedule specific visits? Don't tell the patient to simply contact you for an appointment in a couple of weeks.

☑ Do you keep a record of any appointments a patient fails to keep, however routine the visit? If the patient's condition clearly warrants additional treatment or diagnostic efforts, it's a good idea to write the patient when they fail to show and explain why you need to see the patient. Send the letter by certified mail, return receipt requested.

☑ If you are discharged by a patient, do you confirm this in writing with the patient? Do you make medical records available to the patient's new physician, despite your feelings in the matter?

☑ If you decide to withdraw from a case or discharge a patient from your care, do you notify the patient in writing and provide a reasonable time to find substitute care? If the patient is not hospitalized, be certain to advise the patient if additional care is required and that another doctor should be contacted. Also, tell the patient to contact you again if substitute care cannot be obtained. Care for the patient until substitute care is obtained or a reasonable time has passed. If the patient is hospitalized, a doctor should continue to care for the patient until another doctor has assumed the care.

☑ Before withdrawing from a case, are you certain that a good reason exists in your own mind for doing so? Withdrawing can cause bad feelings and spur a malpractice claim. If there are already bad feelings, you have a better chance to ameloriate them as the patient's physician.

☑ Before withdrawing from a case, do you consider simply referring the patient to a specialist or other doctor? Patients tend to accept referrals much better than withdrawals. If a patient is referred, make certain that it is clear to all concerned that you are no longer to be involved in the patient's treatment.

☑ When possible, do you give notices in person and have the patient acknowledge receipt in writing? If the relationship is already antagonistic this probably won't work. If personal delivery is not possible, send the notice by certified mail, return receipt requested, with delivery restricted to the patient. When certified mail is used, a receipt is returned to the sender. The purpose of certified mail is to obtain a receipt upon delivery and not proof of mailing. That receipt will be signed by any person where delivered unless you designate otherwise. Certified mail can be used without going to a post office. Contact your local post office for the required forms and information on postage charges and how to use certified mail. Because so many people don't pick up certified mail, it's ideal to send the notice by both certified mail and regular mail. If the certified mail is refused or not picked up, follow up with a telephone call to the patient and confirm that the notice was received. Document the conversation in the patient's file.

☑ Are you cautious when asked why you refuse a patient or withdraw from a case? Try to terminate any relationship or dealings on a good tone. Avoid breaches of confidentiality or statements to third persons.

☑ When the patient contacts another doctor, do you consider talking to the doctor and offering to provide whatever information or background needed, if the patient will permit it? Do what you can to avoid having the new doctor tell the patient: "It's sure good you came to me before it was too late!" Swallowing ego at this point can prevent choking on a malpractice judgment later.

Liability for others: borrowed servant

☑ When using equipment in the hospital, do you follow, or are you at least familiar with, the manufacturer's instructions? Hospitals should provide copies of the instructions to all doctors on request.

☑ Do you avoid taking the responsibility to direct someone to fix something this way or that way unless you are an expert? For example, if you are the operating surgeon and discover that the Bovie unit is not functioning properly, under no circumstances tell the nurse to do this or that. If a piece of equipment is not working properly, inform the circulating nurse and direct the nurse to call someone qualified to come and fix it. Don't assume more supervision and control than you must.

☑ If the ancillary personnel supplied by the hospital are not adequate to the matter at hand, do you politely insist on competent assistance? They're your responsibility, too, while they're with your patient.

Disclosure of records or information: privacy

☑ Without written, oral, or a reasonably implied consent, do you allow medical students, interns, residents, or other health care professionals who are not actually involved in the care of the patient to be present when a patient is interviewed or examined, especially if it involves a female or sexual organs? (Except your chaperone.)

☑ Do you avoid taking and publication of photographs, including x-rays, of patients (for use in articles or lectures) without the patient's written consent? The consent must be consistent with the extent of the publication. For example, permission to take photographs doesn't mean you can show them.

☑ Are you careful about release of information as performed or guided by the hospital? Remember that the hospital pays its attorney to protect the interests of the hospital and not necessarily those of the staff members.

☑ If you do employment, insurance, or any other type of examination that requires release of confidential information to a third party, it is advisable to use your own written permit form, although other consent forms may be executed and an implied consent given by the patient in submitting to the examination. Another way to handle this is to give the patient the report and then allow him to send the report to the person to whom it is to be submitted. In some cases the third party may prefer direct submission, particularly if there may be a desire to alter the report. Do you at least keep a copy of the patient's signed release in your file?

☑ If you do not have a patient's consent to disclose confidential information and you are not clearly required by law to release or report the information, do you insist that a subpoena be issued requiring that information be provided? This is particularly important if the doctor is treating the patient while the litigation is ongoing. The only exception to this rule should be when information is discussed by the patient's treating doctors.

☑ Where you are asked for information supposedly under some unfamiliar statutory or regulatory authority, don't hesitate to ask for a citation. Check it out or have your attorney do so. Do you satisfy yourself as to the propriety and legitimacy of all such releases before they go out?

☑ Do you refuse to release information over the telephone except in case of an emergency? Even when an emergency exists, take a telephone number and call back the person requesting the information.

Defamation

☑ Unless a prohibition exists against a patient's reviewing insurance forms or other reports sent to others, or some good reason prevents it, do you show the patient the forms or reports in advance?

☑ Are you careful to document your reasons in reporting possible abuse and neglect cases? Overly zealous health care providers, in their haste and fear of reporting laws, have at times set into motion embarrassing and disruptive legal proceedings. Yet the law clearly favors reporting in close calls. Cases should be reported if there is reason to believe that child abuse has taken place. Don't rely on someone else to do it. Besides being liable to sanctions under child abuse reporting statutes, a doctor who fails to report may be liable to the child who is later reinjured by the parents.

False imprisonment

☑ Are you documenting incompetence and medical justification on all patients restrained under your authority?

HMO's

☑ Are you providing the same level and quality of care to the prepaid plan patients as your others? You give the medical assistance and self-pay/never-pay patients good care; don't sacrifice quality on the altar of cost-control.

Learn about the law

The fact that a doctor reads this book demonstrates a resolve to learn more about medical-legal matters. A doctor should not stop here. A doctor must keep current not only in his or her specialty but also in the law as it applies to the practice. It would frighten most doctors to learn how knowledgeable some attorneys are about medicine and health care. It's time doctors learn more about law.

How does a doctor learn about the law? Well, obviously the best way would be to go to law school. A doctor who lives in or near a city with a law school might investigate the possibility of enrolling or at least of taking some appropriate courses. Some law schools have night sessions that could be conveniently scheduled.

If enrolling in law school is an unaffordable luxury, a doctor should take advantage of law-related continuing education courses. Doctors regularly receive information about courses sponsored by the American Medical Association and other organizations. Doctors should attend them and also consider attending those courses sponsored by attorney organizations, including, among others, the Pennsylvania bar.[31]

Often the most practical way to learn about the law is the way it has been done for years. Read about it.

There are a few musts for a doctor's legal library. We suggest that doctors have these books or publications in their personal library, either for the individual doctor or the group. Other books are more appropriate for the hospital's library or the local medical society:

- ***Textbook of Legal Medicine.*** This C.V. Mosby publication was completed as a project of the American College of Legal Medicine. It is a broad compendium of information not only on malpractice law but also on other areas of law relating to the practice of medicine, such as contracts.
- ***Purdon's Pennsylvania Statutes Annotated.*** This is a good one for the hospital's library. Physicians and administrators, without any legal training at all, are able to carefully read and understand most statutes. The annotations give history and background, but better yet they give one-paragraph synopses of points of each statute taken from law cases. Questions will be raised, of course, and can be taken to an attorney, but reading the law itself will alert the doctor to those questions. The entire set and updates are needed because the applicable laws are found in different sections. A review of citations in endnotes to each chapter of this text will demonstrate how scattered they are.
- ***Pennsylvania Code, Title 28. Health and Safety.*** This is an official publication of the Commonwealth, containing regulations after they have gone through the notice and comment process. The regulations have the force of law, and this title is essential to have available. The hospital probably already has this one. It is published in two volumes by Frey Communications, 800 W. Church Road, Mechanicsburg, Pa. 17055-3198.
- ***The Citation.*** This is available by subscription from the American Medical Association. It is prepared bimonthly by the Office of General Counsel of the AMA and is described as "A Medicolegal Digest for Physicians." It is a synopsis of court cases affecting doctors. Although it covers cases throughout the United States, it is helpful to know what is happening in other states because lawyers look to other states for trends and theories to apply to Pennsylvania next.[32]
- ***Medical Malpractice Prevention.*** Published bimonthly by ASV Communications, this easily read "throw-away journal" contains valuable insights based on true occurrences. More thorough reviews are sometimes included.
- ***American Medical News.*** This tabloid is published by the American

Medical Association and is sent to the association's members. It is useful in letting a doctor know the latest in medical malpractice litigation, as well as other matters affecting doctors.[33]

- ***Medical Economics.*** When attorneys or accountants want to know what doctors are thinking from a business and legal point of view, they sometimes turn to Medical Economics, which is published by the Medical Economics Company.[34] The publication contains numerous articles about the business of medicine, including medical malpractice. Although sometimes a bit sensationalistic and always simplistic, especially helpful are the articles in which doctors tell about their good, and not so good, experiences with the law.
- ***Newspapers.*** The physician should choose one that covers the whole state, either as is, or to supplement the local paper.
- ***Trial.*** This is the official magazine of the Association of Trial Lawyers of America.[35] It routinely includes articles on medical malpractice and the latest theories used to sue doctors. It also has pages of advertisements for medical experts. There is no better way of finding out what patients' attorneys are thinking than by subscribing to this magazine.
- ***Malpractice folder.*** A physician might consider starting a file folder for any articles, notes, or other items of interest regarding medical malpractice, especially regarding his own specialty. While it's better to read these items before they are placed in the folder, they should be kept on file regardless of whether the doctor gets around to reading them immediately. They can be reviewed later if necessary.

Besides these "musts," a doctor should complement the library with other selected publications about the law. There are many from which to select.[36]

Some sets of books that would be helpful also cover many areas of law not to be of particular interest to doctors. Selective reference to the right part of these can be enlightening. Several sets of books fall into this category.[37] We would especially like to note *Bender's Deposition Strategy, Law and Forms*[38] and *American Jurisprudence Proof of Facts.*[39]

Bender's Deposition Strategy, Law and Forms is designed to help attorneys prepare for taking depositions.[40] However, it is helpful in preparing for trials as well. It includes lengthy discussions on particular litigation areas, including medical malpractice. Specific topics are then discussed, ranging from informed consent to otolaryngology. Also provided are strategy suggestions and actual questions and answers to be used. Major headings in the discussion of medical malpractice include:

- ***Introduction.*** An overview of medical malpractice deposition practice is initially provided, including what the patient's and doctor's attorneys should do before a deposition is taken.
- ***Conduct of the deposition: strategy, tactics, and style.*** Practical tips on conducting depositions are provided. This is a how-to discussion and thus would be extremely helpful to review.

- ***Development of defendant doctor's background, training, and experience—plaintiff's inquiry.*** This tells just how the patient's attorney learns about the doctor.
- ***Examination.*** Several sections relate to questioning others or their records. It is helpful to know what other witnesses will be asked.
- ***Treatment.*** Sections also cover pretreatment, treatment, and post-treatment of the patient. Highlighting these discussions are those pertaining to informed consent and other conversations with patients.
- ***Specific areas of medicine.*** Finally, specific areas of medicine are discussed, and questions to be used in very specific cases are provided. For example, questions are provided for a case claiming brain damage suffered by an infant during delivery and a case claiming misdiagnosis of a fractured vertebra.

American Jurisprudence Proof of Facts contains textual discussions of highly specific areas of the law followed by sample testimony to assist in preparing for and proving the facts that are at issue in a case. Many pertain to medical malpractice. For example, one article discusses medical malpractice liability based on negligently giving an injection or an intravenous or subcutaneous infusion. After providing background information, the article provides a checklist of what must be proved in such a case. It concludes with sample testimony—questions and answers—of the patient, the expert witness, and even the doctor sued.[41]

While there is not sufficient reason to purchase these expensive sets, the doctor should ask a personal attorney for permission to look at the attorney's set or review them at an area law library. They are helpful and in some cases may give a virtual script of the questions and answers at the trial.

Anyone who starts buying law books quickly finds out that they are expensive; they are worth the investment, however. A doctor clearly should have access to books such as the *Pennsylvania Statues Annotated,* but could use some alternative to individual purchases. For example, an area hospital or medical society might establish a medical-legal library for the staff. Some law libraries are surprisingly open. Books may alternatively be available through the local public library. The important thing is not how the books are made available, but that they are available.

We realize that medical malpractice is a topic that is to doctors what radical neurosurgery is to patients. This is not to suggest that a brain transplant is required. Besides, the physician's immune system would surely reject a lawyer's brain. But stuffing legal knowledge into the physician's cranial vault is a necessary and rewarding effort.

Reviewing your insurance coverage

Reviewing malpractice insurance coverage won't prevent claims, but it will certainly help protect a doctor if a claim is asserted. Most doctors do not review their insurance coverage until a claim has been made. Obviously, this is a mistake. Coverage differs, so it is important to review policies when they are purchased. It is even advisable for the doctor to go over the coverage with a personal attorney. The doctor thus will be better informed of what protection the policy does and does not offer.

Medical malpractice policies are of two basic types:

- ***Occurrence policies,*** which provide coverage for malpractice committed during the policy term. A doctor who purchases an occurrence policy will be covered for malpractice that occurs during a year the policy is in force regardless of when a lawsuit is filed. This form is less available today.
- ***Claims-made policies,*** which provide coverage for claims first made during the time the policy is in force. Claims-made policies are sometimes referred to as discovery policies. A doctor who purchases a claims-made policy is covered only if the policy is effective in the year the malpractice claim is made or suit is filed *and* the negligence occurred during this time or within an earlier date specified in the policy (for example, since the first date continuous claims-made coverage became effective with the insurance company or some other date mutually agreed upon). This clause may be called a prior-acts endorsement. Claims-made policies may also be offered with extended reporting endorsements, extending the time in which a claim may be reported. What form of claim triggers the coverage may vary, from any notice to only a formal court filing.

These broad categories of malpractice policies can be subject to great variations and hybrids. For example, some places require that suit be filed within the policy period, not merely that an incident be reported. Therefore when buying or reviewing coverage, many questions should be considered. Some major considerations are:

- ***What exposure is insured.*** A doctor's professional liability policy generally insures a doctor against liability because of personal injury arising from rendering or failing to render professional services. It does not insure against other exposure that a doctor may face as a result of being in business, such as workers' compensation, premises liability, and the like. Thus it is important to remember that other coverage may be required. Below are other lists that also suggest other exposures. For example, ask if coverage for those listed below under Who is Insured is required to protect the physician.
- ***Who is insured.*** The person or entity named on a policy is obviously insured. This may not be sufficient, however. Determine who else is or should be insured. Those for whom the doctor may be vicariously liable need coverage as named insureds either on this policy or on other policies. Consider these questions:

  If a partnership is involved, are the individual partners insured?

If a corporation is involved, are the officers, directors, and stockholders insured?

Are employees (doctor or others) insured?

Are associates insured?

Are others whom the law might construe as de facto *or borrowed servants, partners, ancillary personnel, employees, or associates insured?*[42]

Are predecessors insured?

Are former partners, officers, directors, stockholders, employees, or associates insured?

Are retired or semiretired partners, officers, directors, stockholders, employees, or associates insured?

Does the term insured *include any person for whom you are legally responsible, although not technically a partner, officer, director, stockholder, or employee?*

Does the definition of insured extend to the heirs, executors, administrators, successors, assigns, and legal representatives of each insured in the event of death, incapacity, or bankruptcy?

Does coverage extend automatically to any added partner, officer, director, stockholder, employee, or associate?

Is coverage affected by any change in the legal form of practice, such as a change from a partnership to a corporation, or the reverse?

Does coverage differ between the "named insured" and the "insured"?

If you rely on your insurance policy to cover you for acts or omissions of others for whom you may be responsible without naming them, is the coverage clear and adequate?

- ***Type of coverage.*** Review the type of coverage. Consider these questions:

Does the policy provide occurrence or claims-made coverage?

Is unrestricted coverage provided in a claims-made policy for all prior acts to the last occurrence policy or beginning of practice, whichever is earlier? Don't depend on the agent or company to eliminate gaps.

If an individual joins the practice during the policy term, does the claims-made policy cover that individual's prior acts? In other words, what is the retroactive date of the policy?

If a potential claim is reported, although not asserted, will coverage be available even if the formal claim is ultimately made after the policy term?

Is the existence or availability of "tail" or extended reporting coverage assured by the claims-made policy? For what period?

What is the cost of tail coverage and is there a special discount (or no cost) if the insured becomes permanently disabled or dies? Is the cost different for the retiring physician?

- ***Nature and extent of coverage.*** Review the nature and extent of coverage provided. Consider these questions:

  Does the policy provide for coverage in the amount required by Pennsylvania state law—$100,000 per occurrence and $300,000 per annual aggregate?

  Is coverage provided regardless of the theory claimed by the patient—negligence or breach of contract?

  Are claims for defamation, invasion of privacy, assault, battery, wrongful detention, false imprisonment and, in general, intentional torts covered? They may be covered to the extent that the claim arises out of a medical situation.

  Is coverage provided for service on medical staff committees, such as peer review committees?

  What deductible is required?

  Does the deductible include both liability (indemnity coverage) and defense costs?

  Is the deductible payable per policy term or per claim?

  Are defense costs paid in addition to the policy's limits, or do they reduce the limits?

  Is coverage provided worldwide, or only within the United States or a particular state?

  Does the carrier provide any "courtesy" coverage, such as defending an employee or technician named as a co-defendant because of services rendered in the course of their employment with you?

- ***Exclusions of coverage.*** What a policy doesn't cover is often overlooked in reviewing the terms. However, this is particularly important because the doctor is "bare" in these areas. Coverage exclusions are usually general areas of exclusion contained in the body of the policy documents. More specific exclusions usually are contained in policy "riders." Policy riders are additions to policies that, for example, may exclude coverage for any claim made by a particular individual who previously filed suit against you. Consider these questions:

Will defense coverage be provided even if payment of the claim itself is not covered?

Are punitive damages covered in case suit is brought under another state's laws? (Unlike Pennsylvania, a few states may allow coverage of punitive damages.)

Are indemnity agreements you've entered covered?

Are obligations assumed under contract covered, such as a contract retaining your services as an independent contractor?

Are property damages covered?

Is coverage provided for violation of discrimination laws, such as the Civil Rights Act?

- ***Handling claims.*** Review how claims are handled. Consider these questions:

  Under what circumstances must you report a possible, but unasserted claim to the insurer?

  Do you have the right to approve the defense counsel retained by the insurer?

  Can the insurer settle claims without your consent?

  If you refuse to settle a claim, how will that affect your coverage?

  Must the insurer continue to defend a claim until a final judgment is rendered, even if the limits of the policy have been exhausted?

- ***Policy conditions.*** Every policy contains a variety of other technical provisions. Review them carefully. Consider these questions:

  Can the insurer cancel the policy for reasons other than failure to pay a premium or deductible?

  What notice must be given before refusing to renew the policy?

  To what extent may coverage be denied based on misrepresentations or statements made in the application for the policy?

  To what extent may the insurer seek to recover amounts paid on your behalf against others? Stated otherwise, to what extent does the insurer have what is known as the right of subrogation?[43]

  May additional premiums or surcharges be assessed?

  Is there a formula, such as a percentage premium, for limiting what can be charged for tail coverage or tail buy-out?

Perhaps most important is picking the insurance company. The carrier has to be approved by the Commonwealth, the federal Risk Retentive Act notwithstanding.[44] But the blessings of Pennsylvania's Insurance Commissioner are not a guarantee of solvency. Four major malpractice insurance companies have failed in recent memory, leaving their insureds to scramble for prior acts coverage or to pay for already filed claims.

In the series of laws passed in the 1970's regarding medical malpractice, the most important to survive court review is the statute dealing with the catastrophic loss fund.[45] Unlike the arbitration statute, this has been declared constitutionally permissible.[46] Any health care provider (but defined as not including nurses, dentists, and chiropractors) who has more than 50% of his practice in Pennsylvania is required to have coverage in the amount of $100,000 per occurrence and $300,000 per annual aggregate.[47] The fund comes from a surcharge, calculated as a percentage of the insurance costs, and is levied on health providers annually.[48] The amount that the fund will need in any given year is determined by calculating the amount required to reimburse the fund for all claims and expenses paid out in the previous calendar year, plus maintain a $15 million reserve.[49]

The fund's limit of liability stops at $1 million per occurrence for each health care provider and $3 million per annual aggregate for each health care provider.[50] Thus, if a patient wins a suit for over $1 million, the physician will have to pay the excess. The first million-dollar verdict in a personal injury case was rendered in 1962. Between then and 1986, 98 verdicts over a million have been reported in Pennsylvania, 41 between 1983 and 1986.[51] The need for insurance above $1 million, as well as below $100,000, should be apparent.

Seeking constructive legislation

Doctors are typically interested in medicine and health care. They generally are not interested in working with the political system to seek legislation that will address the medical malpractice crisis or, for that matter, other issues affecting medicine and health care. This attitude must change.

The fact that major reform legislation in medical malpractice—the Health Claims Arbitration Process—has been held unconstitutional by the Pennsylvania Supreme Court is clearly discouraging. Other states have found similar legislation appropriate and valid, but the real delays in the process were less in those jurisdictions.

Many elements of the legal system as it pertains to doctors and health care must be addressed. The most immediate concern is to eliminate the avalanche of suits that are frivolous or without merit while expeditiously and reasonably resolving claims that may have merit. Bringing about meaningful change requires doctors' involvement.

Back to medicine? Absolutely—but better prepared!

No one denies that at times claims against doctors, dentists, or other health care providers should be pursued and reasonable compensation provided to those injured by negligence. However, a flood of suits that are frivolous or without merit is destroying the best medical delivery system the world has ever known.

The medical malpractice crisis is a chain reaction. It starts with the threat of frivolous complaints, which causes medical malpractice insurers to increase premiums, which causes health care providers to practice defensively, which causes the cost of medical care to rise, which causes patients to distrust doctors and perceive them as uncaring and greedy, which leads patients to seek a means—often legal—to respond. And then the cycle begins again.

To break the cycle, doctors, dentists, and other health care providers must be allowed to get back to medicine. Medicine has been and should continue to be the priority. Legal and malpractice concerns need to be dealt with, not ignored. But they should then be given the proper perspective, not allowed to overwhelm and spoil the medical system.

The perspective should be that malpractice is a problem and a risk of practice that cannot be completely avoided. But it is a risk that can be managed and reduced. That management and reduction will require time, effort, and expense; it should not require medically unnecessary expense or risk for patients. But the expenditure of that time, effort, and expense will result in a risk that becomes acceptable. Then that risk can be properly regarded as only one part of a wonderful life of healing and caring for others.

Endnotes

1. King Henry VI, Act IV, Scene II.
2. It is hoped that you have not had this experience. I have. HH.
3. U.S. Department of Health, Education and Welfare, *Report of the Secretary's Commission on Medical Malpractice* at 14 (1973).
4. U.S. General Accounting Office: HRD-86-50, 86-112, 86-21, 87-55, and 87-73. Available from the U.S.G.A.O., P. O. Box 6015, Gaithersburg MD 20877.
5. St. Paul Fire and Marine Insurance Co., *Malpractice Digest,* vol. 13, no. 1 (1986). Cases of say, esophageal intubation, might be reported as mistreatment or mismonitoring.
6. The Medical Protective Co., *The Protector,* vol. 1, no. 1 (1984).
7. American College of Emergency Physicians, *Foresight,* Issue 3, December 1986, citing the results of a 5-year closed claim study. *See also* Dunn, J.: Risk Management in Emergency Medicine **5** :51, 1987.
8. The Medical Protective Co., *The Protector,* vol. 2, no. 1 (1985).
9. National Association of Insurance Commissioners, *Malpractice Claims Final Compilation: Medical Malpractice Closed Claims 1975-1978,* vol. 2, no. 2 (1980).
10. The Medical Protective Co., *The Protector,* vol. 3, no. 3 (1986).
11. The Medical Protective Co., *The Protector,* vol. 2, no. 3 (1985).
12. The Medical Protective Co., *The Protector,* vol. 2, no. 1 (1985).
13. The Medical Protective Co., *The Protector,* vol. 3, no. 1 (1986).
14. The Medical Protective Co., *The Protector,* vol. 3, no. 2 (1986).
15. The Medical Protective Co., *The Protector,* vol. 2, no. 2 (1985).
16. The Medical Protective Co., *The Protector,* vol. 3, no. 4 (1986).
17. The Medical Protective Co., *The Protector,* vol. 2, no. 4 (1985).
18. The Medical Protective Co., *The Protector,* vol. 3, no. 3 (1986).
19. The Medical Protective Co., *The Protector,* vol. 3, no. 2 (1986).
20. St. Paul Fire and Marine Insurance Co., *Malpractice Digest,* vol. 13, no. 1 (1986).
21. St. Paul Fire and Marine Insurance Co., *Malpractice Digest,* vol. 13, no. 2 (1986).

22. The Medical Protective Co., *The Protector,* vol. 1, no. 1 (1984) and vol. 3, no. 2 (1986).
23. St. Paul Fire and Marine Insurance Co., *Malpractice Digest,* vol. 12, no. 2 (1985).
24. St. Paul Fire and Marine Insurance Co., *Malpractice Digest,* vol. 12, no. 2 (1985).
25. The "hang together or hang separately" principle applies before the case is filed, too.
26. The Medical Protective Co., *The Protector,* vol. 1, no. 2 (1984). The story was mentioned in an article by Eugene F. Senseny, M.D., medical director of The Medical Protective Co.
27. The Medical Protective Co., *The Protector,* vol. 2, no. 3 (1985).
28. A helpful booklet on this topic is "Office Staff Responsibility in Preventing Malpractice Suits—A Practical Guide," available from the Illinois State Medical Inter-Insurance Exchange, 20 North Michigan Avenue, Suite 700, Chicago, Ill. 60602. The booklet was originally prepared on behalf of The Risk Management Committee—The Doctor's Company.
29. American Medical Association Special Task Force on Professional Liability and Insurance, *Professional Liability in the '80s: Report I* (October, 1984) at 16.
30. St. Paul Fire and Marine Insurance Co., *Malpractice Digest,* vol. 12, no. 2 (1985).
31. A doctor should ask his or her personal attorney to keep him advised of courses when they are advertised. In addition to the Bar, programs are conducted by many organizations. The National Health Lawyers Association and the American College of Legal Medicine have excellent programs.
32. The Citation may be obtained from the American Medical Association, 535 North Dearborn Street, Chicago, Ill. 60610.
33. A similar publication that is also helpful is "Family Practice News," published semimonthly by International Medical News Group, Fairchild Division of Capital Cities Media Inc., 12230 Wilkins Avenue, Rockville, Md. 20852.
34. Subscription information should be directed to Medical Economics Co., Box 55, Oradell, N.J. 07649.
35. Subscription information should be directed to The Association of Trial Lawyers of America, 1050 31st Street, NW, P.O. Box 3717, Washington, D.C. 20007.
36. A partial listing of other publications to consider include: *Defendant, A Psychiatrist on Trial for Medical Malpractice* by Sara C. Charles, M.D., and Eugene Kennedy (The Free Press, a division of Macmillan Inc., New York, N.Y.) *Malpractice: Managing Your Defense* by Raymond M. Fish (Medical Economics Books, Oradell, N.J. 07649). *The Law of Medical Malpractice* by Joseph H. King, Jr. (West Publishing Co., P.O. Box 3526, St. Paul, Minn. 55465). *Health Care Law: A Practical Guide* by Michael G. Macdonald, Kathryn C. Meyer, and Beth Essig (Matthew Bender & Co., Inc., P.O. Box 989, Dept D.M., Albany, N.Y. 12201). This book is written primarily for attorneys and covers a variety of legal issues including medical malpractice, risk management, consent to treatment, confidentiality, and others. *Medical Malpractice* by David Louisell, Charles Dramer and Jules Kalisch (Matthew Bender & Co., Inc., Box 989, Dept. D.M., Albany, NY 12201). This is a three-volume set written for attorneys covering medical and dental malpractice. It includes actual trial transcripts and commentary on each stage of litigation. *Consent to Treatment: A Practical Guide* by Fay A. Rozovsky (Little, Brown, & Co., 34 Beacon Street, Boston, Mass. 02108). This book provides comprehensive coverage of informed consent issues. Sample forms are included. *Medical Malpractice: Guide to Medical Issues* by Lee S. Goldsmith, M.D., LL.B., and others (Matthew Bender & Co., Inc., Box 989, Dept. D.M., Albany, N.Y. 12201). This book is written by doctors for attorneys to tell them how to prepare for medical malpractice litigation involving various medical specialties. *Pattern Interrogatories: Medical Malpractice* by D. Denner (Lawyers Co-operative Publishing Co., Aqueduct Building, Rochester, N.Y. 14694). Although designed to help attorneys prepare written questions, the book is helpful in giving examples of what questions would be asked verbally as well.
37. Other sets include: *American Jurisprudence Trials.* This series provides an encyclopedic guide to modern practices, techniques, and tactics used in preparing and trying cases. Specific topics are addressed, and detailed bibliographies provided. For example, one article is entitled "Defense of Medical Malpractice Cases." *See* **16** Am. Jur. Trials 471. The Publisher is the Lawyers Co-Operative Publishing Co., Aqueduct Building, Rochester, N.Y. 14694. *American Law Reports.* This series selects specific

areas of the law, provides a featured court decision, and then provides a textual discussion of cases on the topic. In an article on a given topic virtually every case available, whether favorable or unfavorable, has been located for the reader. An example of one topic discussed is "Medical Treatment." *See* **20** A.L.R. 4th 1179. This set is also published by The Lawyers Co-operative Publishing Co., Acqueduct Building, Rochester, N.Y. 14694. *Bender's Forms of Discovery.* This set provides sample interrogatories for various areas of the law. Relevant topics include physicians and other medical personnel; dentists; drugs and druggists; hospitals; personal injuries; and x-rays. Although actually designed for preparing written questions, they are helpful in planning or anticipating verbal questions as well. This set is published by Matthew Bender & Co., Inc., P.O. Box 989, Dept. D.M., Albany, NY 12201. *Jury Verdict Research.* This service outlines and analyzes awards in personal injury cases, including medical malpractice. A separate survey is published for Pennsylvania and another on physician and hospital negligence nationally. These services are excellent warnings of why doctors are being sued in Pennsylvania and elsewhere. The publisher is Jury Verdict Research Inc., 5325 Naiman Parkway, Suite B, Solon, Ohio 44139-1065. *Medical Malpractice Verdicts, Settlements & Experts.* As its title indicates, this service provides information regarding medical malpractice verdicts, settlements, and experts. According to the publication, its purpose is "to enhance the likelihood that victims of malpractice will receive adequate compensation for injuries and that health care providers will be protected from fruitless lawsuits brought by uninformed patients." Of particular help to the reader are the names of expert witnesses and the types of cases in which they testify. The publisher also provides a national database of medical malpractice lawsuit filings and, from time to time, special reports on selected areas of malpractice litigation. Like similar services, it tells the doctor what's on the minds of attorneys. The publisher is M. Lee Smith Publishers & Printers, P.O. Box 2678, Arcade Station, Nashville, Tenn. 37219. *Medical Liability Reporter.* This service is designed to provide comprehensive coverage of health care law issues. It discusses individual cases and compares similar cases in the same or other courts. The publisher is Miller Freeman Publications Inc., 500 Howard Street, San Francisco, Cal. 94105. *Lawyers Medical Encyclopedia* is another attorney-oriented, multi-volume publication.

38. This series is published by Matthew Bender & Co., Inc., P.O. Box 989, Dept D.M., Albany, N.Y. 12201.
39. This series is published by The Lawyers Co-operative Publishing Co., Aqueduct Building, Rochester, N.Y. 14694.
40. *See* Chapter 6 regarding depositions.
41. *See* 36 POF2d 637, Medical Malpractice: Liability for Negligent Injection of Infusion. A few other examples include: 36 POF 2d 1, Dental Malpractice; 34 POF 2d 99, Druggist's Liability for Improperly Filling Prescription; 34 POF2d 557, Adequacy of Consent to Autopsy; 26 POF2d 183, Medical Malpractice— Negligence in Postoperative Care of Patient; 26 POF2d 363, Malpractice of Psychiatric Nurse.
42. If a doctor practices in the proximity of other doctors, even if legally separate, this is important but often overlooked coverage.
43. Subrogation is a legal term for the substitution of one person in the place of another with reference to a claim, demand, or right. The person subrogated succeeds to the rights of another. *See* Black's Law Dictionary (ed. 5) at 1279. For example, if a person is involved in a car accident caused by someone else, the person will often have his or her own insurer pay for the damage to the car. The person's insurer is then subrogated to the person's rights and may sue to recover what was paid to its insured from the person who actually caused the accident. More often, the insurer gets subrogation money from the other driver's company without suit.
44. 40 Pa. C.S.A. Section 1301.701 (Purdon 1987).
45. *Id.*
46. McCoy v. Connors, Bd. of Medical Ed. and Licensure, 391 A.2d 723 (Pa. Commonwealth 1978).
47. 40 Pa. C.S.A. Section 1301.701 (Purdon 1987).
48. If the liability insurance is lumped in with other kinds of insurance, the company

has to sort it out. 31 Pa. Code Section 242.4 (1984). Obviously, the physician will want the premium portion attributed to malpractice liability minimized, so as to minimize the surcharge. But the company wants to stay out of trouble with the commissioner.

49. 40 Pa. C.S.A. Section 1301.701 (Purdon 1987).
50. *Id.*, at (d).
51. Personal Injury Verdict Survey, Pennsylvania Edition, p.6, Jury Verdict Research 1986. This includes all personal injury cases, not just medical malpractice.

INDEX

NO POSTAGE
NECESSARY
IF MAILED
IN THE
UNITED STATES

BUSINESS REPLY MAIL

FIRST CLASS PERMIT NO. 135 ST. LOUIS, MO.

POSTAGE WILL BE PAID BY ADDRESSEE

DENNIS CARSON
The C.V. MOSBY Company
11830 Westline Industrial Drive
P.O. Box 46908
St. Louis, Missouri 63146-9934

NO POSTAGE
NECESSARY
IF MAILED
IN THE
UNITED STATES

BUSINESS REPLY MAIL

FIRST CLASS PERMIT NO. 135 ST. LOUIS, MO.

POSTAGE WILL BE PAID BY ADDRESSEE

DENNIS CARSON
The C.V. MOSBY Company
11830 Westline Industrial Drive
P.O. Box 46908
St. Louis, Missouri 63146-9934